West Press introduced the *Great Towns* series of travel guidebooks in 1985. In less than two years, *The Great Towns of The West* (1985) and *The Great Towns of California* (1986) have delighted travelers nationwide and earned critical acclaim.

"The most impressive of the new guides is *The Great Towns of the West.*"
The Denver Post

"Until now none of the big publishers has paid much attention to the cities outside the mainstream, many of which are worthwhile destinations. *The Great Towns of The West* does a fine job of covering towns that make travel off the interstate so fascinating."
Seattle Post-Intelligencer

"An invaluable resource for finding Western vacation spots that combine the best in size, location and natural and urban features, Vokac's organized guidebook also rates each attraction mentioned and provides helpful prices."
American West

"*The Great Towns of California* will appeal to seasoned travelers, urban escapists, and armchair adventurers alike."
The Bloomsbury Review

"The beauty of the guide lies not only in the detailed information about lodging, restaurants, campgrounds, shopping, nightlife, etc., but also in the tips about nearby, unusual off-beat places or attractions generally known only to locals."
Books of The Southwest

"The narrative descriptions that accompany each entry, unlike the tired prose of many guidebooks, inspire confidence and sometimes delight. This is an uncommonly fresh, useful resource."
American Reference Books Annual

"Vacation planners will appreciate the wealth of revealing insights provided in a concise, well-organized format."
Booklist

"This is an excellent guide . . . one that you can use again and again."
The Province, Vancouver, B.C.

Now, there is also

THE GREAT TOWNS OF THE PACIFIC NORTHWEST

Published in 1987, this all-new guide is the most comprehensive yet to natural, civilized places throughout Oregon and Washington that you can enjoy for vacations . . . or for the rest of your life.

THE
GREAT TOWNS
OF THE
PACIFIC NORTHWEST

A Guide To
Exciting Destinations
In
Oregon and Washington

David Vokac

Library of Congress Cataloging-in-Publication Data

Vokac, David, 1940-
     The great towns of the Pacific Northwest

     Includes index.
     1. Oregon—Description and travel— Guide-books. 2. Washington (State)—
Description and travel— Guide-books. 3. Cities and towns—Oregon—Guide-books. 4.
Cities and towns — Washington (State)—
Guide-books.   I. Title.
F874.3.V64   1987   917.95'0433   87-2130
ISBN 0-930743-02-4

First Printing April 1987
Second Printing August 1987
Manufactured in the United States of America

Preface

Natural grandeur is the essence of the Pacific Northwest. Here, between California and Canada, is an awesome landscape filled with majestic, untamed scenery that can make any spirits soar. Two states, Oregon and Washington, share this vast region of endless shorelines and tranquil waterways, luxuriant forests, and glistening peaks.

Much has been written about landmarks like Crater Lake and Mt. Rainier National Parks, and about Seattle and Portland—the vibrant metropolises where a majority of the people live. However, detailed information about special places apart from the renowned attractions remains scarce. Towns rich in both human charms and scenic splendors—like Ashland and Port Townsend—are treated casually in guidebooks. Yet, these and other out-of-the-way towns that successfully blend inspiring natural settings with the comforts and artistry of civilization are among the region's greatest achievements—and most appealing leisure destinations.

My abiding interest in such places began as a result of growing up in Cody, Wyoming (the eastern gateway to Yellowstone Park). It was nurtured by a career in urban planning when I lived and worked in various locations throughout Western America. In 1985, I wrote *The Great Towns of The West* to give the most appealing, remote Western towns the careful attention they deserve. That premier work became the foundation for this guidebook.

The Great Towns of the Pacific Northwest is intended to serve as the essential guide to extraordinary towns and their surroundings in Oregon and Washington. Toward that goal, communities throughout those states were re-examined during the last half of 1986 and early 1987. All eight originally-included towns were found to be as desirable as ever. In addition, eight more towns met the criteria first developed three years earlier. The full range of leisure pursuits in and around the sixteen "great" towns was field-checked and evaluated. Attractions, restaurants, lodgings, shops, nightlife, campgrounds, special events, and the weather were systematically addressed in each locale.

During eight months of full-time, entirely independent effort, I personally visited each feature anonymously. No payments or favors were accepted. Thus, every listing is described and rated on merit alone. I believe that this guide is as honest, accurate, and complete as possible.

For everyone who wonders what special places and pleasures await beyond the cities of Oregon and Washington, *The Great Towns of the Pacific Northwest* has the answers. All the information you need to create a visit perfectly tailored to your time, finances, and interests is in this guidebook.

To Joan

THE PACIFIC NORTHWEST

VANCOUVER

NORTH CASCADES
NATIONAL PARK

VICTORIA

La Conner

Port Townsend

OLYMPIC
NATIONAL
PARK

Chelan

SEATTLE

Leavenworth

SPOKANE

Ocean

TACOMA

Olympia

WASHINGTON

Long Beach

MOUNT
RAINIER
NATIONAL PARK

Seaside

Cannon Beach

PORTLAND

Pacific

SALEM

OREGON

Lincoln City

Newport

Bend

Florence

EUGENE

Bandon

CRATER LAKE
NATIONAL PARK

Scale in miles

Gold Beach

Grants Pass

0   100

Ashland

One inch equals approx. 85 miles

6

Contents

Introduction

This is a travel guide to the Pacific Northwest's "other" desirable destinations—scenic, civilized locales apart from the famed national parks and bustling cities. It was written to help vacation planners and travelers discover these remarkable out-of-the-way towns and their splendid surroundings, and enjoy them to the fullest.

A wealth of new information is presented in two ways that set this guidebook apart from others. Attention is focused on a wide range of leisure pursuits primarily of interest to adventurous individuals and couples. As a result, premium wineries and isolated hot springs receive as much attention as famous museums and amusement parks. Second, the subject matter is concentrated on the most appealing of the Pacific Northwest's towns and their environs. It was therefore possible to identify, evaluate, and describe all of the special places and pleasures in each locality. Subjects normally included in guidebooks—attractions, restaurants, and lodgings—are presented in careful detail. In addition, several topics that are seldom found in a single book—weather, shopping, nightlife, camping, and special events—are given the same thorough attention.

This book is designed to provide all of the information you'll need to get the most out of these exciting places within your time, finances, and interests.

The Selection Process

A "great town" is defined in this guidebook as an independent, unspoiled community rich in human-scale charms and scenic splendor. It is a locality that possesses the things that make both an ideal hometown and a vacation paradise.

This general concept provided the basis for developing specific factors to be used in selecting the great towns of the Pacific Northwest. Five measures—population size, independence, natural setting, freedom from environmental problems, and leisure appeal—were used in a sequential process of elimination involving the 1,700-plus named urban places in Oregon and Washington. Each was assessed during the search for great towns throughout a vast 165,000 square mile area reaching from California to the Canadian border, and from the Pacific Ocean to the Rocky Mountains.

Population size was the first factor to be considered. The Census Bureau treats urban places as "metropolitan statistical areas" or "cities" once they have more than 50,000 people. At the other extreme, villages with less than one thousand people are almost always too small to have all essential urban services and facilities. After eliminating cities (like Salem, Oregon) and tiny villages (like Winthrop, Washington) from further consideration, 430 towns were left.

These were then evaluated in terms of independence. All towns less than ten miles from the nearest small city (with at least 50,000 population), and farther (up to at least forty miles) from the largest metropolitan centers were excluded. This was done because suburban communities are inevitably dependent on, and assume some of the characteristics of, the nearby city. Edmonds, Washington and Forest Grove, Oregon are examples of towns eliminated because they are suburbs.

The natural setting of each remaining town was then assessed. Mountains and the coastal rim of the Pacific Ocean are the outstanding landforms and the ultimate attractions of the Pacific Northwest. All towns lacking an impressive setting, i.e. more than a few miles from one or the other of these features, were omitted. Examples include Walla Walla and Ellensburg, Washington; and Cottage Grove and Pendleton, Oregon.

Next, environmental problems like oil refineries, pulp and paper mills, or smokestack industries near downtown caused a disappointingly large number of additional towns to be rejected. Anacortes and Port Angeles, Washington and Astoria and Coos Bay, Oregon are examples.

Finally, the remaining towns were evaluated for their overall leisure appeal as vacation destinations and hometowns. The quality and quantity of both lodgings and leisure facilities were used to measure each locality's desirability to visitors as well as residents. Waldport and Redmond, Oregon and Cashmere and Omak, Washington are among towns dropped from further consideration at this point in the research.

All towns that survived the process of elimination through this step were field-checked. During a detailed survey, the setting (water features, landforms, vegetation), in-town assets (landmarks and landscapes), and downtown characteristics (parks, vistas, condition and quality of buildings, shops, and nightlife, parking, etc.) were systematically reviewed. A few additional towns, like Mt. Vernon and Ocean Shores, Washington and Brookings and Enterprise, Oregon were set aside because the on-site survey revealed problems that weren't apparent from the earlier research. Every community that had high scores in both the factor evaluation and the field survey is featured in this book.

The Great Towns

There are now sixteen great towns in the Pacific Northwest. Included are all eight of the original towns selected when the process was first used in 1984. Ashland, Bend, Cannon Beach, Grants Pass, Newport, and Seaside in Oregon; and Chelan and Port Townsend in Washington were each found to be as desirable as ever. Almost all of the attributes that caused these localities to be singled out for the first time three years ago are as vital as before. In addition, notable new facilities contribute to the unique character and distinctive local flavor of each of these premier great towns.

It was a pleasure to find that eight additional localities now meet all of the selection requirements. Bandon, Florence, Gold Beach, and Lincoln City in Oregon; and La Conner, Leavenworth, Long Beach, and Olympia in Washington joined the ranks of the great towns of the Pacific Northwest in 1987. This exciting development is clear evidence of a renewed emphasis throughout Oregon and Washington on diversifying the region's economy—and welcoming travelers. During the past three years, each of these towns made major public and private improvements to enhance the civilized and natural charms of its setting, while contributing to the area's desirability for both residents and visitors.

Collectively, these sixteen towns are the prime sources of leisure-time excitement in the Pacific Northwest apart from the famous natural landmarks and thriving metropolises. Individually, each offers unique enchantment that makes it a worthy destination for a weekend—or a lifetime.

How To Use This Guidebook

The sixteen great towns are listed alphabetically by state. A chapter is devoted to each town, with all information organized sequentially by categories described below. The brief remarks about each category, and explanations of location, ratings, and prices can help you use this book more effectively. As an added reference, page numbers for all towns, named features, and general kinds of attractions and diversions included in this book are provided in the detailed index.

Weather Profile

Weather plays a crucial role in recreation and leisure. Because of this, a great deal of care was taken in obtaining and presenting detailed weather information. The weather profiles for each town are intended to be the most complete in any travel guidebook.

Numeric data includes average high and low temperatures, rainfall, and snowfall for each month. The "Vokac Weather Rating"© (VWR) uses all of this (plus the frequency of precipitation) to measure the probability of "pleasant weather"—i.e., warm, dry conditions suitable for outdoor recreation by anyone dressed in light sportswear. The typical weather that can be expected each month is rated from "0" to "10." A "0" signifies the most adverse weather with almost no chance that shirt-sleeves and shorts will be appropriate. Every increment of one on the VWR represents a 10% greater chance of pleasant weather. For example, a "5" is used where there is a 50% chance that any given day in the month will be pleasant. A "10" pinpoints "great" weather, with warm, dry days almost 100% assured. An easy-to-follow line graph is used to display the month-to-month VWR. Generally, ratings of "7" or above indicate a high probability of desirable conditions for outdoor activity. Ratings of "6" or less suggest an increasing likelihood that the weather may restrict outdoor ventures and/or require special clothing. As an added convenience, each month on the graph has been subdivided into four segments roughly corresponding to weeks. Readers interested in "fine-tuning" the VWR may find the smaller segments helpful. For example, if the ratings for September and October are "10" and "6," the position of the connecting line during the last week (segment) of September indicates an "8" rating. The implication is that weather during the last week in the month is normally still "very good," but no longer "great," as it was earlier in the month. The data are also translated into concise narrative forecasts that describe what the weather will probably be like in each month, and in each season, of the year.

Attractions & Diversions

Every notable attraction in each town is described and rated. Included are leisure-time destinations of special interest to adults—like wineries, golf courses, and libraries—that are typically missing from guidebooks. In addition, all kinds of diversions like bicycling, ballooning, horseback riding, river running, and sportfishing are described, and sources for equipment rentals and guides are named. As a convenience, popular categories of attractions and diversions are always listed alphabetically under general headings such as "boat rentals," "warm water features," and "winter sports."

Shopping

Distinctive shops are among the most popular features of almost every great town. Yet, they are often ignored in travel guidebooks. In this book, all notable shops that emphasize locally produced gourmet foods or unusual items (especially those reflecting local artistry or craftsmanship) are described under "Food Specialties" and "Specialty Shops" for each town. The desirability of each downtown as a place to shop and browse is also discussed.

Nightlife

Life after dark is of particular interest to most adults. For each of the Pacific Northwest's great towns, the overall quality of places to go and things to do for an evening is summarized. Then, all first-rate live theaters, nightclubs, pubs, historic saloons, and other sources of nightlife are named. Each is described in terms of featured entertainment as well as furnishings and decor.

Restaurants

Both the quantity and quality of dining places are discussed, along with predominant food styles, for each town. All noteworthy restaurants are described in terms of food and atmosphere. Service is not mentioned because it can vary so much over time—or even on a given evening. Prices are summarized in categories from "low" to "very expensive" (see the discussion of "prices" later in this chapter). Meals served (B=breakfast, L=lunch, D=dinner) are identified under the restaurant's name, along with days closed, if any. Specific hours of operation and special services (like approved credit cards) are not described, because they change frequently in restaurants. Places that cater especially to families, fast-food shops, and themed chain restaurants are generally excluded because of the adult orientation and emphasis on distinctive dining in this book.

Lodging

A systematic effort was made to identify and describe all of the best and all of the bargain accommodations in and around each town. Conventional motels and other sanitized lodgings clustered along highway strips and near freeway off-ramps are also described. These places seldom reflect the charms of an area and are even less frequently bargains. But, they might come in handy on nights when better accommodations and bargain motels have no vacancies. Every town is summarized in terms of the number and quality of its lodgings, and the average percentage by which rates are reduced apart from summer.

Each notable lodging is portrayed in terms of amenities, both natural (like a lakeside location or an oceanfront beach) and man-made (i.e., outdoor pool, whirlpool, tennis courts, etc.). Also, wherever toll-free reservations are possible, the numbers are provided. Room decor and generally available room features—phones, TV, etc.—are mentioned. A highlight of this guidebook is that hundreds of individual rooms with special views and/or furnishings are singled out. Thus, every exceptional room (starting with the best) in the foremost resorts, inns, etc. in each town is identified by a room number (or name), described, and priced. In addition, every effort was made to include and depict all of each town's safe and clean bargain accommodations (priced at $30 per night or less per couple). The "regular room" price which completes each listing is the lowest price charged during prime time—on a summer weekend—for two people in a room with one bed.

Campgrounds

Two kinds of campgrounds are included: all places within reasonable driving distance from town that have a special natural setting (by a river or an oceanfronting beach, for example), and places with complete facilities (including hot showers) that are convenient to a great town. Natural and man-made attractions, as well as sanitary and individual site features, are consistently described. The base rate that ends each listing is the minimum price charged for two people occupying a tent site during prime time.

Special Events

Most of the great towns offer special events at various times. The most popular or unusual events that take place annually are identified, along with the reason for each celebration. Features and entertainment are briefly described.

Location

It is hard to be lost for very long in any of the great towns because of their compact "human scale." This also explains why it's usually easy to find your destination, since most features are either downtown or along the few major streets through town. To help the reader locate features without a map, listings are addressed according to a street number and both mileage and direction from downtown. The term "downtown" covers all features within approximately one-quarter mile of the busiest, most intensely developed portion of the business district. Because this definition is used for each town, it is easy to compare quantities and kinds of features within and among downtowns, and to quickly estimate distances between any listings in each town.

Ratings

Every feature listed in each town is rated. Three levels of quality are reflected in the ratings. (1) A star preceding an entry indicates an especially notable example or source of a product or service. It is worth going out of the way for, if you are interested in that thing. (2) An entry is included, but not starred, if it is a good (but not exceptional) example or source of the product or service. (3) Other features and activities were rated but not included if they were judged to be: of only average or lower quality, readily available in many other places, or lacking in some important characteristic.

Evaluations of each feature were made personally and anonymously, and no payments or favors were accepted. As a result, each listing is rated on merit alone, and solely reflects the judgment of the author. A special effort was made to assure that ratings are comparable among all features and towns. For example, if a restaurant is starred, it is not merely one of the finest available locally. It is a place that would be a special dining experience in any city or town lucky enough to have it. Each individual feature was consistently evaluated both in terms of its overall quality and how well it succeeds in being what it purports to be. Thus, if a restaurant proclaims that it is a temple of haute cuisine, its rating was based both on the quality of the food and decor and on its ability or failure to live up to a lofty aspiration.

Rating information is somewhat perishable in any guidebook. After all, chefs move on, bed-and-breakfast inns change ownership, shops discontinue certain merchandise, and so on. However, ratings are offered throughout this book as summary opinions to help make your selection of features easier.

Prices

Information is provided about the cost of all lodgings, campgrounds, and restaurants. Because prices change along with the economy and whims of management, there can be no assurance that specific dollar numbers quoted in the lodging and campgrounds sections will be in effect. However, the prices shown will continue to illustrate comparable values, since relative price levels usually remain constant. For example, a "bargain" motel (with rooms costing $30 or less in 1987) can be expected to remain a relative bargain in later years when it is compared to other lodgings—even though the price of a room increases—because other lodgings in that area will typically increase their prices by about the same percentage as the bargain motel.

All quoted prices are projected for the summer ("high season") of 1987. They were obtained for every lodging listed in this book through field work and a telephone survey conducted the previous winter. Each price is a per-night rate for two people in a room with one bed. Rates for one person are usually a few dollars less, and rates for two beds (or more than two people) may be a few dollars more per night. Prices are for "European plan" accommodations (no meals) except as noted in the text for "American plan" lodgings that include one or more meals in their daily rates. Campground prices are the lowest forecast for 1987 per car with two persons for a site without electrical or other special hookups. It should be assumed for both lodgings and campgrounds that the use of on-premises facilities (like swimming pools, saunas, etc.) is included in the price of a room or campsite, unless fees or rental charges are noted in the description.

A basic price code was designed to provide a capsule summary of the cost of an average meal in each restaurant. The same code is used for all listed restaurants. As a result, the cost of different kinds of fine dining can be compared within any great town, or contrasted with the cost of similar restaurants in any other great town. Four categories are used to define the cost per person for a "normal" dinner (soup or salad, average-priced entree, and beverage) not including wine, tip, or tax. The categories and related prices are:

Low : less than $8
Moderate : $8 - $14
Expensive : $14 - $20
Very Expensive : $20 - $30

Food and lodging cost substantially less in the great towns of the Pacific Northwest than in cities or in California. Resort prices are relatively lower, and bargain lodgings are more plentiful. So are low-priced restaurants, and there are no extremely expensive ($30 or more) dining rooms, yet.

Some Final Comments

All information has been carefully checked, and is believed to be current and accurate. However, the author cannot be responsible for changes since these are beyond his control. No malice is intended or implied by the judgments expressed, or by the omission of any facility or service, from this guide.

As with any guidebook, this one will be challenged about towns and features that were included, and those which were left out. A reader may disagree with the absence of a favorite town, or the fact that a place remembered fondly in one of the great towns has been excluded. Regardless, *The Great Towns of the Pacific Northwest* will achieve its purpose if it encourages you to go beyond the cities and famous landmarks to discover and experience the special pleasures of these enchanting locales.

The author welcomes your comments and questions.

c/o West Press
P.O. Box 99717
San Diego, CA 92109

Ashland, Oregon

Ashland is a preeminent Western crossroads of culture and recreation. One of the nation's finest theatrical complexes and Shakespearean festivals is the driving force. The location is also special. Sequestered in a luxuriant mixed forest of broadleaf and evergreen trees high on the southern rim of the Rogue River country, the town overlooks a broad, pastoral valley surrounded by impressive peaks.

Complementing the lovely natural setting is one of the mildest climates in the Northwest. Temperatures are pleasant from spring— when blossoms cover the orchards in the valley below—through fall, when roadside stands offer the bountiful harvest. During summer there is almost no rainfall to mar enjoyment of all kinds of outdoor recreation at nearby rivers, lakes, and mountains. Warm evenings normally complement both the downtown Shakespearean Festival and the nearby Peter Britt Music Festival which are staged outdoors under star-studded skies. Enthusiastic theater-goers usually fill the area to capacity throughout the summer season. In winter, snowfall is light in town, but there is plenty of snow on nearby Mt. Ashland to support a major skiing complex.

Gold was first discovered in Oregon in 1851 in the Jacksonville area a few miles northwest of town. Ashland was founded a year later. It never experienced a gold boom, or bust. Instead, it grew slowly at first with conventional businesses—a sawmill, flour mill, and general store. Passenger train service began in 1884. By the turn of the century, the diversified local economy included railroading, fruit growing, and lumbering. Pursuit of the town's ultimate destiny began inauspiciously during the Great Depression. In 1935, a local professor, Angus Bowmer of Southern Oregon State College, won support for using an abandoned Chatauqua site for a Shakespearean production as part of a Fourth of July celebration. Success soon led to the organization of the Oregon Shakespearean Festival Association.

Today, the Festival runs from February to early November in a complex of three fine theaters, and tourism and education are the principal local industries. Lithia Park (superbly landscaped by the designer of Golden Gate Park in San Francisco) adjoins the Festival grounds, and lends great charm to the heart of town. Distinctive galleries featuring local and regional arts and crafts, and numerous specialty food stores, line tree-shaded streets in the compact and handsome downtown shopping district. Nightlife is similarly plentiful, and remarkably diverse. Choices in addition to the festival include "off-Shakespeare" theater, cabarets, sports bars, friendly locals taverns, live music lounges—and a candlelit movie theater. Restaurants are abundant. Among them are several gourmet dining rooms serving outstanding international specialties. Thanks to a recent proliferation of bed-and-breakfast inns, travelers can now opt for a delightful change of pace in artistically converted residences a short stroll from the theaters and park. Several newer motels, a resort, and a restored landmark hotel also accommodate visitors, as do several lakeside campgrounds nearby.

Elevation:

1,950 feet

Population (1980):

14,943

Population (1970):

12,342

Location:

280 miles South
of Portland

Ashland, Oregon
WEATHER PROFILE
Vokac Weather Rating

V.W.R.*		Jan.	Feb.	Mar.	Apr.	May	June	July	Aug.	Sep.	Oct.	Nov.	Dec.
Great	10												
Fine	9												
Very Good	8												
Good	7												
Moderate	6												
	5												
	4												
	3												
Adverse	2												
	1												
	0												

	Jan.	Feb.	Mar.	Apr.	May	June	July	Aug.	Sep.	Oct.	Nov.	Dec.
V.W.R.*	0	0	2	7	8	10	10	10	10	8	2	0
Temperature												
Ave. High	45	51	56	64	70	77	86	85	78	66	53	46
Ave. Low	30	32	34	37	43	48	51	51	45	40	35	31
Precipitation												
Inches Rain	2.8	2.1	2.0	1.4	1.7	1.2	0.3	0.3	0.8	1.6	2.5	3.0
Inches Snow	5	3	2	-	-	-	-	-	-	-	-	3

*V.W.R. = Vokac Weather Rating: probability of mild (warm & dry) weather on any given day.

Forecast

	V.W.R.*	Temperatures Daytime	Temperatures Evening	Precipitation
Jan.	0 Adverse	chilly	chilly	frequent rainstorms/snow flurries
Feb.	0 Adverse	cool	chilly	frequent showers/snow flurries
Mar.	2 Adverse	cool	chilly	frequent showers
Apr.	7 Good	cool	cool	occasional showers
May	8 Very Good	warm	cool	occasional showers
June	10 Great	warm	cool	infrequent showers
July	10 Great	hot	warm	negligible
Aug.	10 Great	hot	warm	negligible
Sep.	10 Great	warm	cool	infrequent showers
Oct.	8 Very Good	warm	cool	occasional showers
Nov.	2 Adverse	cool	chilly	frequent rainstorms
Dec.	0 Adverse	chilly	chilly	frequent rainstorms/snow flurries

Summary

Ashland is near the upper end of a broad tributary valley of the Rogue River. It is nestled along the fringe of a lush mixed-forest of pines and shade trees in low hills at the base of beautiful Mt. Ashland. The area enjoys the mildest four season climate in the Northwest. **Winter** is chilly and damp, with frequent rainfalls and a few snow flurries. Several miles away and thousands of feet higher, a well-regarded winter sports complex offers fine conditions for skiing. In **spring**, good weather arrives in April, heralded by a fragrant profusion of blossoms in nearby orchards. Days are warm and rainfalls are light by May. **Summer** is faultless. Warm-to-hot days, warm evenings, and negligible showers are perfect for enjoying the lovely surroundings during the day and outdoor theaters at night. In **fall**, mild weather continues through Halloween and provides ideal conditions for savoring fall colors and the bountiful nearby fruit harvest.

19

ATTRACTIONS & DIVERSIONS

Applegate River Canyon
starts 25 mi. W via OR 99 & OR 238
Near the town of Ruch, the highway forks south and winds for several miles along the scenic reaches of the upper Applegate River Canyon near the California border. Clear pools in idyllic settings are plentiful. Several along this remote portion of the river are popular for nude bathing.

★ *Bicycling*
Bicycles may be rented at the following locations by the hour or longer. Miles of paved scenic byways beckon bicyclists to the lush, gentle valley below town, and dirt bike enthusiasts will enjoy the twenty-four-mile loop road to Mt. Ashland.
  Ashland Mountain Supply *downtown at 31 N. Main St.* *488-2749*
  Siskiyou Cyclery *1.7 mi. SE on OR 99 at 1729 Siskiyou Blvd.* *482-1997*
Boat Rentals
  Hobie House Marina
  5 mi. S on OR 66 *488-0595*
Catamarans, sailboats, and windsurfer rentals and lessons are offered at the marina on scenic Emigrant Lake, or at Howard Prairie Lake.

★ **Crater Lake National Park**
80 mi. NE via I-5 & OR 62
Oregon's only national park features one of the world's most beautiful lakes. It lies nestled in a huge bowl created when volcanic Mt. Mazama collapsed into a caldera hollowed out by climactic eruptions about 6,000 years ago. The mountainous rim of Crater Lake rises more than 2,000 feet above the water in places, and the lake is nearly 2,000 feet deep (America's deepest). A magnificent thirty-two-mile rim drive around the lake doesn't open until about the Fourth of July, except in years of light snowfall. The highway (OR 62) to Rim Village is kept open year-round, however, in spite of normal snowfalls totalling fifty feet each year. Daily boat tours in summer are another way to experience the lake and see majestic Wizard Island up close. Scenic spur roads and well-marked trails extend from many viewpoints along the rim drive.

★ **Emigrant Lake**
5 mi. S on OR 66 *776-7001*
The nearest major water body to town is a reservoir with a swimming area, plus windsurfing, sailing, boating (rentals available), water-skiing, and fishing. There is also a waterslide. Several shaded picnic areas with barbecues and an improved campground have been provided.

★ *Hiking*
  Mountain Supply of Oregon
  downtown at 31 N. Main St. *488-2749*

20

Forests and mountains surrounding Ashland offer an endless variety of hiking and backpacking opportunities. The local representative of an Oregon chain of outdoor stores is a fine place to get the right clothes and gear, and they carry U.S.G.S. topographic maps of the region.

Horseback Riding
Painted Sky Stables
2.5 mi. SE at 2727 E. Main St.   488-0280
All gear and meals are provided for guided trail rides into the scenic foothills near Ashland. Hour rides, all day, or overnight rides can be reserved.

★ **Howard Prairie Lake**
24 mi. E via Dead Indian Rd.   482-1979
This six-mile-long lake, surrounded by a pine forest, has several county parks on the western shore. Boats may be rented at the marina. Rainbow trout fishing, boating, water-skiing, sailing, swimming, picnicking, and camping are popular.

★ **Jacksonville**
15 mi. NW via OR 99 & OR 238
Gold was discovered here in 1851 in one of the state's first strikes. But the town was bypassed later when the first railroad went through Medford. When the gold played out in the 1920s, Jacksonville even lost its county seat (in 1927) to Medford. In 1967 the whole town was nominated as a National Historic Landmark. Many carefully restored original buildings house specialty stores, galleries, and restaurants. The 1884 County Courthouse, now a museum displaying Oregon history, is one of six museums operated by the Southern Oregon Historical Society in the area. A self-guided walking tour of town is detailed on a brochure available at the old Rogue River Valley Railway Depot Information Center at Oregon and C Streets.

★ *Library*
downtown at Siskiyou Blvd./Gresham St.   482-1151
The Ashland Public Library occupies a classic 1912 Carnegie Library building regally positioned in a parklike setting above the main street. Armchairs and a fireplace (much used in winter) are thoughtfully positioned near a good selection of magazines and newspapers. Closed Fri.-Sun.

★ **Lithia Park**
downtown along Ashland Creek on Pioneer St.   482-9215
One of the West's grandest achievements among town parks (a national historic landmark) borders the theater complex downtown and extends for nearly a mile along Ashland Creek. An enchanting forest shelters formal rose and rhododendron gardens, a landscaped pond with resident swans, meandering pathways, a band shell, lighted tennis courts, imaginative play equipment, emerald-green lawns and playing fields, and secluded picnic sites.

★ **Lithia Spring Water**
  downtown at Winburn Way/N. Main St. in Town Plaza
For about sixty years, drinking fountains on the plaza have provided Lithium water from the nearby mountains. It **is** different.

★ *Orchards*
  starts 3 mi. N via OR 99
Pear and peach orchards commingle with other fruit and nut trees to transform the Bear Creek valley below Ashland into a blossom-time spectacle in April. In late summer and fall, the delectable harvest is displayed and sold at roadside stands.

★ **Rogue River**
  19 mi. N on I-5
The renowned Rogue River offers a greater diversity of outdoor recreation opportunities than any river in the West. In the relatively short length between its spectacular beginnings in the high Cascades near Crater Lake and its broad outlet in the ocean at Gold Beach, the Rogue has a nationally classified Wild and Scenic River section, several pine-clad man-made lakes, and limitless sandy beaches, deep clear pools, riffles, and rapids. It is the primary destination of increasing numbers of river runners, jet boat passengers, cruisers, and sailors in a remarkable variety of watercraft; as well as hordes of swimmers, sunbathers, hikers, picnickers, and campers. Yet, for all of this activity, the Rogue continues to earn its status as a world famous stream for salmon and trout fishing.

★ **Rogue River National Forest**
  NE and SW of town   482-3333
This large forest includes the scenic headwaters of the Rogue River. The Sky Lakes Area features numerous heavily forested lakes. A major winter sports area occupies the upper slopes of Mt. Ashland. A good system of highways and dirt roads plus hundreds of miles of trails, including a picturesque segment of the Pacific Crest National Scenic Trail, provide access for hiking, backpacking, horseback and pack trips, swimming, excellent fishing and boating, camping, and skiing in winter. Information and maps may be obtained at the Ashland Ranger District Office.

★ **Shakespearean Festival Exhibit Center & Backstage Tour**
  downtown at 15 S. Pioneer St.   482-4331
Guided tours let visitors see what goes on behind the scenes at the Festival's theaters. At the exhibit center, you can touch Shakespearean props like thrones, elaborate costumes, broadswords and severed heads, or try on costumes and pose for pictures. Closed Mon.

Warm Water Features
  Emigrant Lake Recreation Area
  5 mi. S on OR 66   776-7001
A 270-foot twin flume waterslide located at the lake is southern Oregon's longest.

Jackson Hot Springs
  2 mi. N at 2253 N. OR 99   *482-3776*
A large (50' by 100') outdoor pool, filled with warm mineral springs
water, is open to the public during the summer. Private rooms
with mineral water tub baths are also available.

Winery
Valley View Vineyard
  23 mi. W via OR 238 at 1000 Applegate Rd. - Ruch   *899-8468*
Several styles of premium grape wine, plus pear wine, are in limited
production at the area's first serious winery. Informal tours are
offered and the tasting room is open daily 11-5. They recommend
a call first during winter. A recently added tasting room (downtown
at 52 E. Main St.) is open daily, except Monday, from 12-6.

Winter Sports
★ **Mt. Ashland Ski Area**
  19 mi. SW via I-5 and Mt. Ashland Rd.   *482-2897*
The vertical rise is 1,150 feet and the longest run is approximately
one mile. Elevation at the top is 7,500 feet. There are two chairlifts.
All essential services, facilities, and rentals are available at the base
for downhill skiing. Night skiing is offered Thurs.-Sat. evenings. There
is a cafeteria and lounge at the base, but no lodging facilities.
The skiing season is December through April.

SHOPPING

Ashland's robust, compact downtown is centered around a
handsome, tree-shaded plaza. Specialty shops are thriving, along
with theaters and an increasing number of distinctive restaurants,
lounges, and lodging places. Parking on the street and in
municipally-owned lots is free.

Food Specialties
Ashland Bakery & Cafe
  downtown at 38 E. Main St.   *482-2117*
A full line of pastries and breads is made here. The whole grain
breads are popular. Everything is served to go or with light fare
in a bright and cheerful room.

★ **Ashland Wine Cellar**
  downtown at 38 C St.   *488-2111*
A fine selection of Northwestern wine is displayed, sold, and offered
for limited tasting, along with many other premium wines, in an
impressive cellar beneath a very complete liquor store. Closed Sun.

★ **Cafe Vanille Ice Cream Parlour**
  downtown at 40 N. Main St.   *482-9764*
Butter-rich ice creams made in the Rogue Valley are featured in
cones, sundaes, shakes, and fanciful creations. Light fare, pies and
cookies, and coffee specialties are also served in the casual parlor
overlooking the plaza, or to go.

★ **Cuppa Joe**
downtown at 60 E. Main St.   *482-5281*
The area's finest selection of gourmet coffees, beans, and related accessories is featured in a well-organized shop. Coffee, espresso, cappuccino, and Italian sodas are served to go, as are selected candies and award-winning homemade ice creams.

★ **Harry and David's Original Country Store**
10 mi. NW at 2836 S. OR 99   *776-2277*
The retail outlet for the Bear Creek Orchards of Harry and David fame showcases gourmet foods and kitchenwares in a large gift shop. The complex also includes a deli, and a market where delicious Comice pears and other kinds of locally grown fruit are packaged in season for purchase or shipment anywhere in gift packs. A comfortable contemporary dining area specializes in locally produced light foods for breakfast and lunch. Tours of the vast facility are available during the fall harvest. In late summer, the adjoining Jackson and Perkins Rose Test Garden is a radiant and fragrant feast for the senses.

★ **Manna from Heaven**
downtown at Main/Gresham Sts.   *482-5831*
Some of the West's best pastries and breads are the tantalizing lure of a bakery that moved downtown in late 1986. In this handsome new showcase, it is more popular than ever.

★ **The Oregon Store**
downtown at 33 N. Main St.   *482-5453*
This independent source of distinctive Oregon-made products opened in the summer of 1986. An excellent selection of arts and crafts and regional gourmet foods has been assembled. In addition, several local premium wines are available for tasting.

★ **Rogue River Valley Creamery**
17 mi. N at 311 N. OR 99 - Central Point   *664-2233*
Delicious extra-sharp cheddar is made here, along with several other cheddar and jack cheeses. This is one of the few places in the country where blue cheese is also made. Samples are served upon request. Closed Sat.-Sun.

★ **Rosie's Sweet Shoppe**
downtown at 303 E. Main St.   *488-0179*
Dozens of flavors of premium ice cream by several manufacturers are served in all sorts of traditional and imaginative treats. Gourmet chocolates and other candies can also be enjoyed in the large, comfortable parlor, or packaged to go.

★ **The Tasting Room**
15 mi. NW via OR 99 & OR 238 at 690 N. 5th St. - Jacksonville 899-1829
Here is one of Oregon's most extraordinary shopping experiences. Regional premium wines, award-winning seasonal fruits, and choice-quality meats, cheeses, and desserts, plus locally crafted gifts,

24

fill a spacious showplace that exudes country charm. Visitors are invited to sample the wines, fruit, beef jerky, smoked sausage, and other gourmet items provided by Valley View Vineyard, Pinnacle Orchards, and Gary R. West Meats.

Specialty Shops

Bloomsbury Books
downtown at 266 E. Main St.   488-0029
This full-line bookstore features works by Northwestern authors. Background music and comfortable chairs contribute to the store's appeal.

★ **Lithia Creek Arts Gallery**
downtown at 31 Water St.   488-1028
All kinds of art work and handicrafts by Rogue River Valley artists are showcased in an inviting gallery that recently moved to a more spacious location.

Myrtlewood Chalet
downtown at 11 N. Main St.   482-5263
Assorted artistic and functional items made exclusively from myrtlewood—the prized hardwood of the Northwest—are showcased here.

Nimbus
downtown at 25 E. Main St.   482-3621
This large, intriguing store features many objects of art in pottery and glassware.

Northwest Nature Shop
downtown at 154 Oak St.   482-3241
A good selection of Northwestern books is a highlight in an engaging shop filled with nature-oriented gifts for all ages.

Paddington Station
downtown at 125 E. Main St.   482-1343
A large old building has been updated into a fascinating two-level gift shop crammed with regional foods and wines, gourmet cookware, and much more.

★ **Sound Place**
downtown at 199 E. Main St.   482-3633
Ashland was given another major cultural boost with the 1986 opening of a state-of-the-art showcase for audiophiles. New age tapes and records are plentiful, ingeniously displayed for easy access, and available for previewing at a well-furnished listener's island.

★ **Tudor Guild Gift Shop**
downtown at 15 S. Pioneer St.   482-0940
In the theater complex is a delightful shop that caters to lovers of Elizabethan lore with many books on Shakespeare and his plays, slides of Ashland productions, patterns for Elizabethan costumes, theater posters, and many Old English items. Closed Mon.

★ **The Von Grabill Collection**
  downtown at 199 E. Main St.   *488-1841*
One of the Northwest's finest showcases for jewelry, ceramics, rugs and other premium-quality handcrafted collectibles opened in the summer of 1986. A casually elegant coffee-and-dessert bar fits perfectly alongside the artistic displays and provides a comfortably detached view of activity on Main Street.

NIGHTLIFE

Live theater is **the** vital force in Ashland, and it is presented in new off-Shakespeare playhouses as well as on Festival stages during most nights of the year. Numerous restaurants, gourmet dessert places and lounges cater especially to after-theater crowds. In addition, several distinctive nightclubs provide a diversity of live entertainment for dancing or listening.

★ **Ashland Hills Inn**
  3 mi. SE on OR 66 at 2525 Ashland St.   *482-8310*
Live music for dancing is provided most nights in the resort's plush contemporary lounge.

Beau Club
  downtown at 347 E. Main St.   *482-4185*
A pool table in the back room, a jukebox, a back bar with stained glass murals, and comfortably padded stools and booths make this a good place to drop in for casual refreshments.

Cooks Tavern
  downtown at 66 E. Main St.   *482-5145*
This lively contemporary tavern offers disco dancing, pool, and electronic games in a rear area, and a good assortment of tap beers in a barroom enhanced by a brick fireplace.

★ **Jazmin's**
  downtown at 180 C St.   *488-0883*
An eclectic mixture of popular live entertainment is showcased in a large, handsome lounge with comfortable seating, a dance floor, and two wood sculpted seals suspended near a skylight. International specialties are served before the live music begins.

★ **Log Cabin Tavern**
  downtown at 41 N. Main St.   *482-9701*
Pool, foosball, and electronic games are provided, but the most notable feature in this handsome tavern with a distinctive back bar and wooden armchairs is that it exudes the elusive feeling of a classic "town bar."

★ **Mark Antony Hotel**
  downtown at 212 E. Main St.   *482-1721*
The landmark hotel's lobby is a favorite rendezvous for theater-goers and actors. A pianist entertains on weekend evenings. The adjoining Stage Door lounge is a comfortable place to enjoy periodic live entertainment, a quiet drink, and a Main Street view.

★ **New Playwright's Theatre**
  downtown at 31 Water St.   *482-9236*
An ambitious assortment of theatrical events is showcased year-round in an intimate theater by Lithia Creek that recently became an equity playhouse. The troupe's productions range from classical to avant-garde, and from tragedies to comedies and musicals.

★ **Oregon Cabaret Theatre**
  downtown at 241 Hargadine St.   *488-2902*
Cabaret-style entertainment is the lively feature of one of Ashland's most delightful playhouses. After two years of painstaking modification, a turn-of-the-century church (listed on the National Register of Historic Places) opened in 1986. Food, wine and beer are served to tables at several levels in the capacious auditorium. Spectacular stained glass windows, a chandelier, and theater organ contribute to the sophisticated ambiance.

★ **Varsity Backstage Theatre**
  downtown at 166 E. Main St.   *482-3321*
Behind the Varsity Theatre (reached by an adjoining walkway off Main Street) is a little cabaret/movie theater with regular and sofa-style seating. Classic films, live theater, poetry readings, and musicals are among the events offered in a candlelit auditorium.

RESTAURANTS

Local restaurants have flourished with Ashland's growing acclaim as a theater town. Some of the Northwest's most exciting and distinguished dining can be experienced in this burgeoning gourmet haven.

Andre's Restaurant
  1 mi. SE on OR 99 at 1209 Siskiyou Blvd.   *482-5092*
  B-L-D.   *Moderate*
Homestyle American dishes include some nice touches—big, sticky cinnamon rolls; biscuits with Oregon fruit preserves; etc. In this well-decorated coffee shop, customers have a choice of padded booths, tables and chairs, or counter service.

Arbor House
  5.5 mi. N via OR 99 at 103 W. Wagner St. - Talent   *535-6817*
  D only. Closed Tues.   *Moderate*
An around-the-world tour of various countries' specialties is the feature in a cozy converted cottage that reflects the spirit of the chef/owner.

★ **Archie's Pizza**
  downtown at 75 N. Main St.   *482-2989*
  D only. Plus L on Sat. & Sun.   *Low*
The area's best pizza recently moved to this downtown location. You get your choice of whole wheat or white flour pizzas, hand-thrown and topped with fresh ingredients. Well-executed murals, a fireplace and an upright piano distinguish the casual decor.

Ashland Hills Inn (Windmill's)
3 mi. SE on OR 66 at 2525 Ashland St.   *482-8310*
B-L-D.   *Moderate*
New owners since 1986 have updated the menu of the resort's Cascade restaurant to include such intriguing specialties as hazelnut chicken, coconut/beer batter shrimp, marinated sirloin with peppercorns, dill/tarragon bread, and homemade desserts. The gracious contemporary dining room still offers a tranquil picture window view of the countryside. A plush lounge and dining deck adjoin.

As You Like It
downtown at 58 E. Main St.   *482-5330*
B-L-D.   *Moderate*
Contemporary American dishes including homemade sweet rolls and pies are served to diners in well-padded booths in a neo-Elizabethan coffee shop that was recently spruced up.

★ **Back Porch BBQ**
downtown at 92 1/2 N. Main St.   *482-4131*
L-D.   *Moderate*
Delicious Texas-style barbecue, with meats smoked fresh daily on the premises and served with all the right trimmings, is an authentic down-home treat. It's served in a relaxed dining room indoors, but best enjoyed on the captivating multilevel patio by Lithia Creek, where patrons have a choice of sunny or tree-shaded tables. Late in the evening, the dining room serves as a nightclub with live music for dancing.

★ **Beasy's Back Room**
downtown at 139 E. Main St.   *482-2141*
D only.   *Moderate*
The steak's the thing here. It's sizzled in lemon butter, Texas hill-country style, and served in a capacious split-level dining room with a choice of booths or tables and chairs. The easygoing decor is a study in rough brick and wood texture, with some Old West bric-a-brac on the walls for accents.

Bella Union
15 mi. NW via OR 238 at 170 W. California - Jacksonville 899-1856
L-D. Sat. & Sun. brunch.   *Moderate*
American-style beef, chicken and fish dishes are offered, with a few innovations like chili in a loaf of bread. Local art adorns the walls in a dining room with a view of a vine-covered patio (used in summer). The adjoining barroom, updated to include comfortable pillow booths along one wall, still has much-trod wooden floorboards that suggest the building's century-long heritage.

The Breadboard
1 mi. N on OR 66 at 744 N. Main St.   *488-0295*
B-L. Closed Sun.   *Moderate*

The sourdough pancakes and homemade baked goods are very good in this cheerful little roadside cafe. A mountain view and a fireplace balance the picnic table decor.

Brother's
downtown at 95 N. Main St.   482-9671
B-L-D. Closed Mon.   *Moderate*

Fresh quality ingredients are used for an extensive assortment of dishes. Breakfast is served all day and homemade cinnamon rolls are a weekend highlight in this cozy, comfortable New York kosher-style deli/restaurant.

Cafe Med
14 mi. N via I-5 at 12 N. Riverside (at Main) - Medford   773-6088
B-L-D. No D on Mon. Closed Sun.   *Moderate*

An appetizing assortment of light dishes (tofu scramble, crepes, omelets, croissant sandwiches, mesquite-grilled chicken, etc.) has gotten Medford's most contemporary restaurant off to a good start. There is a comfortable neo-1950s cafe in front and a sleek dining room and lounge beyond.

Callahan's Lodge
10 mi. S on I-5 (Mt. Ashland exit) at 7100 OR 99   482-1299
D only. Closed Mon.   *Moderate*

Family-style dinners including a relish tray, soup, salad, spaghetti, an Italian pasta or steak entree, and dessert have appealed to visitors for forty years. Many windows provide high country views from the big casual dining rooms and from the adjoining lounge.

★ Change of Heart
downtown at 139 E. Main St.   488-0235
D only.   *Expensive*

Gourmet Continental cuisine is given a light disciplined touch for the half-dozen entrees served each evening in an elegant, romantic setting overlooking the Elizabethan theater, Main Street, and the mountains beyond.

★ Chata
4 mi. N at 1212 S. OR 99 - Talent   535-2575
D only. Closed Mon.-Tues. from Oct. to May. Closed Jan. Moderate

The Eastern European cuisine is some of the best of this style in the Northwest. All dishes including homemade breads and desserts are prepared with skill, discipline, and the freshest possible ingredients in a charming, casually elegant roadside house.

★ Chateaulin
downtown at 50 E. Main St.   482-2264
D only.   *Expensive*

Traditional and Nouvelle French dishes carefully prepared with seasonally fresh ingredients are among the best in town. The polished, wood-trimmed little bistro is inevitably crowded with theater-goers and others here to enjoy delicious food and sophisticated ambiance.

Clark Cottage Restaurant
.3 mi. SE on OR 99 at 568 E. Main St.   *482-2293*
B-L. D in summer only. Closed Mon.   *Moderate*
Casual homestyle cooking is offered by the new owners in a converted cottage with old-time decor jarringly updated by glass-topped tables.

Copper Skillet
2 mi. SE on OR 66 at 2270 Ashland St.   *482-2684*
B-L-D.   *Low*
Breakfasts include homemade cinnamon rolls or biscuits served with unlimited omelet variations. Pies are also homemade. The pleasant, family-oriented coffee shop is enhanced by many plants and picture window views of surrounding mountains.

4 J Country Cafe
5 mi. N at 103-C OR 99 - Talent
B-L.   *Low*
The desserts (try the pear crisp) and biscuits are good, and homemade, in a very plain little roadside cafe that recently changed ownership.

Geppeto's
downtown at 345 E. Main St.   *482-1138*
B-L-D.   *Moderate*
Italian foods are featured, along with some unusual specialties (chicken in currant sauce, scrambled eggs with pepperoncini and cheddar, pesto omelets), plus homemade cinnamon rolls and pies. This casual cafe is a long-time local favorite.

Gourmet Underground Deli
downtown at 125 E. Main St.   *488-2595*
B-L-D.   *Moderate*
Homemade desserts, pastries, and jams are highlights in a well-decorated deli in the basement under Paddington Station.

Greenleaf Grocery & Deli
downtown at 49 N. Main St.   *482-2808*
B-L-D.   *Moderate*
Cannelloni, calzone, and Greek spinach pie are house specialties on a long list of international soups, salads, sandwiches, and desserts. Beyond the deli case is a cheerful split-level dining room and two levels of decks overlooking Lithia Creek. Patrons can also have their selections specially packed to go.

★ **The Immigrant**
downtown at 19 N. First St.   *482-2547*
D only. Closed Mon.   *Moderate*
Food from Afghanistan is the promise, and the results are even better than the helpful descriptions. While everything here is exotic, it is an easily acquired taste because dishes are prepared fresh, from scratch, with authentic talent. The small dining room is casual and simply furnished with accents from the owner's homeland.

★ **Ingram's**
   14 mi. N via I-5 at 1124 Court St. - Medford   *779-0761*
   B-L. Closed Sun.   *Low*
   Here is an American classic. Delicious two or three egg omelets,
   big homemade raisin-filled cinnamon rolls, and enormous fluffy
   biscuits are among the reasons why this roadside cafe is especially
   popular for breakfast. But, it's usually jammed for lunch, too, with
   savvy natives lured by a tantalizing array of superb homemade
   pies. The decor is as uncomplicated as the homestyle meals.

★ **Jacksonville Inn**
   15 mi. NW at 175 E. California St. - Jacksonville   *899-1900*
   L-D.   *Moderate*
   Very complete multi-course American dinners are served amidst
   Victorian elegance in a romantic candlelit cellar or upstairs. The
   skillfully refurbished Civil War-era building also houses a shop with
   an excellent assortment of Oregon wines, and eight hotel rooms
   with Western antiques.

La Burrita
   downtown at 397 E. Main St.   *482-0813*
   D only. Closed Sun.   *Low*
   The house specialties—pork carnitas, fajitas, chicken marinated
   in lime and cilantro sauce, and cactus sauteed with eggs—suggest
   the range of offerings served amidst flamboyant south-of-the-border
   decor.

Marin's Cafe
   5.5 mi. N on OR 99 at 109 Talent Hwy. - Talent   *535-2911*
   B-L-D. Closed Sun.   *Low*
   All-American fare, including several homemade pies and cakes, is
   still offered by the new owners in a casual restaurant that has
   been a local favorite.

Michael's
   .3 mi. SE on OR 99 at 457 Siskiyou Blvd.   *482-9205*
   B-L-D. No D on Sun.   *Low*
   Breakfasts were recently added, and include some delicious
   surprises like bluehazel pancakes, and home potatoes that are some
   of the best anywhere. The handsome little wood-toned dining room
   and an adjoining patio with boulevard-and-mountain views are also
   the right settings for enjoying the featured old-fashioned
   hamburgers.

The Oak Knoll
   3.3 mi. SE at 3070 OR 66   *482-4312*
   L-D. Closed Mon.   *Moderate*
   Homestyle American cooking is featured in a casually elegant dining
   room overlooking the Oak Knoll Golf Course. A cozy view lounge
   adjoins.

★ **Omar's**
   1.2 mi. SE on OR 99 at 1380 Siskiyou Blvd.   *482-1281*
   L-D. No L on Sat. & Sun.   Moderate
The carefully prepared seafood, steak, and homemade desserts
served here have been noted for quality for more than forty years.
There are two casual dining areas and a cozy lounge in this local
landmark.

★ **Plymale Cottage**
   15 mi. NW via OR 99 & OR 238 at 180 N. Oregon - Jacksonville 899-8807
   L only. Closed Sun.   Moderate
Soups, salads, sandwiches and desserts are fresh and made from
scratch. Even the salad dressings, as well as the pies, are homemade.
A tiny Civil War-vintage cottage has been thoughtfully converted
into a cozy luncheon spot.

Tommy's the Restaurant
   downtown at 47 N. Main St.   *482-3556*
   B-L-D.   Moderate
A comprehensive selection of contemporary American fare is served
in a pleasant, wood-brick-and-plant-trimmed restaurant/bistro.

The Wild Plum
   14 mi. N via I-5 at 1528 Biddle Rd. - Medford   *772-5200*
   B-L-D.   Moderate
Humongous cinnamon rolls and sticky buns are featured along with
dozens of different kinds of pies in a big contemporary coffee shop.
This country-themed representative of a small Oregon chain is
oriented toward hungry families, and it's convenient to the freeway.

★ **The Winchester Inn**
   downtown at 35 S. Second St.   *488-1115*
   D only. Sun. brunch.   *Expensive*
Skillfully prepared Continental cuisine is served in a lavishly
restored Victorian mansion that also serves as a charming bed-
and-breakfast inn. Guests are treated to a colorful view of an
adjoining flower garden throughout summer.

LODGING

Good accommodations have proliferated in Ashland. In addition
to contemporary motels, a remarkable number of bed-and-breakfast
places have been added recently. Accommodations anywhere near
the festival complex are relatively expensive in summer. However,
there are still a few bargains on the main highway through town—
OR 99 and OR 66. Most places reduce their summer prices (shown
below) by about 15% in early fall, 30% in late fall and winter, and
15% in spring.

★ **Ashland Hills Windmill Inn**
   3 mi. SE on OR 66 at 2525 Ashland St.   *482-8310*
Ashland's largest accommodation is a contemporary resort hotel

with a big outdoor pool, whirlpool, putting green, two tennis courts and a jogging path, plus an elegant dining room and lounge. Each spacious, well-furnished room has a phone, cable color TV with movies, and a private balcony. For toll-free reservations, call: in Oregon (800)452-5315; outside (800)547-4747.

#271—corner, bay windows, fine mountain view,	K bed...$80
#372,#272,#371—corner, bay windows, fine view,	2 Q beds...$70
standard room—some view,	Q bed...$50
regular room—no windows,	Q bed...$40

Ashland Motel
.9 mi. SE on OR 99 at 1145 Siskiyou Blvd. 482-2561
An outdoor pool is a feature of this small motel. Each room has a phone and cable color TV with movies.

regular room—	Q bed...$43
regular room—	D bed...$33

Ashland's Main Street Inn
downtown at 142 N. Main St. 488-0969
A renovated Victorian house is now a small bed-and-breakfast inn. Each room has some period furnishings, a color TV and a private bath. A complimentary Continental breakfast is served to the room.

"Blue Room"—view downtown, bay window, semi-private deck,	D bed...$55
regular room—	D bed...$55

Bard's Inn - Best Western
downtown at 132 N. Main St. 482-0049
This newer motel has a convenient location, a small outdoor pool, and a whirlpool. Each well-furnished room has a phone and color TV with movies. For toll-free reservations, call: (800)528-1234.

regular room—	K bed...$66

Cedarwood Inn
2 mi. SE on OR 99 at 1801 Siskiyou Blvd. 488-2000
The outdoor pool is notably accented by palm trees in this modern motel. Other amenities include a whirlpool, sauna, and steam room. Each spacious room has a phone and cable color TV with movies. For toll-free reservations outside Oregon, call: (800)547-4141.

courtyard room—wet bar, deck or patio,	K bed...$54
regular room—	Q bed...$42

★ **Chanticleer Inn**
downtown at 120 Gresham St. 482-1919
A 1920s craftsman-style bungalow has been skillfully converted into one of Ashland's most charming bed-and-breakfast inns. Each room is nicely furnished with antiques and fresh flowers (from the inn's lovely gardens), and has a private bath. A full breakfast is served in a sunny dining room, or by request in bed.

"Aerie"—sunny corner room overlooking valley,	T & Q beds...$79
regular room—	Q bed...$69

Columbia Hotel
downtown at 262 1/2 E. Main St.   *482-3726*
A small refurbished turn-of-the-century hotel in the heart of town
is a **bargain.**
"large front room"—share bath,   2 D beds...$36
regular room—private bath,   2 D beds...$44
regular room—share bath,   D bed...$30
Curl Up Motel
3 mi. N at 50 Lowe Rd. by I-5   *482-4700*
This two-level motel was opened in 1985. Each of the spacious,
nicely furnished rooms has a phone and cable color TV.
#232,#231—end, extra window with mountain
view,   Q bed...$44
regular room—   Q bed...$38
Flagship Quality Inn
3 mi. SE on OR 66 at 2520 Ashland St.   *488-2330*
Mountains frame the view beyond the large outdoor pool in one
of Ashland's newest motels. Each comfortably furnished unit has
a bogus fireplace, a refrigerator, phone, and cable color TV. For
toll-free reservations, call: in Oregon (800)332-2330; outside
(800)334-2330.
deluxe unit—spacious, kitchen,   Q bed...$72
regular room—   Q bed...$52
Hersey House
.7 mi. N at 451 N. Main St.   *482-4563*
A turn-of-the-century house has been converted into a handsome
bed-and-breakfast inn surrounded by one of the prettiest gardens
in town. Breakfast is complimentary. Each of the four guest rooms
has attractive period furnishings and a private bath.
"The Eastlake Room"—windows on two sides,
view of Mt. Ashland,   Q bed...$65
regular room—   Q bed...$60
Jackson Hot Springs
2.3 mi. N at 2253 OR 99   *482-3776*
A large outdoor mineral pool is operated (in summer) free to guests.
Private (fee) rooms for hot mineral tub baths are available. Each
of the rustic old cabin units is a **bargain** with a complete kitchen
and private bath. Some have a color TV.
regular room—   D bed...$25
Knights Inn Motel
2.5 mi. SE on OR 66 at 2359 Ashland St.   *482-5111*
This modern **bargain** motel has an outdoor pool. Each nicely
furnished unit has a phone and cable color TV.
regular room—   Q bed...$30
Manor Motel
.7 mi. N at 476 N. Main St.   *482-2246*

This small, old motor court is a **bargain.** Each plainly furnished, small room has a cable color TV.

regular room— D bed...$30

★ **Mark Antony Hotel**
downtown at 212 E. Main St. 482-1721
Ashland's National Historic Landmark hotel in the heart of town was once the tallest building between San Francisco and Portland. Recently renovated, there is a large landscaped outdoor pool, plus a dining room with a grand chandelier, and a comfortable lounge. Each room has a phone, B/W TV, and a private bath. For toll-free reservations outside Oregon, call (800)544-5488.

#911—fine theater/mt. view from top (9th)
    floor corner, K bed...$60
#907,#905—corners, top floor, fine town views, Q bed...$55
regular room— D bed...$50

The Morical House
1.2 mi. N at 668 N. Main St. 482-2254
A century-old home was recently restored to reflect its Victorian heritage and to serve as a stylish bed-and-breakfast inn surrounded by an acre of lawns and gardens. Each room features some antiques and a private bath. A full complimentary breakfast is served.

#5—whole top (3rd) floor, good views, clawfoot tub, Q bed...$65
regular room— Q bed...$65

Palm Motel
.8 mi. SE on OR 99 at 1065 Siskiyou Blvd. 482-2636
This tiny old motel across from the college has a small outdoor pool. Each humbly furnished room has color TV.

regular room—small, Q bed...$36
regular room—tiny, D bed...$32

The Queen Anne
downtown at 125 N. Main St. 482-0220
A century-old Italianate house (listed on the National Register) was skillfully transformed (with no exterior changes) into a picturesque bed-and-breakfast inn in 1986. A Continental buffet breakfast is complimentary. Each of the plush, tastefully furnished rooms has a private bath.

"Queen Victoria Room"—bay window, clawfoot
                   tub, pedestal sink, Q bed...$65
regular room— Q bed...$65

★ **Romeo Inn**
.4 mi. S at 295 Idaho St. 488-0884
A charming Cape Cod-style house has been skillfully transformed into an outstanding bed-and-breakfast inn set amid noble trees on an expansive lawn. Landscaped grounds also include a tranquil outdoor pool and a whirlpool. Each spacious, beautifully furnished bedroom has a private bath. A full complimentary breakfast is served in the morning, and tea is offered in the afternoon.

#1—pvt. entrance, splendid fireplace, windows
    on 3 sides,   K bed...$77
regular room—   K bed...$73
★ **The Stone House**
downtown at 80 Hargadine St.   *482-9233*
From the hot tub behind the distinctive stone house, guests can actually see the actors on stage at the Elizabethan theater. Needless to say, with this feature, the three units in Ashland's best situated **bargain** lodgings are extremely popular in summer.
"Cottage"—refrigerator/wet bar, loft with   Q bed...$30
"Suite"—LR, kitchen,   K bed...$40
regular room—   Q bed...$25
Stratford Inn
.3 mi. SE at 555 Siskiyou Blvd.   *488-2151*
This handsome newer motel has a small indoor pool and whirlpool. Each well-furnished room has a phone and cable color TV. For toll-free reservations in Oregon, call (800)452-5319; elsewhere (800)547-4741.
regular room—   Q bed...$57
Super 8 Motel
2.5 mi. SE on OR 66 at 2350 Ashland St.   *482-8887*
An indoor pool with mountain view windows and an adjoining sunning patio is a feature of Ashland's representative (opened fall 1986) of the national motel chain. Each attractively furnished room has a phone and cable color TV with movies. For toll-free reservations, call (800)843-1991.
regular room—   Q bed...$38
Timbers Motel
1.3 mi. SE on OR 66 at 1450 Ashland St.   *482-4242*
This modern two-level motel has a small outdoor pool. Each spacious, nicely furnished room has a phone and cable color TV with movies.
regular room—   Q bed...$36
Valley Entrance Motel
1 mi. S on OR 99 at 1193 Siskiyou Blvd.   *482-2641*
This modern motel across from the college has a small outdoor pool. Each room offers standard motel decor, a phone and cable color TV.
regular room—   Q bed...$46
Vista-6 Motel
3 mi. SE via OR 66 at 535 Clover Lane   *482-4423*
The freeway adjoins this modern little single-level motel, which has a tiny outdoor pool. Each of the plain little **bargain** rooms has a cable color TV.
regular room—   Q bed...$26

★ **The Winchester Inn**
downtown at 35 S. Second St. *488-1113*
One of Ashland's most luxurious bed-and-breakfast inns is a large, carefully converted century-old home an easy stroll from the theaters. An elegant dining room is used for full complimentary breakfasts exclusively for guests. Fine dinners are served to the public as well. Each beautifully furnished room has a private bath.

"Sylvan Room"—fine view of adjacent oak trees, Q bed...$72
"Garden Room"—windows on 2 sides, Q bed...$72
regular room— Q bed...$72

The Woods House
.5 mi. N at 333 N. Main St. *488-1598*
A 1908 craftsman-style home and carriage house have been converted into a casually elegant bed-and-breakfast inn. Each beautifully decorated room has a private bath. A full breakfast is complimentary.

#6—upstairs, tree views, skylight above Q bed...$68
regular room— D bed...$48

CAMPGROUNDS

An outstanding assortment of water-related campgrounds are within a half hour drive of town. All of the best feature complete facilities in shady locations by a scenic lake or a hot springs pool.

Emigrant Lake Campground
5 mi. SE on OR 66 *776-7001*
The county operates a facility by an attractive little reservoir with lake swimming, boating, fishing, and water-skiing. Flush toilets and hot showers are available, but there are no hookups. Each site has a picnic table, fire ring, and grill. Some sites are tree-shaded. base rate...$6

★ **Howard Prairie Lake Resort**
24 mi. E via OR 66 on Hyatt Lake Rd. *482-1979*
This big, private facility includes a campground in a pine forest by a large reservoir. There is a beach, a boat ramp and dock, and rental boats. Lake swimming, boating, water-skiing, and fishing are popular. Flush toilets, hot showers (fee), and hookups are available. Each site has a picnic table and grill, and some are pine-shaded. There is a separate tenting area. base rate...$5

★ **Hyatt Lake**
20 mi. E: 16 mi. SE on OR 66 & 4 mi. N on Hyatt Lake Rd. *776-3728*
The Bureau of Land Management operates a small campground near a scenic little reservoir. Features include a boat ramp, lake swimming, boating, and fishing, plus marked nature trails. Cross-country skiing and snowmobile trails are attractions in winter. Flush toilets and hot showers are available, but there are no hookups. Each site has a picnic table and grill. base rate...$4

Jackson Hot Springs
2.3 mi. N at 2253 OR 99   *482-3776*
A private motel and trailer park adjoin an Olympic-sized outdoor pool. Sunbathing, swimming, and private hot mineral baths are featured. Flush and pit toilets, hot showers, and hookups are available. Each shaded closely spaced site has a picnic table. Grills are shared. There is a separate tenting area.   base rate...$6

SPECIAL EVENTS

★ **Oregon Shakespearean Festival** *downtown late Feb.-early Nov.*
Classic and contemporary plays are professionally staged outdoors in a uniquely beautiful replica of an Elizabethan Theater (1,200 seats) and indoors in the well-proportioned Angus Bowmer (600 seats) and intimate Black Swan (150 seats) theaters. Backstage tours can also be reserved.

Fourth of July   *downtown*   *4th of July*
Here is a classic old-fashioned fourth of July celebration with a parade; fiddlers' jamboree; food, crafts, and live entertainment in Lithia Park; and a fireworks display.

★ **The Peter Britt Music Festival** *Jacksonville   late July - late Aug.*
Two weeks of full-orchestra concerts are performed on the handsome Peter Britt Pavilion stage before outdoor audiences each evening, and during the day on selected weekends. Benches with backs are provided, but many patrons prefer to bring a blanket to the lovely wooded setting and lie on the grassy slope and stargaze while listening. A three-day bluegrass festival takes place in late July, and there is a three-day jazz festival in late August.

OTHER INFORMATION

Area Code: *503*
Zip Code: *97520*
Ashland Chamber of Commerce
  downtown at 110 E. Main St.   *482-3486*
Rogue River National Forest—Ashland Ranger
  2 mi. SE at 2200 Ashland St.   *482-3333*

Bandon, Oregon

Bandon is an enchanting blend of natural grandeur and urbane renewal. The Pacific Ocean is the western boundary. There, bluffs fall away to a smooth sandy beach accented by the Northwest's most fanciful array of natural rock statues. The most imposing have been given names like Table Rock and Face Rock. Bandon's northern boundary is the Coquille River. At the base of sheltering bluffs by a tiny harbor along the riverfront lies Old Town. This newly restored business district is once again flourishing with historic buildings housing a burgeoning assortment of distinctive shops and restaurants.

During normally sunny summer days, capacity crowds are attracted by an assortment of parks that provides all sorts of recreation opportunities along the beaches and river. Beachcombing, clamming, crabbing, sportfishing, hiking, horseback riding, bicycling, golf, and camping are popular. Even ocean swimming can be enjoyed by a hearty few in clear, relatively calm coves nearby. Temperatures are moderate year-round, so hot spells are rare. Freezes and snow are also unusual in town. But, during winter and spring, almost continuous rainstorms driven by strong winds provide a compelling spectacle. Gigantic surf smashing furiously against ragged coastal outcroppings attracts increasing numbers of visitors to the locally proclaimed "Storm Watching Capital of the World."

Settlers first arrived shortly before the Civil War. They may have been drawn by deposits of black sand gold, but they stayed because of abundant natural resources. Growth quickened a few decades later as demand for lumber, salmon, and livestock boomed. That era ended abruptly when a fire destroyed Bandon in 1914. The town was soon rebuilt, thanks in part to the area's expanding role as a vacation destination. Another fire devastated almost everything in 1936. This time, recovery was slow. Bandon survived, but languished until the 1980s, when—in a remarkably few years—it fulfilled its destiny as a major leisure destination.

Today, with a new boat basin, pier, and other skillfully designed facilities intended primarily for recreational uses, the Coquille River waterfront is more desirable than ever. In the adjoining Old Town, dilapidated buildings have been restored, and compatible new ones added. The whole district projects a newfound vitality. A cheese factory, cranberry candy factory, and fresh seafood markets attest to interest in local gourmet foods, just as in-town studios and showrooms, and numerous myrtlewood factories south of town, reflect a new preoccupation with arts and crafts. Quality and skill are also becoming apparent in restaurants which are now plentiful in and around Old Town. Handsome new lodgings are within a stroll of the historic district, and the area's first major resort recently opened near the ocean. As a final enticement for those interested in being as close to nature as possible, Oregon has provided large, complete campgrounds nearby in sheltered locations a stroll away from picturesque ocean beaches.

Elevation:

60 feet

Population (1980):

2,311

Population (1970):

1,832

Location:

230 miles Southwest of Portland

WEATHER PROFILE
Vokac Weather Rating

V.W.R.*		Jan.	Feb.	Mar.	Apr.	May	June	July	Aug.	Sep.	Oct.	Nov.	Dec.
Great	10												
Fine	9												
Very Good	8												
Good	7												
Moderate	6												
	5												
	4												
	3												
Adverse	2												
	1												
	0												

	Jan.	Feb.	Mar.	Apr.	May	June	July	Aug.	Sep.	Oct.	Nov.	Dec.
V.W.R.*	0	0	0	2	5	8	10	10	8	5	1	0
Temperature												
Ave. High	52	54	56	59	62	65	67	69	67	65	58	54
Ave. Low	38	39	39	41	45	49	50	50	48	45	42	39
Precipitation												
Inches Rain	9.6	7.6	6.9	3.7	2.5	1.4	0.4	0.5	1.6	5.1	8.0	9.1
Inches Snow	1	-	-	-	-	-	-	-	-	-	-	-

*V.W.R. = Vokac Weather Rating: probability of mild (warm & dry) weather on any given day.

Forecast

	V.W.R.*		Temperatures		Precipitation
			Daytime	Evening	
Jan.	0	Adverse	cool	chilly	continual downpours
Feb.	0	Adverse	cool	chilly	frequent downpours
Mar.	0	Adverse	cool	chilly	frequent downpours
Apr.	2	Adverse	cool	cool	frequent rainstorms
May	5	Moderate	cool	cool	frequent showers
June	8	Very Good	warm	cool	occasional showers
July	10	Great	warm	cool	negligible
Aug.	10	Great	warm	cool	negligible
Sep.	8	Very Good	warm	cool	occasional showers
Oct.	5	Moderate	warm	cool	frequent rainstorms
Nov.	1	Adverse	cool	cool	frequent downpours
Dec.	0	Adverse	cool	chilly	continual downpours

Summary

Bandon is sprinkled across a low headland where the Coquille River empties into the Pacific Ocean. Because of the moderating influence of the seaside location, there is seldom a frost of any consequence, and snowfalls are unusual. Continual downpours during the **winter** months keep people indoors, however, and contribute nearly half of the year's precipitation. **Spring** remains cool until June, but the weather is more usable because of diminishing rainfall. **Summer** is delightful, enhanced by the fact that this is the driest coastal section of the Pacific Northwest. An almost assured absence of rain and long warm days are ideal for comfortably exploring the enchanting beaches and countryside. Pleasant weather continues into early **fall**, but by Halloween, cool days and frequent rainstorms have returned.

ATTRACTIONS & DIVERSIONS

★ Bandon Beach
3.8 mi. SW on Beach Loop Rd.
Paved paths from the parking lot provide access to a nearby broad sandy beach punctuated by fantastic offshore rock formations.

★ Battle Rock Park
27 mi. S on US 101 - Port Orford
A splendid coastal panorama can be enjoyed from the parking lot above Battle Rock. Well-worn paths lead to a tiny stand of pines at the top of Battle Rock, a large picturesque seastack that becomes an island only at extreme high tide. A wide sandy beach extending to the south rewards beachcombers with close-up views of all sorts of tiny rocky islands and shoreline monoliths.

Boat Ride
Bold Duck Riverboat Trips
downtown at 1st St./Chicago Av.   347-3942
A two-level sternwheel riverboat leaves twice daily for a six-mile (two-hour) narrated cruise up the Coquille River. On weekends, three-hour dinner cruises are also offered.

★ Bullards Beach State Park
3 mi. N via US 101   347-2209
Miles of ocean beaches, low dunes, and the tranquil north bank along the final mile of the Coquille River before it empties into the ocean distinguish this park. Ocean and river fishing are popular, as are beachcombing and dune hikes. Shaded or sunny picnic facilities on grassy lawns are abundant, and a first-rate campground occupies a sheltered location near the river and ocean.

★ Cape Arago
25 mi. N via US 101 & West Beaver Hill Rd.   888-3732
Rocky nearshore islands are major breeding grounds for sea lions and harbor seals. A paved parking area half a mile before the cape affords the best views of sea lions, seals, and birds. You'll need binoculars to see them well from the northern observation point at Cape Arago, but you can hear them from anywhere in the vicinity. The southern observation deck provides a grand view of the coast to Bandon and beyond—on a clear day. Sunny picnic tables have been given picturesque locations on a bluff high above the sea.

Cape Blanco State Park
23 mi. S on US 101   332-2971
Here is the most westerly park in the continental United States. It includes Oregon's highest lighthouse (250 feet above the sea), a campground, a long section of near-wilderness beach, and a restored historical Victorian house.

★ **Coquille River Lighthouse**
   6 mi. N via US 101 & Bullards Beach Rd.
   This lighthouse was abandoned years ago, but the state has left the main room of the photogenic structure open, and posted interpretive signs.

Face Rock Viewpoint State Park
   .7 mi. SW on Beach Loop Rd.
   Face Rock is the unique highlight of this blufftop viewpoint, but the splendid panoramic seascape in both directions is also memorable.

Horseback Riding
Stone Butte Stables
   18 mi. S on US 101   *348-2525*
   Guided trail rides into the foothills near the Oregon coast take riders through forests, meadows, and streams to viewpoints with the Pacific Ocean in the distance. Horses can be reserved according to your schedule to be ready when you arrive for rides of up to three hours.

★ **Old Town**
   downtown at 2nd St./Chicago Av.   *347-9616*
   The heart of Bandon was established before the turn of the century on a choice level site by the Coquille River near the ocean. In the intervening decades, major fires periodically destroyed the downtown area. During the 1980s, it's coming back with more vitality than ever with arts and crafts shops, restaurants, night spots, lodgings, and sea-oriented businesses. Part of the "rebirth" includes a self-guided walking tour keyed to a series of historic photo displays that capture the essence of the way it was.

★ *Scenic Drive*
   for 6 mi. along Beach Loop Dr.
   Broad sandy beaches, picturesque seagirt rocks, grassy headlands, and low sand dunes are the compelling attractions along this scenic byway. State park viewpoints, beach accesses, and picnic sites abound.

★ **Shore Acres Arboretum**
   24 mi. N via US 101 & W. Beaver Hill Rd.   *888-3732*
   One of the Northwest's most beautiful public gardens has been fully restored, and is being skillfully maintained by the state. Begun near the turn of the century by Lewis Simpson, a lumber baron, the estate grounds include formal, Oriental, and rose gardens. A garden house and exquisitely landscaped pond remain from the original plan. If you are interested in natural rarities, note the bamboo and fan palms—one more than twenty feet high. These plants attest to the "banana belt" micro-climate of sheltered locations near the southern Oregon coast.

★ **South Slough National Estuarine Sanctuary**
  20 mi. N via US 101 & West Beaver Hill Rd.　　888-5558
  A recently expanded interpretive center 300 feet above the South Slough offers a panoramic overlook of the first national estuarial preserve. Well-marked hiking trails of various lengths provide access to the slough far below.

Sportfishing
Coquille River Charters, Inc.
  downtown at Bandon Boat Basin　　347-9406
  You have a choice of fishing for salmon or bottom fish in the ocean, or trolling and crabbing on the Coquille River. Bait, tackle, and crab rings are provided, and you can buy a one-day fishing license on board. Departures are normally in the early morning and afternoon daily.

★ **Sunset Bay State Park**
  23 mi. N via US 101 & W. Beaver Hill Rd.　　888-4902
  Here is a quintessential Pacific Northwest scene—a large cove with a curving beach of fine sand and calm water sheltered by forested bluffs. Beyond, dramatic rock outcroppings complete the picturesque scene. The shallow, protected bay is ideal for swimming. Picnic tables offer a choice of sun or shade in choice locations near the shoreline. Other facilities include a boat ramp, campground, and bathhouse.

★ **West Coast Game Park**
  6.5 mi. S on US 101　　347-3106
  For about twenty years, hundreds of free-roaming animals and birds (over seventy species) have been meeting people face-to-face here. This is the largest privately owned zoo where you can enjoy the experience of both observing and touching wild animals. It is also a fascinating place to observe how people and animals can communicate.

SHOPPING

A compact shopping district is once again flourishing in Old Town—the original heart of Bandon—along the Coquille River. Numerous galleries and studios, gift shops, and gourmet food outlets share picturesque historic buildings (and compatible newer ones) with restaurants and night spots. In addition, myrtlewood fans should not miss the concentration of factory/showrooms on the highway south of town.

Food Specialties
★ **Baghdad's**
  downtown at 170 E. 2nd St.　　347-3924
  Large, tasty cinnamon rolls are a highlight in a small full-line bakery. Pastries, etc. are served to go, or with coffee at tables surrounded by wall hangings, pottery, jewelry, and other works of art for sale.

★ **Bandon's Cheddar Cheese**   *347-2461*
    downtown at 2nd St./Grand Av.
Some of the West's finest cheddar (from mild to extra sharp) and jack cheeses are produced here. Samples are generously offered of each type of cheese. In the well-organized retail shop, visitors can taste, buy cheeses in various sizes, watch cheese being made through picture windows, or enjoy a video description of the cheese-making process. Other Oregon food specialties are also sold in the gift shop.

★ **Bandon Fish Market**   *347-4282*
    downtown at Bandon Boat Basin on 1st St.
Whatever fish and shellfish are in season are sold in this shaped-up little shop. Locally canned and smoked fish are also available. They do a thriving carryout business with their shrimp or crab croissants; seafood cocktails; chowder; and fish and chips.

★ **Cranberry Sweets Co.**   *347-2526*
    downtown at 1st St./Chicago Av.
One of Oregon's most distinctive and delicious regional specialties is the cranberry-flavored candies produced here. Samples of several of the many flavors (including the original favorite—cranberry nut) are offered. Delicious cranberry truffles and different styles of candy are also now made and sold here, along with Oregon food specialties by others.

★ **Misty Meadows**   *347-2575*
    5 mi. S on US 101
Here's the place to buy locally produced cranberry jellies and jams, along with blackberry, raspberry, blueberry, and other locally grown berries and fruits. The roadside stand is open daily.

Specialty Shops

Charleston Pottery   *347-4311*
    downtown at 110 E. 2nd St.
Here is a good example of the community's burgeoning cultural spirit. Artistic and functional pottery of all kinds is produced in a studio that can be viewed from the sales/display room in a converted historic building.

★ **The Continuum Center**   *347-4111*
    downtown at 175 E. 2nd St.
The selection of new age books, tapes, and records is the largest in Oregon, and there is an excellent assortment of children's books. The Center also features an exhibit that addresses immortality from the perspective of great minds down through the centuries.

The Country Merchant   *347-4341*
    downtown at 2nd St./Elmira Av.
Oregon wines and food products, coffees, teas, pottery, myrtlewood, and other gifts and clothing are attractively displayed in a big newer store where you can enjoy a free cup of gourmet coffee while browsing.

Myrtlewood

The most extraordinary concentration of myrtlewood factories and retail showrooms occurs along US 101 between three and seven miles south of town.

The Oregon Myrtlewood Factory
5.5 mi. S on US 101   *347-2500*
A good assortment of decorative and functional myrtlewood pieces and some unusual candles inlaid with shells are displayed in a retail outlet for an adjoining myrtlewood crafts factory. Tours are available.

Out of the Woods Myrtlewood
6.5 mi. S on US 101   *347-2721*
Unique free-form furniture and clocks are the specialty of this factory. Many are on display in an adjoining showroom. Burls and slabs of myrtlewood are also sold.

Pacific Myrtlewood
6.2 mi. S on US 101   *347-2200*
Round salad bowls, plates, serving dishes, and other functional myrtlewood pieces are created in the factory behind the showroom.

★ Seagull Myrtlewood
3 mi. S on US 101   *347-2248*
Resident craftsmen include a woodcarver and a glass sculptor. Visitors can watch them create works of art from rough myrtlewood slabs and molten glass. A large and varied display of aesthetic wood and glass pieces is sold in this roadside factory/showroom.

Zumwalt's Myrtlewood Factory
5.7 mi. S on US 101   *347-3654*
A good selection of the round pieces (dishes, bowls, etc.) made from myrtlewood in the rear of the shop are on display with assorted decorative works produced locally.

★ Northwest Collectors Gallery
6.3 mi. S on US 101   *347-9332*
A large, woodcrafted, hunting lodge-style building became one of the Northwest's most handsome galleries recently. Quality paintings and other wall hangings, sculptures in wood and metal, and intricate small art objects distinguish this outstanding showcase for regional artists. Visitors are invited to enjoy coffee and cookies and to listen to new age music while browsing.

★ 230 Second Street Gallery
downtown at 230 2nd St.   *347-4133*
The premium-quality art and crafts exhibited here reflect the ability of local and regional artists and craftsmen to capture the essence of the area's natural grandeur in aesthetic creations. Wall hangings, sculpture, woven furnishings, and jewelry are all shown to maximum advantage in a large and appealing gallery.

NIGHTLIFE

After dark, it's usually peaceful and quiet in Bandon. In Old Town, however, cultural events are frequently presented at Harbor Hall, and a cluster of casual lounges offers legal gambling and other games, plus live music for dancing on weekends.

Christopher's
downtown at 2nd St./Fillmore Av.   347-4151
There may be live music and dancing on weekends, and legal gambling and pool happen nightly in a sprawling, pecky cedar-walled tavern with two iron fireplaces and a massive myrtlewood bar.

★ **Harbor Hall**
downtown at 210 E. 2nd St.   347-9712
This multipurpose auditorium provides music, live theater, films, lectures, and workshops at different times throughout the year. It is "the" performing arts and meeting center of Bandon.

The Inn at Face Rock ·
2.6 mi. SW at 3225 Beach Loop Dr.   347-9441
A pianist occasionally plays on weekends in the resort's stylish and cozy lounge. As an added attraction, patrons get a picture window view of surf breaking on a sandy beach.

Lloyd's Lounge
downtown on 2nd St.   347-9987
A big dance floor is popular when there's live entertainment (on weekends) in Bandon's biggest night spot. Other features include pool, legal gambling, pinball machines, and a jukebox, and you can belly-up to a massive polished-chestnut bar.

Quarterdeck Lounge
.4 mi. S at 300 US 101   347-9024
Legal gambling is featured in a spacious room comfortably outfitted with padded booths and chairs around a large hooded wood-burning fireplace.

RESTAURANTS

Several restaurants have opened in Bandon in recent years, including two of the best on the southern coast. Homestyle preparation and use of fresh local seafoods and produce distinguish a growing number of dining places. A few dining rooms have views of the ocean or river.

★ **Andrea's Old Town Cafe**
downtown at 160 Baltimore Av.   347-3022
B-L-D.   *Moderate*
Bandon's most famous restaurant is one of the best on the southern Oregon coast. Almost everything is prepared with skill from scratch. Local fruits and vegetables, seafoods (especially crab), and lamb

are emphasized on the short, ever-changing dinner menu, and the baked goods are homemade. The works of local artists are displayed in a casual wood-toned dining room accented by green growing plants.

★ **Bandon Boatworks**
.8 mi. W on S. Jetty Rd.   347-2111
L-D. Closed Mon.   *Moderate*
Local fresh seafoods, fruits, and vegetables are used to create some of the area's finest dishes. For example, the homemade cranberry bread, and the baked fresh salmon, can be sensational when they're available. The little salad bar, stocked with choice fresh vegetables and fruits, is a good alternative to too-thick clam chowder. The wood-toned upstairs dining room is the most romantic in town. Each of the ten tables is set with linen and roses and has a 270° panoramic view of the beach, harbor, and picturesque lighthouse.

Chicago Street Eatery
downtown at 130 Chicago St.   347-4215
L-D.   *Moderate*
Fresh Italian foods with a flair are featured. For example, a bowl of popcorn might be brought to the table when you sit down, and pizza-by-the-slice may be garnished with an orange segment. The quality of preparation is uneven, but it can be very good. Booths are set with linen in the tiny dining room.

Christopher's
downtown at 2nd St./Fillmore Av.   347-4151
L-D.   *Low*
Conventional seafoods and a few beef and chicken dishes are offered, along with homemade desserts. One of the simply furnished dining rooms has an iron stove. A lounge adjoins.

Eat 'n Station
downtown at 635 2nd St.   347-9615
B-L-D. Closed Sun.   *Low*
Uninspired breakfasts are served all day, and there is a salad bar in this very plain, family-oriented restaurant.

Fraser's Restaurant
.4 mi. S on US 101   347-3141
B-L-D.   *Low*
Delicious homemade ice cream in several flavors is the highlight—not the homemade pies ordinaire — in this popular short order restaurant. An interesting "Bandon mural" adorns the no-frills dining room. A lounge adjoins.

★ **Hurry Back**
23 mi. N via US 101 at 100 Commercial - Coos Bay   267-3933
B-L-D. No D on Sun.   *Moderate*
The splendid homemade pies (lemon chiffon, French apple, etc.),

cheesecake, and cakes (chocolate truffle, carrot, etc.) are worth a long drive by any true believer in decadent desserts. More wholesome, yet also delicious, are the homemade breads, soups, fresh garden salads, and local seafood—all skillfully prepared with first-rate fresh ingredients. In Coos Bay's top-rated restaurant, the desserts are on display, there is a tiny lunch counter, and wood tables and chairs match the handcrafted wood-trimmed interior.

The Inn at Face Rock
2.6 mi. SW at 3225 Beach Loop Dr.   *347-9441*
B-L-D.   *Moderate*
The menu is conventional, but the view is extraordinary. From the resort's casually elegant dining room, guests can watch surf breaking on a sandy beach where a tiny stream empties into the ocean.

Lloyd's Restaurant & Lounge
downtown on 2nd St.   *347-9987*
B-L-D.   *Low*
Breakfast is served all day, and the menu is oriented toward American-style fast foods in a no-frills restaurant adjoining a lounge.

Minute Cafe
downtown at 145 E. 2nd St.   *347-2707*
B-L-D.   *Low*
Here's the best bet in town for an early breakfast, with all kinds of omelets, and fine cinnamon rolls from the bakery across the street. In addition to hearty American dishes, a salad bar, and homemade pies, Szechwan-style food is served Wed.-Fri. nights. The tiny dining room and lunch counter is comfortably homespun, and an adjoining patio is also used when weather permits.

★ **The Portside Restaurant**
20 mi. N via US 101 at the Boat Basin - Charleston   *888-5544*
L-D. Sun. brunch.   *Moderate*
The owner's fishing boat provides local fresh halibut, salmon, and bottom fish in season, and the restaurant is only a few miles from a large oyster farm. For a tasty change from thick clam chowder, try the oyster stew or bouillabaisse (the house specialty). Well-prepared entrees are broiled, poached, and sauteed—as well as fried. Diners are seated in a large, comfortably furnished room where stylish wood trim is used to frame an expansive window wall view of the harbor.

Three Gables Restaurant
1.3 mi. SW on Beach Loop Rd./11th St.   *347-2649*
B-L-D. No D on Fri. Closed Sat.   *Moderate*
In addition to an eclectic assortment of chicken, fish, and steak dishes, a soup-and-salad bar and homemade desserts are available in this casual, family-oriented restaurant with some ocean view.

The Truculent Oyster Restaurant
27 mi. S on US 101 - Port Orford   332-9461
L-D.   Moderate
Fresh oysters and steamer clams are the specialty. These and other
seafoods, the best in Port Orford, are served in comfortably
furnished rooms with wood-toned nautical atmosphere.

The Wheelhouse
downtown at Chicago Av./1st St.   347-9331
L-D.   Moderate
The portions of seafood, Oregon lamb, chicken, and beef are
generous, but the preparation is uninspired. In a two-level dining
room that opened in 1986, tables are set with linen, grass placemats,
and fresh flowers. Diners have a view of the boat harbor across
the street.

LODGING

There are relatively few places to stay in Bandon, and most have
opened in the last three years. Standard motels predominate, and
there are some bargains (even in summer). A full range of lodgings,
from resort to bed-and-breakfast, are sprinkled along the coast
and river. Rates are usually reduced at least 20% apart from summer.

Bandon Beach Motel
1.3 mi. SW on Beach Loop Dr. at 1110 11th St. SW   347-2103
Some of the units in this **bargain** motel have a view of Bandon
Beach. Each simply furnished room has cable color TV.
  regular room—no view,   Q bed...$28

Bandon Wayside Motel
.7 mi. E on OR 42-S   347-3421
The new owners are doing a nice job of refurbishing and maintaining
this older **bargain** motel. Each of the small, simply furnished rooms
has a B/W TV.
  regular room—   D bed...$22

Caprice Motel
.6 mi. S on US 101   347-3208
Most of the units in this modern, single-level motel are set back
from the highway. Each has a phone and cable color TV with movies.
  regular room—   Q bed...$35

Harbor View Motel
downtown at 355 2nd St. (Box 1409)   347-4417
The best Bandon views are from the rooms in this motel, which
was built in 1985. In addition to a panoramic backdrop that includes
the historic Old Town district and harbor, each well-furnished unit
has a refrigerator, phone, and cable color TV with movies. A
Continental breakfast is complimentary.
  #38,#31—top floor, end rooms with extra
           window, small private balcony, fine
           view from   K bed...$52

#28,#21—end rooms, extra window, fine view from   Q bed...$48
   regular room—no view,   Q bed...$36

★ **The Inn at Face Rock**
  2.6 mi. SW at 3225 Beach Loop Dr.   *347-9441*

Bandon's first resort opened during the 1980s on a bluff across the highway from a superb ocean beach. In addition to a stylish view restaurant and lounge, a 9-hole (fee) golf course adjoins. Each spacious, handsomely furnished unit has a phone and cable color TV.
  second floor suite—1 BR, fireplace, kitchenette,
                private deck with good
                   ocean view,   Q bed...$90
  regular room—meadow/trees view,   K bed...$43

La Kris Motel
  .3 mi. S on US 101 at 9th St. (Box 252)   *347-3610*

This small, single-level motel has a phone and cable color TV in each of the rooms.
  regular room—   Q bed...$32

Lamplighter Motel
  .7 mi. E at junction US 101/OR 42S   *347-4477*

This modern single-level motel has nicely furnished rooms with a phone and cable color TV.
  regular room—   Q bed...$32

Lighthouse Bed and Breakfast
  .4 mi. W at 650 Jetty Rd. SW (Box 24)   *347-9316*

A plush, contemporary residence on the river overlooking the lighthouse and ocean is now the finest bed-and-breakfast inn in Bandon. It's a short walk (or use a complimentary bicycle) to either the beach or Old Town after the hearty complimentary breakfast.
  deluxe room—greenhouse-bath and whirlpool,
                view toward Old Town,   K bed...$65
  regular room—fine view of sunsets at the jetty,   Q bed...$55

Old Town Guest House
  downtown at 370 1st St.   *347-9632*

There are only two units, but they are on the second floor of a newer building across the street from the Boat Harbor. Each has a semi-private deck, skylight, and cable color TV with movies.
  #1—kitchen, harbor view, loft with   Q bed...$47
  regular room—harbor view,   Q bed...$35

Sunset Motel
  1.8 mi. SW at 755 Beach Loop Dr. (Box 373)   *347-2453*

Some of the units in this newer **bargain** motel are built into a slope facing the ruggedly beautiful rocks along Bandon's spectacular beach. Each well-furnished unit has a phone and cable color TV.
  #17—studio, kitchen, fireplace, semi-private
            deck, splendid ocean view,   2 D beds...$50
  regular room—small, no view,   D bed...$27

Table Rock Motel
1.2 mi. SW on Beach Loop Dr.   347-2700
This well-maintained old single-level motel has some no-frills
bargain rooms, some larger units with kitchens, and some distant
ocean views.
regular room—small, no view,   D bed...$25

CAMPGROUNDS

Two campgrounds with complete facilities are beautifully sited near
the ocean north of town.

★ **Bullards Beach State Park**
3 mi. N on US 101   347-3501
The state operates a sheltered campground approximately a mile
from a long ocean beach backed by low grassy dunes. It also adjoins
the mouth of the Coquille River. Shore fishing and beachcombing
are popular. Hot showers, flush toilets, and full hookups are
available. Each well-spaced grassy site is tree-shaded, and has a
picnic table and fire ring. For toll-free reservations in Oregon, call
(800)452-5687. Non-Oregonians add $2 surcharge to base
rate.   base rate...$7

★ **Sunset Bay State Park**
23 mi. N via US 101 & W. Beaver Hill Rd.   888-4902
Oregon operates a superb campground in a forest a stroll inland
from tranquil Sunset Bay beach, and a scenic hike from Shore
Acres—the coast's most spectacular gardens. Flush toilets, hot
showers, and full hookups are available. Each of the spacious grassy
sites is pine-shaded, and has a picnic table and fire ring. For toll-
free reservations in Oregon, call (800)452-5687. Non-Oregonians
add $2 surcharge to base rate.   base rate...$6

SPECIAL EVENT

★ **Cranberry Festival**   *in and around town*   *mid-September*
A lot of activities are crammed into this three-day celebration of
Bandon's most distinctive crop. Highlights include cranberry food
fairs, harvest exhibits, and historical exhibits; plus a parade, queen's
coronation and ball, arts and crafts fairs, and a barbecue in the
park.

OTHER INFORMATION

Area Code: *503*
Zip Code: *97411*
Bandon Chamber of Commerce
downtown at 2nd St./Chicago Av. (Box 1515)   347-9616

Bend, Oregon

Bend is the heart of a year-round recreation wonderland. Nearby, majestic glacier-clad peaks of the central Cascade Range tower over an evergreen forest. A seemingly endless assortment of crystal-clear lakes and streams grace the sylvan landscape. Symmetrical cinder cones, lava tubes and flows, and other bizarre remnants of recent volcanism also punctuate the unspoiled countryside.

Coupled with these dramatic surroundings is a surprisingly pleasant four season climate. Winters are relatively mild in town. But, heavy snowfall is close by on Mt. Bachelor, where ideal conditions for both downhill and cross-country skiing have fostered the finest snow sports complex in the Pacific Northwest. In spring, skiing remains excellent on the mountain even after warm weather begins to attract crowds to golf courses, tennis courts, swimming pools, and other outdoor recreation facilities in Bend. Summer is the area's busiest season, when uniformly warm and sunny weather attracts throngs of visitors to a remarkable diversity of outdoor recreation opportunities.

The town's name is attributed to an early immigrant who said "Farewell, Bend!" as he reluctantly continued westward across the Deschutes River that runs through town. The lush pine forest and the good water at this bend in the river were the first that pioneers from the east saw after hundreds of miles of dry, open prairie. Although the initial exploration of the area was by John C. Fremont in the

1840s, Farewell Bend wasn't founded until 1900. (Postal authorities soon dropped the "Farewell.") A railroad arrived in 1911 and lumber milling became the dominant industry. Meanwhile, as roads and recreation equipment improved, Bend gradually developed as a tourist destination. With the recent completion of several major resort complexes in and near town, and the development of a superb skiing complex highlighted by a lift to the top of beautiful Mt. Bachelor, Bend's ultimate destiny as a year-round leisure center is being fulfilled.

Today, a bend of the Deschutes River is showcased in one of the West's loveliest parks. The center of town is only a block away. An increasing number of distinctive specialty shops and galleries, restaurants, lounges, and theaters have settled into the compact district which has recently been outfitted with a wealth of public improvements. Colorful landscaping, eye-catching supergraphics, a minipark with a major water sculpture, and one of the most whimsical statues anywhere have helped to restore downtown Bend to preeminence following a decline caused by years of rampant shopping center development. Accommodations both in and around town are plentiful. Choices range from one of the West's largest selections of budget motels to some of the most lavish resorts anywhere. Many of the best facilities feature picturesque riverside locations and views of distant volcanic peaks. Lakeside and riverfront campgrounds are also numerous in the forests near town.

Elevation:

  3,630 feet

Population (1980):

  17,263

Population (1970):

  13,710

Location:

  160 miles Southeast
  of Portland

WEATHER PROFILE

Vokac Weather Rating

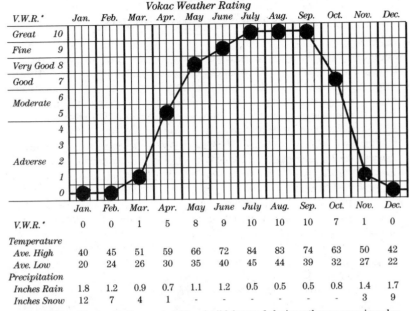

V.W.R.*	Jan.	Feb.	Mar.	Apr.	May	June	July	Aug.	Sep.	Oct.	Nov.	Dec.
V.W.R.*	0	0	1	5	8	9	10	10	10	7	1	0
Temperature												
Ave. High	40	45	51	59	66	72	84	83	74	63	50	42
Ave. Low	20	24	26	30	35	40	45	44	39	32	27	22
Precipitation												
Inches Rain	1.8	1.2	0.9	0.7	1.1	1.2	0.5	0.5	0.5	0.8	1.4	1.7
Inches Snow	12	7	4	1	-	-	-	-	-	-	3	9

*V.W.R. = Vokac Weather Rating: probability of mild (warm & dry) weather on any given day.

Forecast

	V.W.R.*	Temperatures Daytime	Evening	Precipitation
Jan.	0 Adverse	chilly	cold	occasional snow flurries
Feb.	0 Adverse	chilly	chilly	occasional snow flurries
Mar.	1 Adverse	cool	chilly	infrequent snow flurries/showers
Apr.	5 Moderate	cool	chilly	infrequent showers
May	8 Very Good	warm	cool	infrequent showers
June	9 Fine	warm	cool	infrequent showers
July	10 Great	hot	cool	negligible
Aug.	10 Great	hot	cool	negligible
Sep.	10 Great	warm	cool	negligible
Oct.	7 Good	cool	chilly	infrequent showers
Nov.	1 Adverse	cool	chilly	infrequent showers/snow flurries
Dec.	0 Adverse	chilly	cold	occasional snow flurries

Summary

Bend straddles the Deschutes River on a vast pine-forested plain accented by volcanic hills and distant glacier-capped peaks. The rugged grandeur of the setting, matched by a surprisingly mild four season climate, has resulted in one of the West's most desirable year-round playgrounds. In **winter**, bitter cold or heavy snowstorms are rare. Instead, days are typically chilly, but sunny. While occasional snowfalls are relatively light in town, they are heavy enough on nearby Mt. Bachelor to support the Northwest's finest winter sports complex. **Spring** arrives with cool temperatures that increase rapidly. Warm days begin in May. Light sportswear is appropriate in town while good skiing continues through spring on the mountain. **Summer** is splendid, with dry, warm-to-hot days balanced by inevitably cool evenings. Brisk sunny weather in early **fall** contributes to carefree enjoyment of all kinds of outdoor recreation through Halloween.

ATTRACTIONS & DIVERSIONS

★ *Bicycling*

Scenic, relatively level terrain abounds in the pine forests around Bend. Two bicycle paths with a combined distance of more than nine miles start downtown and extend westward to recreation areas. Many additional miles of picturesque separated bikeways are available to guests and bicycle renters at Sunriver Resort. Bicycles can be rented by the hour or longer at:

Century Cycles *.6 mi. W at 1135 NW Galveston Av.* *389-4224*
Sunriver Village Mall *16 mi. SW off US 97 - Sunriver* *593-8214*

Boat Rentals

★ **Sunriver Marina**
19 mi. S off US 97 - Sunriver *593-2161*

For nearly forty miles, the crystal-clear Deschutes River meanders slowly through luxuriant forests and meadows. Canoes may be rented here by the hour or longer, and downstream pickups can be arranged.

★ **Cascade Lakes**
start 25 mi. SW via Century Drive Hwy.

Dozens of small, clear lakes are nestled in a vast pine forest near the base of glacier-shrouded volcanic peaks along a thirty mile section of the Century Drive Highway (a 100-mile paved loop). Cultus and Elk Lakes are the most picturesque and best developed, with rustic resorts, launching ramps, sandy beaches, swimming areas, picnic facilities, and campgrounds.

★ **Cove Palisades State Park**
39 mi. N off US 97 *546-3412*

One of central Oregon's most popular parks borders the southern shore of Lake Billy Chinook near the confluence of the Crooked and Deschutes Rivers. Volcanic cliffs tower above narrow watery fingers that stretch back to shaded campgrounds, picnic and swimming areas, and a marina (546-3521 for reservations) where visitors can rent catamarans and motorboats. Fishing and water-skiing are also popular on the reservoir.

★ **Deschutes National Forest**
S & W of town *388-5664*

This giant forest includes Century Drive—a 100-mile paved scenic loop past some of the Northwest's finest peaks and lakes; several notable volcanic areas; parts of the Mt. Jefferson, Mt. Washington, Three Sisters, and the Diamond Peak wilderness areas; and the state's biggest winter sports facility—the Mt. Bachelor Ski Area. A good system of paved and dirt roads is backed by hundreds of miles of trails. The Pacific Crest National Scenic Trail lies along part of the western boundary of the forest. Hiking, backpacking, horseback and pack trips, boating, fishing, swimming, river running, and camping are popular. All kinds of snow sports are enjoyed in winter. Information and maps may be obtained at the Supervisor's Office in town.

★ **Drake Park**
downtown on Riverside Blvd.
Pine-shaded lawns slope to a placid stretch of the Deschutes River and frame splendid views of distant peaks. This is an enchanting place for a picnic by the heart of town. Canoeing is also popular. A half mile downstream is another picturesque haven, Pioneer Park, with shaded lawns, rock gardens, and flower beds by the river.

Golf
Bend Golf and Country Club
3.5 mi. S at 20399 Murphy Rd.   *382-7437*
This attractively landscaped, private 18-hole golf course does allow visitor play. A pro shop, club and cart rentals, and a restaurant and lounge are available.

★ **Sunriver Resort**
16 mi. SW off US 97 - Sunriver   *593-1221*
Two scenic 18-hole championship courses have been built into broad meadows and forests near the Deschutes River. All facilities are open to the public, including a pro shop, driving range, putting green, club and cart rentals, plus view restaurants and a lounge.

★ *Hiking*
Crystal-clear lakes, streams, and waterfalls are shaded by luxuriant pine forests beneath glacier-capped peaks to the west of town. To the east, eerie lava formations of every kind invite exploration. In this setting are hiking trails for every adventurous spirit. In town, two places rent and sell clothes and gear suitable for hiking and backpacking, and they sell detailed U.S.G.S. topographic maps of the area:

Mountain Supply of Oregon *.9 mi. N at 2104 NE Division*   *388-0688*
Tri-Mountain Sports   *downtown at 815 NW Wall St.*   *382-8330*

★ *Horseback Riding*
Several area stables rent horses by the hour or longer. Some will also arrange extended pack trips into the national forest wilderness areas. For information and reservations, contact:

High Cascade Stables   *25 mi. NW - Sisters*   *549-4972*
Inn of the Seventh Mountain *7 mi. SW on Century Dr. Hwy.* *389-9458*
Lake Creek Lodge (unguided, too) *25 mi. NW - Sisters* *595-6158*
Sunriver Resort   *16 mi. SW off US 97 - Sunriver*   *593-1221*

★ **Lava Lands**
12 mi. S on US 97   *382-5668*
The Lava Lands Visitor Center has automated displays and slide shows describing the remarkable geology of the area. There are also interpretive trails. A road winds to the top of Lava Butte, a cinder cone more than 500 feet high, just north of the center.

At the top, an observation tower rewards visitors with breathtaking panoramic views of the central Cascades. About 1.5 miles south, across the highway, another paved road leads to the lava river caves, where the highlight is a lava tunnel a mile long. Lanterns may be rented. There are also ice-filled caves. Two miles further south on US 97 and east on Forest Road 195 is the eerie lava cast forest, a fascinating collection of tree molds—or casts—which were formed when flowing molten lava surrounded and destroyed living trees some 6,000 years ago. It can be viewed from a mile-long paved interpretive trail.

Library
downtown at 507 NW Wall St.   388-6677

The Deschutes County Library is a modern facility with upholstered chairs in a spacious, well-stocked periodical reading area. Closed Sun.

★ Metolius River Recreation Area
35 mi. NW: 31 mi. on US 20 & 4 mi. on (paved) Camp Sherman Rd.

A river abruptly appears out of the side of a pine-shaded hill by the end of a paved trail from a well-marked parking lot/picnic area. The Metolius River flows crystal-clear for a distance of about ten miles. It is one of the nation's most popular fly-fishing-only streams with a variety of trout, plus kokanee. Several cabin complexes, a campground, and a general store line the banks of this picturesque stream in a ponderosa pine forest.

★ Newberry Crater
39 mi. S: 25 mi. S on US 97 & 14 mi. E on Forest Rd. 2129

Within the caldera (giant crater) of an enormous volcano that collapsed upon itself are waterfalls, streams, and two pretty little lakes. Boat ramps and rentals, campgrounds, rustic resorts, and hiking trails have been provided. A magnificent panoramic view is enjoyed from the easily reached summit of Paulina Peak. One of the world's largest obsidian (volcanic glass) flows is accessed by a short interpretive trail.

★ Oregon High Desert Museum
7 mi. S on US 97   382-4754

The cultural and natural history of the arid region of central and eastern Oregon is the focus of an impressive "living museum" opened in 1982. Among unusual features, visitors experience a variety of different tactile sensations at "touch tables," and they are encouraged to take part in demonstrations like wool-carding, and grinding corn with an ancient mano. There are several buildings in addition to the large orientation center, including a Forestry Learning Center where a tree's entire root system dangles dramatically overhead. A highlight among wildlife exhibits is an otter pond with both underwater and den viewing areas.

Bend, Oregon

★ **Pilot Butte State Park**
1 mi. E on US 20
A paved road circles up symmetrical slopes to the summit of an extinct cinder cone. There, visitors have a 360° unobstructed view across town to all of central Oregon, including most of the majestic volcanic peaks of the central Cascade Range.

★ *River Running*
Several river guide services offer two hour, all day, or longer rafting trips on the river near town, and on other nearby streams, during the summer. All equipment and meals are provided for scenic, whitewater, and moonlight trips. For information and reservations, contact:

The Factory Outlet (sells/rents rafts) *3 mi. S at 61297 S. US 97* 389-6070
Hunter Expeditions   (guided trips)   389-8370
Inn of the Seventh Mountain   (guided trips)   382-8711
Sun Country Tours   (guided trips)   382-6277

★ **Sisters**   923-5191
21 mi. NW on US 20
Deep in a ponderosa pine forest on a broad valley floor is a bustling little community that has decided to recapture some of its own past. Behind turn-of-the-century frontier-town facades are a growing number of Western-themed specialty shops, nightspots, and restaurants.

Warm Water Features

★ **Juniper Aquatic Center**   389-7665
.6 mi. E at 800 NE 6th St.
Big adjoining indoor and outdoor pools are the centerpieces of an imposing recreation complex that also includes a sauna, whirlpool, and gym. In the surrounding park are tennis courts and attractively sited picnic tables.

★ **Sunriver Resort**   593-1221
16 mi. SW via US 97 - Sunriver
An Olympic-sized pool with a beautifully furnished scenic deck is open to the public daily.

Winter Sports

★ **Mt. Bachelor**   382-8334
22 mi. SW on Century Drive Hwy.
With a chairlift to the mountain's 9,065-foot summit, the vertical rise in Oregon's biggest skiing complex is 3,100 feet and the longest run is several miles. There are eleven chairlifts, including five triple chairs. All services, facilities, and rentals are available at the base for both downhill and cross-country skiing. Restaurant and lounge facilities have been provided at the area, but no lodgings. The skiing season is one of the longest in the West—from November into June. For toll-free information (outside Oregon) call (800)547-6858.

★ **Mt. Bachelor Nordic Sports Center**
22 mi. SW on Century Drive Hwy.   *382-8334*
Nearly thirty miles of cross-country ski touring trails are marked, patrolled, and maintained in quiet forests and meadows at the base of Mt. Bachelor. Rentals and classes are offered from November through May.

Snowmobiling
The Yamaha Store
.8 mi. N at 1841 NW Division St.   *389-8686*
Snowmobiles can be rented here, and guided tours are available.

SHOPPING

The compact downtown, centered just east of the Deschutes River and Drake Park, still primarily serves the everyday needs of residents and visitors. But, a growing number of galleries, gourmet food stores, and other distinctive shops are opting for this especially picturesque location instead of the big ordinary shopping malls that have proliferated in recent years.

Food Specialties
The Bagel Stop
.6 mi. E at 661 NE Greenwood Av.   *389-3363*
A good variety of bagels is made at this small shop daily. Closed Sun.-Mon.

Coffee & Company
downtown at 835 NW Wall St.   *389-6464*
Coffee and tea are served by the glass at a coffee bar. All kinds of coffee beans and products, teas, and Italian sodas are sold.

★ **Flanagan's**
downtown at 801 NW Wall St.   *382-1455*
Many flavors and styles of premium ice cream are served in an inviting parlor with greenery and wooden tables and chairs. Other desserts and sandwiches are also served here, or to go.

Gelato Primo
downtown at 839 NW Wall St.   *388-4981*
This small takeout shop features a half dozen flavors (including some unusual flavors in season such as huckleberry) of gelato, and several kinds of cookies.

★ **La Strada**
downtown at 114 NW Minnesota Av.   *388-0222*
A good selection of wines and well-made pate, pastas, calzone, and filo triangles qualify this appealing little shop as a gourmet takeout. Selected wine tasting is usually available. Closed Sun.-Mon.

Pastries by Hans
downtown at 915 NW Wall St.   *389-9700*
The variety of Continental pastries is impressive, but the preparation is usually uninspired in this bright and cheerful main street bakery. Closed Sun.-Mon.

★ **Pi's**
   1.1 mi. SE on US 97 at 325A SE Wilson Av.   *382-2747*
Outstanding breakfast and dessert pastries (including Old World Kolaches) are served to go, or with their own excellent coffee blend at booths or tables in the area's best bakery.

★ **Strictly Oregon Tasting Room**
   .9 mi. N at 2205 NE Division St.   *388-2766*
One of Bend's best culinary attractions opened in late 1986 in a fascinating little roadside building (don't miss a close look at the outside walls). Wines made by Hood River Winery and other premium Northwest wineries are generously offered for tastings and available for sale. Open 12-8 (approx.) daily.

★ **Sweetheart Donuts**
   .4 mi. E on US 97 at 505 NE 3rd St.   *389-7928*
Donuts in a remarkable assortment of flavors, textures, fillings, and styles are sold fresh daily in this tantalizing tiny takeout shop.

Specialty Shops

★ **Blue Sky Gallery**
   downtown at 147 NW Minnesota Av.   *388-1877*
Bend's finest arts and crafts gallery is a well-organized showcase for premium-quality wall hangings, ceramics, wood carvings, and jewelry. Most of the pieces reflect the special flavor or scenic grandeur of the area and were created by regional talent. Closed Sun.

Blue Spruce Pottery
   4.4 mi. S at 61021 S. US 97   *389-7745*
Handcrafted pottery items ranging from dinner sets to sinks are showcased in a roadside studio/gallery. Closed Sun.

The Book Barn
   downtown at 124 NW Minnesota Av.   *389-4589*
A good selection of books about the Northwest is an attraction of this well-organized two-level store. A rental library, collectible older books, and background music are also featured.

★ **Marty's**
   downtown at 61 NW Oregon Av.   *388-1122*
One of the Northwest's most distinctive jewelry and gift stores uses a jungle of luxuriant greenery as a backdrop for handsome showcases displaying the latest styles of jewelry, clocks, crystal chandeliers, and other distinctive art objects. Closed Sun.

Sunbird Gallery at Frame Design
   downtown at 836 NW Wall St.   *389-9196*
A good display of photographic wall hangings and bins filled with Northwestern and other scenic prints are features in this picture and frame shop. Ceramic and hardwood objects of art are also well displayed. Closed Sun.-Mon.

★ **Sunriver Village Mall**
   16 mi. SW via US 97 - Sunriver   593-2166
   Nestled unobtrusively in a ponderosa pine forest near the resort's
   lodge is a surprisingly complete specialty shopping complex. Well-
   landscaped wood-toned buildings house a first-rate bookshop,
   Northwest specialty foods store, bakery, sporting goods store, and
   others.

NIGHTLIFE

There is plenty of life after dark in Bend. Places to go for the fun
of it are scattered, but numerous. In addition to live entertainment,
music, and dancing, Bend has the distinction of being one of the
West's cinema centers, both in number of theaters and in unusual
facilities offered to patrons.

★ **B-Bar-B Saloon**
   21 mi. NW on US 20 - Sisters   549-2601
   Sisters' major contribution to area nightlife offers occasional live
   music for dancing, plus pool tables and darts anytime in a rough-
   wood saloon with a fireplace.

★ **Black Butte Ranch**
   29 mi. NW on US 20 - Sisters   595-6211
   Luxurious ranch-style decor enhances the resort's dramatic two-
   level lounge at the top of the main lodge building. Features include
   a piano, a large stone fireplace, and a deck with memorable views
   of the Cascades beyond the well-tended grounds.

Brandy's
   .8 mi. SE on US 97 at 197 NE 3rd St.   382-2687
   Live entertainment for dancing and listening is especially popular
   on weekends in this big and stylish cabaret with an adjoining
   restaurant.

China Ranch Bar
   1.3 mi. SE on US 97 at 1005 SE 3rd St.   389-5888
   Country/western and other live music for dancing is featured
   several nights weekly in a large casual bar next to a Chinese
   restaurant.

Community Theatre of the Cascades
   downtown at 134 NW Greenwood Av.   389-0803
   Live theatrical productions with an emphasis on comedies or
   musicals are offered in a comfortably furnished little playhouse.
   Closed Mon.-Wed.

Grover's Pub
   1.3 mi. SE at 939 SE 2nd St.   382-3754
   One area is dominated by pool tables, electronic darts, and
   comfortable sofas before a large open fireplace. A conventional
   salad bar and basic booths outfit the other area, where good pizza
   and short order fare are served, along with several tap beers.

★ **Inn of the Seventh Mountain**
   7 mi. SW at 18575 Century Drive Hwy.   *382-8711*
Live entertainment and dancing are offered several nights each
week in the resort's strikingly contemporary lounge. A delightful
fireplace/conversation area is the centerpiece.

★ **Pat & Mike's Cinema Restaurant**
   downtown at 918 NW Wall St.   *382-5006*
Film classics are screened and there are occasional live concerts
and comedy shows in an intimate theater/dining room where
patrons sit at tables with director's chairs, or in traditional theater
seats. Light meals, tap beer, wine, and homemade desserts can
be enjoyed with the movie or performance, or in an adjoining dining
area. Closed Sun.

Players
   downtown at 61 NW Oregon Av.   *388-1288*
Handsome neo-art deco surroundings help make Players a favorite
place for meeting people anytime. The comfortably furnished wood-
and-brass-trimmed lounge has seating on two levels and an island
bar with premium beer on tap. A fine new restaurant adjoins.

★ **Riverhouse Motor Inn**
   1.3 mi. N at 3075 N. US 97   *389-3111*
At the Riverhouse Lounge, live music and dancing are featured
nightly in a spacious room with plush contemporary furnishings.
Outside, drinks are served on an umbrella-shaded view deck
overlooking the picturesque Deschutes River.

★ **Sunriver Lodge**
   16 mi. SW via US 97 - Sunriver   *593-1221*
The Owl's Nest features live entertainment for dancing on weekends.
Plush seating and fine views of the Cascades make this a special
place for conversation and a drink during daylight hours, too.

RESTAURANTS

Bend has recently become a regional gourmet capital. Hearty,
homestyle American fare is still abundantly available, but diners
can now enjoy illustrious examples of New American, Old World,
Continental, and Oriental cuisines as well. Restaurant decor ranges
from plain and casual to elegant and formal. Several dining rooms
also offer picture window views of the area's natural grandeur.

Beef and Brew
   1.4 mi. N at 3194 N. US 97   *389-4646*
   D only.   *Moderate*
Steaks and prime rib are featured, along with a salad bar, in Bend's
representative of a popular small chain.

Black Butte Ranch
   29 mi. NW on US 20 - Sisters   *595-6211*
   B-L-D.   *Moderate*
Updated American treatments of steaks and seafoods complement

the contemporary ranch-style decor of the resort's dining room. Tall picture windows frame views across a lake to the Cascades.

★ **Black Forest Inn**
1 mi. SW at 25 SW 14th St.   389-3138
D only.   *Low*
German specialties, delicious homemade pastries, and Continental dishes are served in a charming Bavarian-style dinner house.

★ **The Brass Wok**
1.3 mi. N at 3081 N. US 97   389-7579
L-D. No L on Sat.   *Moderate*
Flavorful Szechwan, Hunan, and Mandarin-style dishes are skillfully prepared in traditional Chinese woks, and served in generous quantities in pleasingly understated Oriental surroundings complemented by plush booths and classical and new age background music.

★ **Cafe South Center**
2.5 mi. SE at 61419 S. US 97   382-5946
B-L-D. No D on Sun. & Mon.   *Low*
The homemade biscuits and cinnamon rolls are delicious when fresh. They accompany generous portions of all-American dishes made from scratch. Green plants and padded wood booth decor provide one of the most pleasant settings in the area for breakfast.

Chata
downtown at 118 NW Greenwood   389-1878
D only. Closed Sun.   *Moderate*
Eastern European specialties and stuffed pizzas are featured in a new restaurant (related to the Chata near Ashland). The colorful decor includes patterned rugs, unusual wall hangings, many plants, and a choice of padded-wood booths or chairs with pillow cushions at tables set with linens and lamps.

★ **Cyrano Restaurant**
downtown at 119 NW Minnesota St.   389-6276
B-L-D. No D on Mon. Closed Sun.   *Moderate*
Five-course international gourmet dinners, skillfully prepared from fresh ingredients, are served on Fri.-Sat. nights. During the rest of the week, updated dishes derived from regional American to Mexican and Chinese specialties are served in spiffy neo-art deco dining rooms outfitted in hardwood-and-brass trim and bentwood chairs.

D & D Bar & Grill
downtown at 927 NW Bond St.   382-4592
B-L-D.   *Low*
The homemade biscuits are big and fluffy, and most of the other dishes are fresh and generously served in a rustic little grill in the front room of a tavern.

★ **Dandy's Drive-Inn**
.6 mi. NE on US 97 at 1334 NE 3rd St.   382-6141
L-D. Closed Sun.   Low
For nostalgia buffs, the 1950s linger on in this classic burger-and-milkshakes drive-in. The food and prices are better than in latter-day mass-produced versions, and the service—by roller skating car hops—is a real pleasure.

Demetri's Greek Restaurant
1.1 mi. NE on US 97 at 1841 NE 3rd St.   388-0383
B-L-D. Closed Mon.   Moderate
An ambitious assortment of Greek specialties, pizzas, pastas, and American dishes is served in a comfortable contemporary coffee shop that opened in early 1986.

Frieda's Restaurant
.7 mi. N at 1955 NE Division St.   382-3790
L-D. No L on Sat. Closed Sun.   Moderate
American dishes and some German specialties such as potato pancakes and apple fritters are served in this long-established, casual dinner house.

The Gallery
21 mi. NW on US 20 at 230 Cascade - Sisters   549-2631
B-L-D   Moderate
Homemade pies are featured on an all-American menu in a comfortable coffee shop with a fireplace, Old West wall hangings, and an arresting gun collection.

The Gandy Dancer
downtown at 942 NW Wall St.   389-2068
B-L.   Low
Here is the only place in town for light-and-fluffy steamed egg omelets prepared with your choice of ingredients. A casual coffee shop has been built into a large upstairs space with rough-brick walls and skylights.

★ **Giuseppe's**
downtown at 932 NW Bond St.   389-8899
L-D. No L on Sat. & Sun.   Moderate
New in 1986, this classy little Italian trattoria offers an appealing range of skillfully prepared Italian dishes including hand-rolled pastas made fresh daily. Guests are served in a cheerful wood-and-plant-trimmed front room with a handsome hardwood bar, or in cozy, private padded wood booths.

Hotel Sisters
21 mi. NW on US 20 at Cascade & Fir - Sisters   549-7427
B-L-D. No B in winter.   Moderate
A historic hotel has been skillfully converted into a restaurant where barbecued ribs are a highlight among American specialties. Diners have a choice of wooden booths downstairs, or a table in one of the converted bedrooms upstairs. An inviting Western-style saloon adjoins.

Juniper Cafe
1.1 mi. SE on US 97 at 603 SE 3rd St.   *382-6873*
B-L   *Low*
Plentiful plain homestyle breakfasts are the highlights in this unassuming, locally popular cafe that has been here since 1959.

★ **Kayo's**
2.4 mi. S at 61363 S. US 97   *389-1400*
D only.   *Moderate*
Classic Continental specialties are given stylish personalized updates, and presented in a handsome dining room where each table is outfitted with full linen, fresh flowers, and candles.

★ **Le Bistro**
.5 mi. NE on US 97 at 1203 NE 3rd St.   *389-7274*
D only. Closed Sun.-Mon.   *Moderate*
Skillfully prepared French cuisine is served in a remodeled church that now sports casually elegant sidewalk cafe atmosphere with an open kitchen. Downstairs, an intimate lounge has been comfortably furnished in posh velvet-backed armchairs.

McKenzie's Ore House
downtown at 1033 NW Bond St.   *388-3891*
D only.   *Moderate*
Steaks are the dependable specialty among contemporary American dishes offered with a soup and salad bar in this comfortably furnished wood-toned restaurant. The lounge has live music on weekends.

★ **Orion's Restaurant**
3 mi. SE at 61525 Fargo Lane   *388-3990*
D only.   *Expensive*
New York steak is featured in half a dozen different styles, and there is an interesting assortment of other steaks plus seafoods on an updated Continental menu. The comfortable contemporary dining room overlooks lush green fairways.

Papandrea's
.7 mi. N at 1854 NE Division St.   *388-4645*
L-D.   *Moderate*
Fresh ingredients and crust from dough made fresh daily are still offered in Bend's representative of a burgeoning pizza parlor chain that started in nearby Sisters (Cascade Av. on east side of downtown) and is now contemplating major expansion. Bend's outlet recently took over a historic building. Booths and tables are on several levels in an airy interior surrounded by old-brick walls with interesting wall hangings.

Pine Tavern Restaurant
downtown at 967 NW Brooks St.   *382-5581*
L-D. Sun. brunch.   *Moderate*
Sourdough scones are a specialty served with American dishes in

a beautifully refurbished historical landmark. Two giant living ponderosa pines have been incorporated into the decor of the main dining room. Diners have an outstanding view of Drake Park and the Deschutes River.

★ **Players**
downtown at 61 NW Oregon Av.　　　　　*382-5859*
L-D.　　　　　*Moderate*
Since the summer of 1986, Bend has had a temple for true believers in New American cuisine. Virtually everything is made from scratch here from the freshest/best available ingredients. The chef's skill and flair are present in dishes as diverse as red onion soup, blueberry chicken, or Grand Marnier/chocolate pie. The dining rooms are showcases of neo-art deco decor—exposed pipes and skylights, soft-colored walls hung with spot-lighted brass instruments, etc. A very popular lounge adjoins.

The Riverhouse Motor Inn
1.3 mi. N at 3075 N. US 97　　　　　*389-3111*
B-L-D.　　　　　*Moderate*
Continental dishes are served in a handsome contemporary dining room overlooking the Deschutes River. A lounge and deck with a fine view adjoin the hotel's restaurant.

Roszak's
.6 mi. NE on US 97 at 1230 NE 3rd St.　　　　　*382-3173*
L-D. No L on Sat. Closed Sun.　　　　　*Moderate*
Prime rib is a highlight on a contemporary menu in this modish restaurant.

★ **Sandi's Soups**
downtown at 930 NW Brooks　　　　　*389-7385*
L only. Closed Sat.-Sun.　　　　　*Moderate*
This relatively new place is the kind of discovery that makes dining out a pleasure. Both the homemade soups and the fresh-baked bread served with it are outstanding. The tiny eat-in or carryout soup kitchen is tucked away by a parking lot next to Drake Park.

Snow Bunny Restaurant
.8 mi. W at 635 NW 14th St.　　　　　*389-3995*
B-L-D.　　　　　*Low*
Here's one of the best deals in town for breakfast. The homemade muffins and cinnamon rolls are tasty, and the assorted omelets, pancakes, french toast, and other dishes come in generous portions. Blue and white decor also contribute to the bright, cheerful spirit of this cozy cafe.

★ **Sunriver Lodge and Resort**
16 mi. SW off US 97 - Sunriver　　　　　*593-1221*
D only.　　　　　*Expensive*
The resort's main dining room (The Meadows) was thoroughly upgraded in 1986 to reflect management's intention to provide both

gourmet dining and a world-class setting. New American cuisine, emphasizing the finest and freshest available Northwestern produce, is expertly prepared, and presented amidst formal elegance in a spacious dining room with an inspiring view of landscaped grounds backed by snow-capped volcanic peaks. The Provision Co. offers moderately priced breakfasts, lunches, and dinners in an informal dining room with warm marketplace decor and a panoramic view.

Tumalo Emporium
6 mi. NW at 64619 US 20 — *382-2202*
L-D. Sun. brunch. — *Moderate*
Homestyle food is prepared for a short list of house specialties, and a conventional buffet is also displayed in a large, family-oriented restaurant furnished in Victorian rococo decor. A very comfortable Old Western-style piano bar is in the next room.

Victorian Pantry
.8 mi. W at 1404 NW Galveston Av. — *382-6411*
B-L. — *Moderate*
Homestyle dishes, including all kinds of mix-n-match omelet possibilities, are served with whole wheat scones or other pastries in a recycled house with booths and homey decor.

LODGING

There are plenty of places to stay. Most of the area's finest facilities are on the Deschutes River in or near town. One of the West's greatest concentrations of bargain motels lines 3rd Street (US 97) which is the main north-south highway through town. Most places reduce their rates by 15% or more apart from summer. A few increase their rates during the prime skiing season.

★ **Bend Riverside**
.4 mi. N at 1565 NW Hill St. — *389-2363*
A choice of motel rooms or condominium units is available in this big complex on a choice site by the Deschutes River next to Pioneer Park. Landscaped grounds include a large indoor pool, whirlpool, saunas, and a tennis court. Each spacious unit has a phone and cable color TV with movies. For toll-free reservations, call: in Oregon (800)452-6833; elsewhere in the Northwest (800)547-0892.
#258,#257,#253—in one-level building, superb
    falls/rapids view,   K bed...$44
#321—kitchen, gas fireplace, fine view over
    rapids/falls,   Murphy Q bed...$48
#238,#242,#237,#241—balcony, next to falls,
    kitchen, gas fireplace,Murphy Q bed...$48
regular room—   Q bed...$32

★ **Black Butte Ranch**
29 mi. NW on US 20 (Box 8000) - Black Butte Ranch 97759 595-6211
A small spring-fed lake in a high country meadow, surrounded

by a ponderosa pine forest ringed with tall peaks, is the picturesque site of an extraordinary resort. The lodge by the lake, and nearby condominium townhouses and private homes, were carefully sited to blend with the forest and maximize panoramic views. Recreation facilities include a large outdoor pool by the lake (plus three others for guests), whirlpools, saunas, a recreation center, and (for a fee) golf (two 18-hole courses), nineteen tennis courts, bicycles (18 miles of paths), horseback riding, and canoes. The handsome wood-toned lodge has a well-furnished dining room and lounge. Each attractively appointed unit has a phone, cable color TV, and a private deck. For toll-free reservations in Oregon, call (800)452-7455.

"lodge condominium"—1 BR, spacious, kitchen,
      fireplace, (many have)
      lake & mountain view,   Q bed...$90
"deluxe bedroom"—spacious, fireplace,   Q bed...$60
regular room—   Q bed...$45

Blue Spruce Motel
  3.9 mi. SE at 61265 S. US 97   *382-5491*
This old single-level **bargain** motel offers spacious, plain rooms with old-fashioned kitchenettes, a distant view of the Cascades, and cable color TV.
  regular room—   Q bed...$21

Cascade Lodge
  .9 mi. SE on US 97 at 420 SE 3rd St.   *382-2612*
An outdoor pool is a feature of this modern single-level **bargain** motel. Each room has a phone and cable color TV with movies.
  regular room—   Q bed...$28

Chaparral Motel
  1.5 mi. SE at 1300 S. US 97   *389-1448*
The highway is close by this modern little motel with an outdoor pool. Each **bargain** room has a phone and cable color TV.
  regular room—   Q bed...$22

Cimmaron Motel
  .8 mi. E on US 97 at 201 NE 3rd St.   *382-8282*
This is a newer **bargain** motel with an outdoor pool. Each room has a phone and cable color TV with movies.
  regular room—   Q bed...$27

City Center Motel
  downtown at 509 NE Franklin Av.   *382-5321*
This modest little **bargain** motel has plain rooms with cable B/W TV.
  regular room—   Q bed...$19

Entrada Lodge - Best Western
  4 mi. SW at 19221 Century Drive Hwy. (Box 975)   *382-4080*
A pine forest surrounds this appealing motel with an outdoor pool,

whirlpool, and sauna. Each well-furnished room has a phone and cable color TV with movies. For toll-free reservations, call (800)528-1234.

#32—end of single-level bldg., good view of Mt.

Bachelor,	Q bed...$45
regular room—	Q bed...$40

Hill Crest Motel

2.3 mi. SE at 61405 S. US 97   *389-5910*

In this little single-level **bargain** motel, each simply furnished room has a cable color TV with movies.

regular room—	Q bed...$22
regular room—	D bed...$20

Holiday Motel

1.2 mi. SE on US 97 at 880 SE 3rd St.   *382-4620*

An outdoor whirlpool is a feature of this single-level older **bargain** motel. Each small, plainly furnished room has a phone and cable color TV with movies.

regular room—	Q bed...$23

★ **Inn of the Seventh Mountain**

7 mi. SW on Century Drive Hwy. (Box 1207)   *382-8711*

One of Bend's largest resort hotel/condominium complexes has an extensive array of leisure facilities and services, including two large outdoor pools, whirlpools, saunas, seven tennis courts, a putting green, miniature golf, a recreation room, jogging and nature trails, and (for a fee) an outdoor roller/ice rink, rental bicycles, moped tours, guided river rafting, and guided horseback riding. There are also dining rooms and a lounge with live entertainment. Each well-furnished unit has a phone and cable color TV. For toll-free reservations in Oregon, call (800)452-6810; elsewhere (800)547-5668.

#719,#701—1 BR, kitchen, pressed-wood fireplace, balcony, mountain view,	Q bed...$102
#724,#706—deluxe room, private balcony, mt. view,	Q bed...$64
regular room—forest view,	Q bed...$44

Maverick Motel

.6 mi. E on US 97 at 437 NE 3rd St.   *382-7711*

An outdoor pool is available at this newer **bargain** motel. Each room has a phone and cable color TV with movies.

regular room—	Q bed...$27

Motel West

.5 mi. E at 228 NE Irving Av.   *389-5577*

In this newer **bargain** motel, each room has a phone and cable color TV.

regular room—	Q bed...$28

★ **Mt. Bachelor Village**

3 mi. SW at 19717 Mt. Bachelor Dr.   *389-5900*

On a bluff above the Deschutes River is an imposing condominium complex that includes a large outdoor pool, whirlpool, six tennis courts (two lighted), and a nature trail to the river. Each nicely decorated, spacious unit has a phone, color TV, kitchen, and a fireplace.

#244—2 BR suite, balcony, loft with Q beds, fine mountain views,	3 Q beds...$80
#144—1 BR suite, balcony, good views,	2 Q beds...$65
regular room—1 BR suite,	Q bed...$60

Pilot Butte Motor Inn
   downtown at 1236 NW Wall St.   382-1411
This older single-level **bargain** motel offers simply furnished rooms with a phone and cable color TV with movies.

regular room—	Q bed...$21

Plaza Motel
   .4 mi. N at 1430 NW Hill St.   382-1621
Across from Pioneer Park is an older single-level **bargain** motel. Each well-equipped room has a phone and cable color TV with movies.

regular room—	Q bed...$21

Poplar Motel
   .8 mi. SE on US 97 at 163 SE 3rd St.   382-6571
In this little old one-level **bargain** motel, each cozy, humble unit has cable color TV and a kitchen.

regular room—	Q bed...$15

Rainbow Motel
   .4 mi. E at 154 NE Franklin Av.   382-1821
This small single-level motel is a **bargain**. Each room has a phone and cable color TV with movies.

regular room—	Q bed...$21

Red Lion Motel
   .5 mi. E on US 97 at 849 NE 3rd St.   382-8384
This modern two-level motel by the highway has an outdoor pool and a whirlpool. There are no views worth noting, but each nicely furnished room has a phone and cable color TV with movies. For toll-free reservations, call (800)547-8010.

deluxe room—spacious,	K bed...$54
regular room—	Q bed...$41

★ **The Riverhouse Motor Inn**
   1.3 mi. N at 3075 N. US 97   389-3111
One of Bend's largest and finest lodgings is a contemporary hotel delightfully located by the Deschutes River. Amenities include a large scenic pool, whirlpool, and saunas, plus a fine Chinese dining room, a view dining room, and a lounge with entertainment. Each spacious, attractively furnished unit has a phone and cable color TV with movies. For toll-free reservations, call: in Oregon (800)452-6878; other Western states (800)547-3928.

#322,#324—in-room spa, fireplace, river view,
      pvt. balc.,   K bed...$69
#244,#243—fireplace, fine river view,   Q bed...$49
#223 thru #226—pvt. window wall & balc. over
      rapids,   2 Q beds...$49
"Spa Suite"—spacious, mirrored whirlpool room,
      wet bar, no view,   K waterbed...$95
regular room—no river view,   Q bed...$39
Royal Gateway Motel
.9 mi. SE on US 97 at 415 SE 3rd St.   *382-5631*
Each modest room in this modern single-level **bargain** motel has a phone and cable color TV with movies.
regular room—   Q bed...$24
regular room—   D bed...$23
Sonoma Lodge
1 mi. SE on US 97 at 450 SE 3rd St.   *382-4891*
This is a small modern **bargain** motel. Each room has a phone and cable color TV.
regular room—   Q bed...$21
Sportsman's Motel
2 mi. N at 3705 N. US 97   *382-2211*
An outdoor pool and whirlpool are features of this modern **bargain** motel. Each room has a phone and cable color TV with movies.
regular room—   Q bed...$26
regular room—   D bed...$24
★ **Sunriver Resort**
16 mi. SW via US 97 - Sunriver 97707   *593-1221*
One of the West's outstanding contemporary resorts is at the edge of a large meadow surrounded by a vast pine forest. Many of the lodge/condominium units have panoramic views of distant snow-capped peaks. A remarkable assortment of leisure facilities includes two large scenic outdoor pool complexes, several whirlpools, saunas, a recreation room, exercise room, hiking trails, dock and fishing on the Deschutes River, and (a fee for) five racquetball courts, bicycles (24 miles of paved scenic bikeways), golf (36 holes), twenty-two tennis courts (three indoors), horseback riding, and canoes. The Meadows is a posh dining room with a spectacular view, and there are several other restaurants, plus lounges with entertainment. Each spacious, handsomely appointed suite has a phone, cable color TV, a large stone fireplace, and a private deck. For toll-free reservations in Oregon, call (800)452-6874; elsewhere (800)547-3922.
#104,#110—fine meadow/mountain views,   K bed...$79
#208—good view,   K bed...$79
"suite condominium"—(some have) meadow/
      mountain views, kitchen,   2 T or K bed...$105
regular room—lodge bedroom,   2 T or K bed...$79

Westward Ho Motel
1.3 mi. SE on US 97 at 904 SE 3rd St.   *382-2111*
A large enclosed swimming pool and whirlpool are features of this modern **bargain** motel. Each nicely furnished room has a phone and cable color TV with movies.

#166—impressive stonework fireplace in full
     view of   Q bed...$34
regular room—   Q bed...$29

Woodstone Inn - Best Western
.6 mi. E at 721 NE 3rd St.   *382-1515*
New in 1986, this two-level motel has a large outdoor pool and a whirlpool. Each attractively furnished room has a phone and cable color TV with movies. For toll-free reservations, call (800)528-1234.

#129,#130—in-room whirlpool,   K bed...$65
regular room—   Q bed...$40

CAMPGROUNDS

Numerous campgrounds are in the forest west of town. The best of these offer primitive facilities on picturesque little lakes with all kinds of water and high country recreation. In addition, one of the West's finest campgrounds, beautifully sited by the Deschutes River near town, offers complete camping and recreation facilities in a luxuriously furnished park.

★ **Cultus Lake**
45 mi. SW via OR 46 & Forest Rd. 2025   *382-6922*
This Deschutes National Forest campground is located near a beautiful little high country lake in a lush pine forest. Boat launching and rental facilities are nearby. Swimming, fishing, boating water-skiing, and hiking are deservedly popular. There are pit toilets only— no showers or hookups. Each pine-shaded site has a picnic table and a fire area.   base rate...$4

★ **Elk Lake Recreation Area**
30 mi. W on OR 46   *382-6922*
This Deschutes National Forest facility is in a heavily wooded area by a spectacular snow-capped peak. Rental boats and a boat ramp are nearby, and swimming, fishing, and boating are enjoyed. There are pit toilets only—no showers or hookups. Many of the pine-shaded sites have a picnic table and fire area.   base rate...$5

★ **Tumalo State Park**
5.5 mi. NW via US 20 & County Rd.   *382-3586*
The state operates this superb facility by the pretty little Deschutes River. The beautifully landscaped park features a large picnic area by the river, grassy play areas, an outdoor theater, and nature trails in addition to a campground. Swimming and fishing in the river, and hiking, are popular. Flush toilets (B Loop), solar-powered

hot showers, and hookups are available. Each of the well-spaced, shady sites has a picnic table and fire grill/pit. Several sites are by the river. Non-Oregonians add $2 surcharge to base rate.

base rate...$6

SPECIAL EVENT

★ **Cascade Festival of Music**   *Drake Park*   *late June*
Shady lawns on the banks of the Deschutes River in Drake Park provide an idyllic setting for this week-long celebration of classical music. Programs include full symphonies, choral music, and American musical theater.

OTHER INFORMATION

Area Code: *503*
Zip Code: *97701*
Bend Chamber of Commerce
  downtown at 164 NW Hawthorne Av.   *382-3221*
Deschutes National Forest—Supervisor's Office
  1 mi. E at 1645 E. US 20   *388-2715*

Cannon Beach, Oregon

Cannon Beach is an artistic haven in a glorious coastal setting. Whitewashed and weathered-wood cottages and shops are surrounded by a captivating landscape. One of the world's largest free-standing monoliths—Haystack Rock—lies just beyond miles of broad "singing sands" beaches and low coastal dunes. Inland, a natural amphitheater of sylvan hills extends in a graceful curve to a massive seaward headland. State parks and forests that encircle the village assure preservation of the wealth of scenic attractions in the area, while providing an impressive variety of recreation opportunities.

During summer, beachcombing, clamming, shore fishing, horseback riding, hiking, and camping attract capacity crowds. Sunbathers flock on clear warm days, and ocean swimming and surfing are popular enough to justify lifeguards on the town's beaches. Temperatures are surprisingly moderate year-round. Freezes and snow are scarce. However, almost continuous rainstorms and the drama of wind-whipped storm surf provide a compelling spectacle throughout winter and spring. Increasing numbers of visitors come to experience the phenomenon—usually from the comfort of firelit oceanfront lodgings.

The attributes of this superb coastal setting were first admired by American explorers with the Lewis and Clark expedition of 1805. But, the potential for a townsite was ignored for nearly a century. The tiny village was named after a cannon loosed from the shipwrecked

Cannon Beach, Oregon

U.S. schooner "Shark" was hauled to high ground here in 1898. Settlement was very slow for many years, with an economy based almost exclusively on serving vacationers. Growth has accelerated since the 1960s, when increasing numbers of artists and craftsmen, attracted by the spectacular location, began to work and live here year-round.

Cannon Beach is still a village. The special kind of boom that has occurred recently has been one of quality, not quantity. The artistry of the residents is apparent everywhere. Outdoors, it is displayed in details of human-scaled architectural craftsmanship; in an abundance of flowers and carefully tended landscapes; and in memorable public sculptures. Within handsome wood-toned buildings, many studios and galleries display first-rate locally handcrafted products and artwork inspired by the setting. Other winsome shops feature Oregon-made gourmet food specialties. Restaurants are numerous, and a few of the newer places display culinary talent to match the lovely surroundings. Nightlife is scarce, atmospheric, and reflects the tranquility of the setting. Picture window views of memorable sunsets along this sublime section of the Oregon coast can be enjoyed in a couple of comfortable lounges. Accommodations range from carefully maintained tourist cabins that have been here for decades to luxurious contemporary ocean-view rooms in facilities loaded with amenities. All of the best lodgings (and campgrounds) are close to the beach, and several are also within an easy stroll of the center of town.

Elevation:

20 feet

Population (1980):

1,187

Population (1970):

779

Location:

80 miles Northwest
of Portland

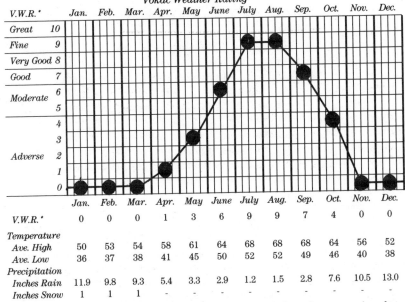

Cannon Beach, Oregon
WEATHER PROFILE
Vokac Weather Rating

V.W.R.*		Jan.	Feb.	Mar.	Apr.	May	June	July	Aug.	Sep.	Oct.	Nov.	Dec.
Great	10												
Fine	9												
Very Good	8												
Good	7												
Moderate	6 5												
	4 3												
Adverse	2 1												
	0												

	Jan.	Feb.	Mar.	Apr.	May	June	July	Aug.	Sep.	Oct.	Nov.	Dec.
V.W.R.*	0	0	0	1	3	6	9	9	7	4	0	0
Temperature												
Ave. High	50	53	54	58	61	64	68	68	68	64	56	52
Ave. Low	36	37	38	41	45	50	52	52	49	46	40	38
Precipitation												
Inches Rain	11.9	9.8	9.3	5.4	3.3	2.9	1.2	1.5	2.8	7.6	10.5	13.0
Inches Snow	1	1	1	-	-	-	-	-	-	-	-	-

*V.W.R. = Vokac Weather Rating: probability of mild (warm & dry) weather on any given day.

Forecast

	V.W.R.*		Temperatures		Precipitation
			Daytime	Evening	
Jan.	0	Adverse	cool	chilly	continual downpours
Feb.	0	Adverse	cool	chilly	continual rainstorms
Mar.	0	Adverse	cool	chilly	continual rainstorms
Apr.	1	Adverse	cool	chilly	continual rainstorms
May	3	Adverse	cool	cool	continual showers
June	6	Moderate	cool	cool	frequent showers
July	9	Fine	warm	cool	infrequent showers
Aug.	9	Fine	warm	cool	infrequent showers
Sep.	7	Good	warm	cool	frequent rainstorms
Oct.	4	Adverse	cool	cool	frequent downpours
Nov.	0	Adverse	cool	chilly	continual downpours
Dec.	0	Adverse	cool	chilly	continual downpours

Summary

Tiny ocean-fronting Cannon Beach is sequestered within a luxuriant pine-forested amphitheater dramatically anchored by a massive headland jutting into the Pacific Ocean north of town. Because of the tempering coastal influence, the area enjoys one of the longest growing seasons in the West outside of California while it endures one of the nation's heaviest annual rainfalls. **Winter** is uniformly cool and very wet. Snowfall is rare because the temperature seldom drops to freezing. Continual rainstorms, however, preclude casual enjoyment of outdoor recreation. **Spring** remains cool and damp with gradually increasing temperatures and diminishing rainfall through June. Fine weather finally arrives in **summer** when, for two very special months, warm days, cool evenings, and infrequent showers make exploring this wonderfully scenic hideaway easy. **Fall** is accompanied by the return of cool days, and frequent heavy rainstorms.

ATTRACTIONS & DIVERSIONS

★ **Bicycling**
Coastal highways and byways give bicyclists access to countryside that
is relatively gentle and remarkably scenic. Bicycles or three-wheeled
"brikes" may be rented by the hour or longer at these shops.
Manzanita Fun Merchants *.7 mi. S at 1235 S. Hemlock St.* 436-1880
Mike's Bike Shop *downtown at 248 N. Spruce St.*   436-1266
★ **Cannon Beach**
borders downtown on W side
One of the most magnificent beaches in the Northwest—or anywhere—
forms the town's three-mile-long western boundary. Above the broad
flat beach, low dunes of dry and powdery "singing sands" provide a
picturesque backdrop.
★ **Ecola State Park**
1 mi. N via Ecola Park Rd.   436-2844
This large natural park occupies most of the southern slopes of
Tillamook Head—the massive promontory between Cannon Beach
and Seaside. Several well-spaced picnic tables overlook breathtaking
coastline views from a pine-bordered highland meadow. Two
picturesque sandy beaches line the southern portion of the park's
nearly six miles of protected coastline. Rock fishing, tide pool
exploring, sunbathing, and surfing are popular. Hiking trails lead to
secluded beaches and coves, and to coastal overlooks where sea lion
and bird rookeries can be observed on offshore rocks. Tillamook Rock
Light, a century-old lighthouse abandoned in 1957, can also be seen
offshore.
★ **Haystack Rock**
.6 mi. S - just offshore
The third largest coastal monolith in the world rises 235 feet from the
surf adjacent to Cannon Beach. Its natural scenic beauty is a major
source of local pride. While the rookery and tide pools around the
base of the rock are protected, observing the small marine life that
abounds there is a favorite pastime.
★ **Horseback Riding**
Sea Ranch Stables   *.3 mi. N on Beach Loop*   436-2815
Guided rides along the beach or into the mountains are offered daily
from mid-May to mid-September.
Library
downtown on Hemlock St. near 1st St.
The Cannon Beach Library is housed in a contemporary wood-toned
building on the main street. A fireplace dominates a charming reading
area with an interesting display of oversized volumes, pictures, and
information about the town and region. Closed Sun.

★ **Manzanita Area**
  15 mi. S on US 101
  Where a broad sandy beach abuts Neahkahnie Mountain, the tiny village of Manzanita is developing as an artisans and sportsmens center. The picturesque main street includes several good restaurants, galleries, a bookstore, and an unusual nursery. Inland two miles, where US 101 crosses the picturesque Nehalem River, another appealing village has developed. Nehalem sports a few art galleries, antique shops, and restaurants, and (along with other tiny riverfront communities) caters to sportfishing. Nehalem Bay State Park occupies much of a large sandspit between the river and the ocean. It is a popular destination for fishermen, beachcombers, and campers.

★ **Oswald West State Park**
  10 mi. S on US 101   *238-7488*
  This state park memorializes the farsighted governor who, in 1912, preserved Oregon's coastal beaches for all of the people. An outstanding walk-in campground one-quarter mile from the parking lot provides tent sites set in a lush coastal rain forest. A sheltered cove and tide pools are a short walk beyond.

Winery
  Nehalem Bay Winery
  19 mi. SE: 18 mi. S via US 101 & 1 mi. E on OR 53   *368-5300*
  Fruit, berry, and grape wines are produced and sold in a building that was one of the original Tillamook cheese factories. The tasting room is open daily 10-5.

SHOPPING

A compact downtown area, centered along Hemlock Street just inland from the beach, is housed in a picturesque cluster of weathered-wood buildings. Collectively, the low-profile cottage-style architecture and numerous fanciful handcrafted touches reflect the town's artistic charm and intimate scale. Galleries and shops emphasizing locally produced fine arts and crafts in all media, plus stores specializing in regional gourmet foods, set the tone for this flourishing district.

Food Specialties

★ **Blue Heron French Cheese Factory**
  42 mi. S on US 101 - Tillamook   *842-8281*
  French-style brie cheese is produced, sold, and available for sampling here daily. A fine assortment of international cheeses is also featured, and samples are generously offered. Knudsen-Erath wines, jams, and other gourmet specialties are displayed, sampled, and sold.

★ **Bruce's Candy Kitchen**
  downtown at 256 N. Hemlock St.   *436-2641*
  A variety of fancy hand-dipped chocolates including some shaped like the famed "haystack" is made on the premises. Visitors can also watch saltwater taffy being made here, as it has for almost a quarter-century. All candies are sold to go, or they will be shipped anywhere.

★ **C & W Meats (Art and Dick's)**
34 mi. S on US 101 - Bay City   377-2231
Sausage, pepperoni, jerky, and smoked salmon are made and sold here
every day. Samples are provided on request.

★ **Cafe Gelato**
.7 mi. S at 1235 S. Hemlock St.   436-1537
Homemade gelato in an assortment of flavors, plus pastries and cakes,
are offered in this new shop. In Manzanita (194 Ladera Av.) is a branch
that serves the same fine gelato and pastries—and offers Sunday
brunch in a lovely alfresco garden setting.

★ **Cannon Beach Bakery**
downtown at 144 N. Hemlock St.   436-2592
Famous for its bread loaf in the shape of Haystack Rock, this
outstanding bakery offers a full line of fine breads, pastries, cookies,
and some unusual treats like Chinese fruit pockets. There are a few
tables, and coffee is available. Closed Tues.-Wed.

★ **Cannon Beach Cookie Company**
downtown at 239 N. Hemlock St.   436-2832
Fresh-baked cinnamon rolls, plus muffins, cookies, and other baked
specialties are sold, with hot cider or coffee, to go or to be enjoyed on a
bench facing main street.

Cannon Beach Seafood Co.
downtown at 123 S. Hemlock St.   436-2272
Fresh Dungeness crab and smoked salmon are specialties. The little
carryout shop also has a good selection of seasonally fresh and smoked
fish and shellfish, plus seafood cocktails.

★ **Hane's Bakerie**
1.9 mi. S at 3116 S. Hemlock St.
Delicious muffins, croissants, and other pastries and breads are
enticingly displayed in this small, new (in 1986) bakery. Closed Mon.

★ **Laurel's Cannon Beach Wine Shop**
downtown at 263 N. Hemlock St.   436-1666
Wines can be purchased by the taste, glass, or bottle in a
well-organized little shop full of premium wines of the Northwest
and elsewhere.

Mariner Market
downtown at 139 N. Hemlock St.   436-2442
In this unusual grocery store a checker board is set in a corner beside a
pot-bellied stove; a museum-load of memorabilia hangs overhead;
unique signwork and handcrafted furnishings are used throughout;
and books are sold along with magazines, newspapers—and groceries.

★ **Old Trapper Sausage**
42 mi. S on US 101 - Tillamook   842-2622
Jerky, pepperoni, beer sausage, and other fine beef sausages are made,
displayed, and sold in a tantalizing takeout shop by the Blue Heron
Cheese Factory. Samples are offered.

★ **Osburn's Grocery Store Delicatessen**
   downtown at 240 N. Hemlock St.   436-2234
Here in one of Cannon Beach's few remaining original buildings is a
fine place to assemble a gourmet picnic with pate, local fruits and
berries, fresh pasta salad, premium cheeses and wines, whole wheat
fruit bar cookies, and more. The adjoining ice creamery is easily
located by the lineup of contented customers in chairs on the porch
and sidewalk savoring cones, shakes, and sundaes.

★ **Phil and Joe's Crab Co.**
   31 mi. S on US 101 - Garibaldi   322-3410
Different sizes of carryout crab and shrimp cocktails star in an
extensive display of fresh, smoked, and canned seafoods to go in a
large, well-organized shop.

Schweitert's Picnic Basket
   downtown at Cannon Beach Mall   436-1470
Many flavors of Tillamook ice cream in a waffle cone, homemade
butter cream fudge, and dozens of kinds of saltwater taffy are the
highlights of this carryout shop.

★ **Tillamook Cheese Factory**
   41 mi. S on US 101 - Tillamook   842-4481
One of the world's largest cheese-processing plants produces the
West's most renowned cheddar cheese. Visitors can watch through
picture windows. Samples are offered. A large regional food and gift
shop and a coffee shop featuring Tillamook dairy products adjoin.

Specialty Shops

Cannon Beach Book Co.
   downtown at 132 N. Hemlock St.   436-1301
A good selection of books is augmented by attractive decor and
classical background music in this small bookstore.

Dueber's for Variety
   downtown (at Sandpiper Square) on N. Hemlock St.   436-2271
If you'd like to see what a souvenir shop with class looks like, stroll
amongst the skillfully displayed mementoes in this big, engaging
variety store.

Gift Galleon
   downtown at 182 N. Hemlock St.   436-1714
A nice selection of Oregon-made specialty foods like mustard,
chutney, and preserves is featured along with other gifts in this small
upstairs store.

★ **Hannen Stained Glass**
   .6 mi. S at 987 S. Hemlock St.   436-2761
A picturesque cottage has been artistically converted into a studio/
gallery featuring superb exhibits of stained glassworks with a
Northwestern theme. Closed Tues.-Wed. in winter.

Haystack Gallery
downtown at 183 N. Hemlock St.   436-2547
This little gallery features artworks in several media that attempt to
capture the essence of Haystack Rock and the local environs.

★ **The Weathervane Gallery**
downtown at 130 N. Hemlock St.   436-2808
Graceful and unusual three-dimensional wire sculptures are
produced and sold in this studio/gallery.

★ **White Bird Gallery**
downtown at 251 N. Hemlock St.   436-2681
The largest gallery in town showcases multimedia fine arts—weaving,
pottery, etc.—by established artists, and newcomers, from all over the
Northwest.

★ **Worchester Glassworks**
.5 mi. S at Hemlock/Gower Sts.   436-2377
Unique objects and functional pieces in glass are produced here by
well-known glassblowers, and displayed in a big, personalized studio/
gallery.

NIGHTLIFE

After dark, the loudest noise in town is usually the sound of waves
breaking on Cannon Beach. Casual live entertainment is available,
however, and more elaborate "action" can be found a few miles north
in Seaside.

★ **Bill's Tavern**
downtown at 188 N. Hemlock St.   436-2202
The quintessential Cannon Beach tavern features woodcrafted decor
with skylights, a pot-bellied stove, pool, and darts. A patio was
recently added out back. Half a dozen beers are on tap to wash down
the homemade chili and hamburgers.

Coaster Theater
downtown at 108 N. Hemlock St.   436-1242
Live theatrical productions, concerts, ballet, lectures, and films are
presented at various times in a versatile little auditorium in the heart
of town.

Harpoon Room Lounge
downtown at 200 N. Hemlock St.   436-2821
Behind the Whaler Restaurant, live piano and/or organ music are
occasionally played for dancing. The cozy, nautical bar has
comfortable booths and armchairs by an unusual raised fireplace.

★ **Tolovana Inn**
2 mi. S at 3400 S. Hemlock St.   436-1111
Live music and dancing are offered several nights weekly in Daggett's,
a comfortably furnished lounge with an ocean view.

RESTAURANTS

Restaurants are relatively numerous. Most feature seafood. Artistic handcrafted decor and ocean views are plentiful, and several places offer notable cuisine.

Bernardo's Restaurant
.6 mi. S at 1116 S. Hemlock St.   *436-1392*
B-L-D.   *Moderate*
The light, contemporary dishes served here are perfectly matched to the cheerful decor in a cozy restaurant that opened in late 1986.

The Bistro
downtown at 263 N. Hemlock St.   *436-2661*
L-D. No L on Mon.-Thurs.   *Moderate*
The bistro-style fare is hit-or-miss in this congested little dining room tucked away in a cottage off the main street.

★ **The Brass Lantern**
.6 mi. S at 1116 S. Hemlock St.   *436-2412*
D only. Closed Wed.-Thurs.   *Moderate*
Traditional dishes receive light, novel treatments that culminate in delicious homemade desserts—like mango pie. Classical music and fresh flowers accent the simply furnished dining room.

★ **Cafe de la Mer**
.7 mi. S at 1287 S. Hemlock St.   *436-1179*
D only. Closed Mon.   *Expensive*
Fresh regional seafoods are prepared in the classic manner, while support dishes like salmon pate, carrot/orange soup, and marionberry/chocolate pie suggest the innovative artistry of the area's best chef. Chairs in the tiny dining rooms are relatively uncomfortable, but the tables are outfitted with full linen napery and fresh roses.

The Driftwood Inn
downtown at 179 N. Hemlock St.   *436-2439*
L-D. No L on Wed.-Fri. Closed Mon.-Tues.   *Moderate*
Fresh seafood and homemade specialties including bread and pies are served in a popular family restaurant.

★ **Food for Thought Cafe**
15 mi. S at 154 Laneda Av. - Manzanita   *368-6240*
B-L.   *Moderate*
Fresh ingredients are carefully prepared for omelets, blue corn waffles, huevos rancheros with homemade salsa, blintzes, and other international favorites. The inviting little coffee house is accented by a fireplace and an adjoining room has a good selection of books to browse and buy between bites.

Grandma Lee's Chowder House
.7 mi. S at 1235 S. Hemlock St.   *436-1762*
B-L-D.   *Low*
The fresh homemade pie (not the chowder) is the reason to visit this very plain deli/dining room.

★ **Kitchen Table Restaurant**
17 mi. S at 12870 US 101 - Nehalem   368-5538
B-L. Closed Tues.-Wed.   Low
Homemade sourdough specialties, cinnamon rolls, and salsa, plus fresh fruits in season are highlights among a limited selection of all-American fare prepared with skill and quality ingredients. Plants, prints, and a fireplace lend warmth to the tiny homespun dining room.

★ **Lazy Susan Cafe**
downtown at 126 N. Hemlock St.   436-2816
B-L. Closed Tues.   Moderate
Breakfast omelets using Tillamook cheese are featured, and there are some unusual specialties like oatmeal waffles and fresh seasonal fruit. Seating is on two levels in a romantic handcrafted wood-toned dining room where classical music, fresh bouquets of local flowers, and fine raspberry jam in glass jars suggest the attention paid to details in one of the best restaurants of coastal Oregon.

Lemon Tree Inn
downtown at 140 N. Hemlock St.   436-2918
B-L-D.   Moderate
Everyday American dishes are served amid family-oriented contemporary surroundings.

Morris Fireside Restaurant
downtown at 207 N. Hemlock St.   436-2917
B-L-D.   Moderate
Homestyle American fare—stuffed pork chops, pot roast, and local seafoods, plus homemade pie—is perfectly complemented by a hand-hewn log cabin-style dining room with a huge central stone fireplace.

Surfview Too Restaurant
.7 mi. S at 1371 S. Hemlock St.   436-2225
B-L-D.   Moderate
Local seafoods and steaks are emphasized on a conventional American menu. The sunny dining room is decorated in a pleasing blend of wood tones and soft pastel colors. Diners have a choice of padded booths or director chairs, or alfresco dining on an adjoining deck. Upstairs is a handsome contemporary lounge.

Tolovana Inn
2 mi. S at 3400 S. Hemlock St.   436-1111
B-L-D.   Moderate
Daggett's, the large restaurant at the Tolovana Inn, features seafood as an accompaniment to an expansive beachfront view that includes Haystack Rock from every seat in the plush contemporary dining room. A contemporary view lounge adjoins.

Uptown Supper Club
14 mi. S at 165 Laneda Av. - Manzanita   368-6189
D only. Closed Tues.   Moderate
The Continental menu features several regional specialties in this casually elegant little dining room.

Wayfarer Restaurant
.6 mi. S at 1190 Pacific Dr.   *436-1108*
L-D.   *Moderate*
An appealing selection of regional seafood specialties—like Dungeness crab casserole—is served in a dining room that features a fine window-wall view of Haystack Rock and the beach. A large lounge adjoins.

The Whaler
downtown at 200 N. Hemlock St.   *436-2821*
B-L-D.   *Moderate*
Extra-small oysters, steamed littleneck clams, and bouillabaisse are among dinner specialties, as cinnamon rolls are for breakfast, in this casual nautically-furnished dining room.

LODGING

Many accommodations in town are convenient to both downtown and the beach. All but two are small and well-scaled to the intimate, romantic setting. Behind weathered wood exteriors are some remarkably elegant furnishings in rooms decorated with artistry and craftsmanship to match the town's aesthetic spirit. Most lodgings reduce their rates by at least 20% apart from summer, when some require a three day or longer minimum stay.

Bell Harbor Motel
.3 mi. N at 208 5th St. (Box 562)   *436-2776*
An ocean view is the feature of a small **bargain** motel near the mouth of Ecola Creek. Each of the older, spacious units has cable color TV.
  #8—1 BR, unusual round kitchen with a fine
      ocean view, fireplace,   Q bed...$60
  regular room #21 & #20—small, some ocean
                            view,   D bed...$28

Blue Gill Motel
.3 mi. S at 632 S. Hemlock St. (Box 660)   *436-2714*
The beach is an easy stroll from this old, single-level motel. Each simply furnished unit has a cable color TV with movies.
  #14—large, knotty pine decor,   Q bed...$32
  #16—old kitchen, brick fireplace,   Q bed...$45
  regular room—   2 T or Q bed...$32

The Cove
downtown at W. 2nd & N. Larch Sts. (Box 86)   *436-2300*
The Cove is a conveniently located little oceanfront cottage colony. Several units have views, kitchens, and fireplaces. All of the comfortably furnished units have cable color TV.
  "Surf Crest"—1 BR, fronts on ocean/forest, brick
                  fireplace, kitchen,   Q bed...$65
  regular room—kitchenette, no view,   D bed...$36

Ecola Inn
.6 mi. S at 1169 Ecola Court (Box 515)   436-2457
Haystack Rock is near this modern oceanside motel. Each spacious
unit fronts on the beach, and has a color TV.
  #2—corner, Franklin (presto log) fireplace,
      kitchen, fabulous many-window beach view,   2 Q beds...$51
  #3—Franklin (presto log) fireplace, kitchen, fine
      beach view from several windows,   2 Q beds...$46
  regular room—   Q bed...$39
Hidden Villa Motel
.4 mi. S at 188 E. Van Buren St. (Box 426)   436-2237
A beautifully landscaped garden enhances this tiny older cottage
colony. Each modest unit is a **bargain** with cable color TV with movies.
  regular room—   D bed...$28
★ **Lands End Motel**
downtown at 263 W. 2nd St. (Box 475)   436-2264
This contemporary beachfront motel has an outdoor whirlpool.
Several rooms have fine oceanfront views. Each unit has a refrigerator,
(pressed wood) fireplace, and cable color TV. Most have a kitchen.
  #6—1 BR, fine ocean view from LR and BR,   Q bed...$74
  #5,#4—1 BR, fine ocean view from LR,   Q bed...$74
  regular room—some ocean view,   Q bed...$55
Major Motel
1.6 mi. S at 2863 Pacific St. (Box 457)   436-2241
The beach adjoins this small modern **bargain** motel. Each plainly
furnished unit has a cable color TV.
  #18—corner, raised brick fireplace, private
      balcony, kitchen, ocean view,   K bed...$60
  #17—raised brick fireplace, private balcony,
      kitchen, ocean view,   Q bed...$55
  regular room—no ocean view,   Q bed...$30
McBee Court
.4 mi. S at Hemlock/Van Buren Sts. (Box 231)   436-2569
This tiny, single-level, older motel is a recently redecorated **bargain**
only a block from the beach. Each simply furnished unit has cable
color TV.
  #10—end unit, fireplace, kitchen, partial ocean
      view,   D bed...$48
  regular room—   D bed...$30
Quiet Cannon Lodgings
downtown at 372 N. Spruce St.   436-1805
The tranquility of this tiny lodging near the mouth of Ecola Creek and
the ocean can't be beat. Each of the well-outfitted units has a
complete kitchen; a living room with a fireplace; bedroom; and bath.
Seaviews from the rooms and (shared) sheltered patio are
memorable.
  regular room—   Q bed...$53

Sea Sprite Motel
1.4 mi. S on Nebesna St. (Box 66) - Tolovana Park 97145 436-2266
The beach adjoins this tiny motel overlooking Haystack Rock. Each unit has a fully equipped kitchen and color TV.

#2,#3—1 BR, Franklin fireplace in living room,
    rocking chair, superb ocean view,   T & Q bed...$75
regular room—mountain & some ocean view,   Q bed...$45

★ **Surfsand - Best Western**
.5 mi. S at W end of Gower St. (Box 219)   *436-2274*
This modern beachfront motor hotel has a large indoor pool and a whirlpool, plus an ocean view restaurant and lounge. Each unit has a phone and cable color TV with movies. For toll-free reservations in Oregon, call (800)452-4470; elsewhere (800)547-6100.

#316—end unit, fireplace, refrigerator, private
    balcony, oceanfront view,   K bed...$89
#216—end unit, fireplace, private balcony,
    refrigerator, oceanfront view,   K bed...$84
#221—end unit, fireplace, private balcony,
    oceanfront view,   2 Q beds...$84
#220,#219—as above, but not end units,   Q bed...$84
regular room—no ocean view,   Q bed...$44

★ **Surfview Resort**
.7 mi. S at 1400 S. Hemlock St. (Box 547)   *436-1566*
A beachfront bluff overlooking Haystack Rock provides a dramatic locale for one of the finest resort motels in the Northwest. A beautifully enclosed big indoor pool, a whirlpool, a sauna, and an exercise room, plus a restaurant and lounge are housed in recently constructed woodcrafted buildings that favor the site. Each unit in the large, three-level complex has lavish contemporary furnishings, a wood-burning fireplace, a balcony overlooking the ocean, cable color TV with movies, a refrigerator, and a phone. For toll-free reservations in Oregon, call (800)452-7132; elsewhere (800)547-6423.

#333,#233—spacious, wet bar, raised fireplace,
               in-room spa, private balcony, floor-
               to-ceiling window wall with
               Haystack/ocean view,   K bed...$139
#342,#320,#220—spacious, corner, raised
               fireplace, private balcony,
               floor-to-ceiling window wall
               with a fine ocean view,   K bed...$92
#242—as above,   Q bed...$90
#343—raised fireplace, ocean/town view,   Q bed...$70
regular room—some ocean view,   Q bed...$51

★ **Tolovana Inn**
2 mi. S at 3400 S. Hemlock (Box 165) - Tolovana Park 97145 436-2211
Wood-trim and shingles distinguish the three-story buildings of this

large motor hotel. In addition to a choice location on the beach, amenities include a big indoor pool, a whirlpool, saunas, and a well-furnished game room with table tennis and pool tables, plus a view restaurant and lounge. Each spacious, nicely refurbished unit has a phone and cable color TV. For toll-free reservations in Oregon, call (800)452-9402.

#328,#327,#332,#330—studio, kitchen, glass-front (pressed log) fireplace, private balcony, great beach/ ocean view,   Murphy Q bed...$65

#323,#322,#320,#319—studio, kitchen, glass-front (pressed log) fireplace, private balcony, nice ocean view,   Murphy Q bed...$65

regular room—mountain view,   Q bed...$35

The Viking Motel

1.5 mi. S off Hemlock St. (Box 219)   *436-2269*

This small oceanfront motel has a newer complex with some excellent units. Each has a phone, cable color TV with movies, and a small refrigerator. For toll-free reservations in Oregon, call (800)452-4470; elsewhere (800)547-6100.

#16,#13—studio, raised fireplace, kitchen, awesome beach & Haystack Rock view from large corner windows,   Q bed...$72

#14,#11—studio, as above but no Haystack Rock view,   Q bed...$72

regular room—older, ocean view,   Q bed...$44

★ **The Waves Motel**

downtown at 2nd/Larch Sts. (Box 3)   *436-2205*

Artistically handcrafted newer units are featured in the loveliest little cottage colony on the beach next to the heart of town. Each beautifully decorated and furnished unit has a cable color TV. Most have a wood-burning fireplace and an electric kitchen.

"South Flagship"—free-standing metal fireplace, kitchen, private ocean view balcony,   Q bed...$83

"North Flagship"—metal fireplace, kitchen, pitched roof, great ocean view,   Q bed...$73

"Sunscoop" #3 & #4—split-level, fireplace, kitchen, many view windows, skylights, private decks,   Q bed...$89

regular room—no view,   D bed...$46

Webb's Scenic Surf
downtown on Larch St. N of 2nd St. (Box 67)   *436-2706*
Near the heart of town on the beach is a small motel with some fine ocean views. Each plainly furnished unit has a refrigerator and cable color TV with movies.

#6—brick fireplace, kitchenette, private beach-
view deck,   2 T & Q beds...$92
#11—gas fireplace, patio, beach view,   Q bed...$83
regular room—oceanfront deck,   Q bed...$73

CAMPGROUNDS

There are few campgrounds near town. Visitors have a choice of either a rustic, private campground with complete facilities a stroll from town and the beach, or a wonderfully picturesque walk-in campground with relatively primitive facilities near the ocean an easy drive south of town.

★ **Oswald West State Park**
10.1 mi. S on US 101   *238-7488*
This state owned facility includes a tenting campground located in a luxuriant rain forest near a secluded ocean beach. It can only be reached by a quarter-mile trail from a parking lot where wheelbarrows are provided to transport your gear. Sunbathing, beachcombing, cold-ocean swimming, and shore fishing are popular. There are flush toilets, but no showers or hookups. Each of the well-spaced pine-shaded sites has a picnic table and a fire area. Non-Oregonians add $2 surcharge to base rate.   base rate...$7

Sea Ranch Trailer Village
.3 mi. N on US 101A   *436-2815*
This privately owned campground is by an attractive stream a short walk from a superb ocean beach. Fishing in Ecola Creek, plus guided horseback rides on the beach, are features at the site. Flush toilets, hot showers, and hookups are available. Each of the closely spaced sites has a rustic picnic table and a fire area. Some are shaded.   base rate...$8

SPECIAL EVENT

★ **Sand Castle Contest**   *on the beach in town*   *early June*
More than 20,000 spectators watch hundreds of participants from all over the country produce short-lived architectural masterpieces and fanciful sculptured figures from wet sand during this one-day celebration of Cannon Beach's greatest attraction.

OTHER INFORMATION

Area Code: *503*
Zip Code: *97110*
Cannon Beach Chamber of Commerce
downtown at 201 E. 2nd St.   *436-2623*

Florence, Oregon

    Florence is the hub of the most diverse outdoor recreation wonderland in the Pacific Northwest. To the north, luxuriant forests cover slopes of promontories and mountains that rise precipitously from the sea. The lovely little Siuslaw River estuary adjoins the heart of town. Sand dunes along the far side of the river extend to Pacific Ocean beaches a mile to the west. Southward along the coast for more than forty miles are some of the world's most spectacular sand formations—including dunes up to five hundred feet high. Numerous small freshwater lakes with sandy or pine-forested shorelines are tucked into the surrounding countryside.

    The sand dunes, beaches, mountains, forests, river and lakes can easily accommodate the increasing numbers of visitors who arrive each summer, when all of the year's balmy weather normally occurs. The Oregon Dunes National Recreation Area, Siuslaw National Forest, and a wealth of state parks protect the remarkable assortment of natural attractions and provide unlimited recreation opportunities. Among the more distinctive activities are: swimming in clear and warm freshwater lakes sheltered by enormous mounds of fine sand; taking a fat-tired vehicle tour into the dunes; playing golf on a scenic course where the sand traps are the real thing; visiting one of the world's largest sea grottoes—which also serves as the only mainland shelter for wild sea lions; or riding a camel. Temperatures are moderate year-round. It is seldom hot or rainy in summer or cold and snowy in winter. As a result, thousands of wild rhododendron bushes bloom throughout the area in late spring. Unfortunately, rainfall is almost continuous from late fall through early spring.

The area was first opened for settlement during the 1870s. Florence grew slowly along the banks of the Siuslaw River. A bridge was completed in 1936 as one of the final links in the Oregon coast highway. Businesses gradually relocated along the busy thoroughfare, and nearly abandoned the original heart of town. The beguiling old business district was finally rediscovered during the 1970s. Dilapidated buildings were refurbished and compatible new buildings were added, along with a minipark, colorful landscaping, and major waterfront renovations. More recently, the estuary was reopened to navigation.

Old Town is flourishing again as the hub of a recreation wonderland. The moorage adjoining the district serves increasing numbers of both pleasure and commercial boats. Diners can enjoy river views or nostalgic decor in historic buildings. New specialty shops and nightlife are thriving. Lodgings, limited until recently to highway-fronting motels, now include motor hotels overlooking Old Town or ocean beaches. Campgrounds are unusually plentiful. The best—Honeyman State Park—may be the finest all-around campground in the Pacific Northwest. There is no doubt that its endless dunes, warm lakes, pine forests, and miles of ocean beaches epitomize what this special region is all about.

Elevation:

30 feet

Population (1980):

4,411

Population (1970):

2,246

Location:

160 miles Southwest
of Portland

V.W.R.*		Jan.	Feb.	Mar.	Apr.	May	June	July	Aug.	Sep.	Oct.	Nov.	Dec.
Great	10												
Fine	9												
Very Good	8												
Good	7												
Moderate	6												
	5												
	4												
	3												
Adverse	2												
	1												
	0												

	Jan.	Feb.	Mar.	Apr.	May	June	July	Aug.	Sep.	Oct.	Nov.	Dec.
V.W.R.*	0	0	0	2	4	7	9	10	7	4	0	0
Temperature												
Ave. High	50	53	55	59	62	65	68	68	67	64	56	51
Ave. Low	37	38	39	41	46	48	50	50	49	46	41	38
Precipitation												
Inches Rain	12.0	8.7	8.0	5.0	3.5	2.3	1.0	0.8	2.6	7.0	10.2	12.5
Inches Snow	1	1	-	-	-	-	-	-	-	-	-	-

V.W.R. = Vokac Weather Rating: probability of mild (warm & dry) weather on any given day.

Forecast

	V.W.R.*	Temperatures Daytime	Evening	Precipitation
Jan.	0 Adverse	cool	chilly	continual downpours
Feb.	0 Adverse	cool	chilly	continual rainstorms
Mar.	0 Adverse	cool	chilly	continual rainstorms
Apr.	2 Adverse	cool	chilly	continual rainstorms
May	4 Adverse	cool	cool	frequent showers
June	7 Good	warm	cool	occasional showers
July	9 Fine	warm	cool	infrequent showers
Aug.	10 Great	warm	cool	infrequent showers
Sep.	7 Good	warm	cool	occasional rainstorms
Oct.	4 Adverse	cool	cool	frequent rainstorms
Nov.	0 Adverse	cool	chilly	continual downpours
Dec.	0 Adverse	cool	chilly	continual downpours

Summary

Florence occupies the last bend of the Siuslaw River before it cuts through a mile of large sand dunes and empties into the Pacific Ocean. Because of the moderating marine influence, freezes and snowfalls are unusual. Continual downpours during the **winter** months keep people indoors much of the time, however, while contributing nearly half of one of the nation's heaviest annual rainfalls. **Spring** remains cool and damp until May, when wild rhododendrons in fullest bloom throughout the area herald the return of warm weather. **Summer** is perfect for exploring the natural grandeur of surrounding sand dunes, beaches, lakes, forests, and mountains. Warm sunny days are only infrequently marred by showers. Early **fall** weather is pleasant, but cool days and continual rainfall become the norm for the next several months after Halloween.

ATTRACTIONS & DIVERSIONS

★ **Boat Rentals**
Boat rentals can be arranged for freshwater fishing near town on Siltcoos and Woahink Lakes. (Highway signs identify where the lakefront facilities are located.) For salmon and trout fishermen, there are two marinas with boat launch and moorage, plus boats, motors, and tackle for rent or sale year-round.

Cushman Store   *3 mi. E at 6750 OR 126*   997-2169
Siuslaw Marina *3.2 mi. E at 6516 OR 126*   997-3254

Camel Riding
★ **Lawrence of Florence**
4.6 mi. S at 83435 US 101   997-2922
Did you ever wonder what it would feel like to ride a camel on a sand dune? The only place in the Northwest where you can get the answer is on the very short guided trip at Lawrence of Florence. Open only in summer.

★ **Cape Perpetua**
24.3 mi. N on US 101   547-3289
The Cape Perpetua Visitors Center features movies and exhibits explaining the geography and marine features of this section of the Oregon coast. Well-marked hiking trails fan out from the Center to tidepools, blowholes, and churning surf and sandy coves bordering the dramatic shore; along a heavily forested creek; and up to the summit of Cape Perpetua—the highest point along the Oregon coast. The easiest way to get to the top is via a paved road that winds and climbs 1.8 miles to a parking area, from which a short trail leads to a magnificent panoramic view of the coast far below.

★ **Captain Cook's Chasm**
24.1 mi. N on US 101
The chasm is a deep cleft in the coastal volcanic basalt rock next to the highway. When conditions are right, a blowhole (spouting horn) sends flumes of sea water forty feet in the air.

Darlingtonia Botanical Wayside
6 mi. N on US 101
A paved hiking trail offers a short stroll to a bog filled with Darlingtonia, commonly known as cobra lilies. This rare, carnivorous plant native to southwestern Oregon and northwestern California traps and eats bugs.

★ **Dune Buggy Rentals**
The most exhilarating way to explore the vast rolling seas of sand that border the ocean south of Florence is on a three-wheeled dune buggy. Two places in the area rent these by the hour or longer.

Gary's A.T.C. Rental   *.3 mi. N at 586 US 101*   997-6755
Odyssey Rental   *3.5 mi. S on US 101*

★ *Dune Tours*
Sand Dunes Frontier
3.5 mi. S at 83960 US 101   *997-3544*
Balloon-tired open-air buses are used for approximately half-hour tours into some of the world's highest sand dunes at the heart of a vast sandy "frontier" that begins just south of Florence and continues for forty-one miles along the coast. The tour is a unique experience. Private tours can be arranged for longer excursions. There is also a miniature golf course, trout fishing in a small pond, and a game room and souvenir shop at this deservedly popular roadside attraction by the dunes.

Flying
Flying R Flight Service
4 mi. S via US 101 at 2001 Airport Way   *997-8069*
Scenic overviews of the central Oregon coast and sand dunes can be reserved here.

Golf
★ **Florence Golf Course**
3 mi. NE via OR 126 at 3315 Munsel Lake Rd.   *997-3232*
This public 9-hole golf course is in a unique setting—bordered by one of the world's biggest sand traps. Thanks to a sand base and automatic irrigation, dry play conditions are normal year-round. Features include a pro shop, driving range, club and cart rentals, and a snack bar.

★ **Heceta Head Lighthouse**
13 mi. N on US 101
High on a precipitous slope of a massive headland, a lighthouse stands watch over a ruggedly beautiful section of the Oregon coast. In use since 1894, the picturesque landmark is not open to the public, but (thanks to the setting) it is one of the most photographed buildings in the West.

★ **Honeyman State Park**
2.5 mi. S at 84505 US 101   *997-3851*
Tiny Cleawox Lake is the gem-like center of a peerless recreation wonderland. Picnic tables are well-spaced along a pine-shaded shoreline. In sharp contrast, a few hundred feet away on the other side of the small lake, majestic sand dunes plunge into crystal-clear waters. The clean, soft-sand beach is an idyllic place for sunbathing, and the lake is warm enough for swimming in summer. A road and hiking trails lead to nearby Woahink Lake—popular for boating, fishing, waterskiing, and swimming.

Horseback Riding
C & M Stables
8.8 mi. N at 90241 US 101   *997-7540*
They only offer guided group rides. But, this is one of a relatively

few places where you can enjoy the feeling of riding a horse across sand dunes, and through the surf on hard sand beaches.

★ **Indian Forest**
5.2 mi. N at 88493 US 101   *997-3677*
This roadside attraction has a surprisingly authentic cluster of full-sized Indian-oriented dwellings, and exhibits, plus a well-organized trading post featuring dolls, jewelry, and other handmade Indian collectibles.

★ *Moped Rentals*
 Gary's A.T.C. Rental
.3 mi. N at 586 US 101   *997-6755*
A good way to enjoy the salt air and rhododendron-bordered backcountry roads to freshwater lakes and dune areas is by mopeds, which can be rented here by the hour.

★ **Oregon Dunes National Recreation Area**
starts .8 mi. S on US 101
A remarkable mixture of sandy beaches, clear freshwater lakes and streams, and islands of pine forests mingle with some of the biggest sand dunes in the world. Fishing, beachcombing, hiking, dune buggy riding, swimming, and camping are popular activities in this unique recreation area which extends along the coast for more than forty miles.

★ **Sea Lion Caves**
12 mi. N at 91560 US 101   *547-3111*
Here is the only year-round natural habitat for wild sea lions on the American mainland. A scenic walkway and an elevator take visitors down to a mammoth wave-carved grotto, more than three hundred feet long, and one hundred feet high, in the base of the cliff. Hundreds of sea lions can usually be seen from the viewing area, which is open during daylight hours all year. There is also a large gift shop, and a dramatic life-sized bronze sculpture of the "Stellar Sea Lion Family."

★ **Siltcoos Park**
8 mi. S via US 101 and park access road
This large coastal park provides trailheads for hikers interested in exploring dozens of miles of coastal sand dunes to the south, and staging areas for ORV'ers interested in ridge-and-ravine romping on several miles of dunes from the park northward. Several campgrounds and scenic picnic areas are also available.

★ **South Jetty Dune and Beach**
.8 mi. S on US 101
ORV staging areas, hiking trailheads, and sand dune and beach access parking lots are positioned along a six-mile paved road that extends to the south jetty—where the Siuslaw River empties into the ocean. There are also boat launching and shore fishing sites, and a crabbing pier, on the Siuslaw River.

★ *Sportfishing*

Sportfishing boats can be chartered daily year-round for deep sea fishing, and for salmon fishing in the summer months. All of the following operators provide all necessary equipment.

Estabrook's *downtown at Bay Bridge Marina*   997-6828
Gee Gee Charters *25 mi. S at Winchester Bay*   271-3152
Hobo Jack's (river drift fishing) *22 mi. E at 13987 OR 36* 268-4889
Shamrock Charters *25 mi. S at Winchester Bay*   271-3232
Thompson Charters *25 mi. S at Winchester Bay*   271-3133

SHOPPING

The historic commercial heart of Florence—Old Town—has begun to reassert itself in an exciting new direction in recent years. A small but flourishing cluster of galleries and specialty shops now fills historic buildings with first-rate arts, crafts, foods, and wines largely produced in the Northwest. Other notable stores offering handcrafted and gourmet goods with a regional bent are sprinkled along US 101 north and south of town.

Food Specialties

★ **B.J.'s Ice Cream Parlor**
   1.9 mi. N at 2930 US 101   997-7286
Several dozen flavors of ice cream, including some of the finest on the Oregon coast, are manufactured here. All of the flavors are displayed and sold in a variety of fountain treats in the roadside shop's small serving area, or to go. An annex is in Old Town.

Florence Donuts & Deli
   .3 mi. N at 529 US 101   997-2550
Delicious thinly wrapped cinnamon rolls and other breakfast pastries are the specialty of this little takeout bakery.

★ **Incredible Edible Oregon**
   downtown at 1336 Bay St.   997-7018
An impressive assortment of all-Oregon food and wine specialties, plus selected Oregon arts and crafts, distinguish this shop on the main street of Old Town. Custom gift packs, and a catalog, are available.

Krab Kettle
   downtown at 280 US 101   997-8996
When crabs are in, this roadside shack comes to life with outdoor kettles bubbling and cooked crabs on display. Assorted smoked salmon and other fresh and smoked seafoods are also sold in season.

★ **Old Sarajevo Bakery**
   downtown at 185 Maple St.   997-3320
The biggest culinary surprise in Florence is an authentic Yugoslavian bakery tucked away on a side street. A limited assortment of delicious European breads and pastries is sold to go or to eat in an attractive little coffee shop. Closed Sun., plus Mon. in winter.

★ **Sportsmen's Cannery**
    25 mi. S via US 101 - Winchester Bay   271-3293
Highest quality salmon, tuna, and shellfish are hand-packed and processed here with no preservatives or artificial additives. Fresh, smoked, and canned gourmet seafoods are displayed and sold in an inviting shop, along with seashore gifts and local artworks. The knowledgeable staff will tell you where the fishing is best, rent and sell crab rings and tackle, and custom can your catch.

Woodsman's Native Nursery
    2.8 mi. N at 4385 US 101   997-2252
A nursery specializing in native coastal plants and trees is also the outlet for assorted jams and jellies produced from local berries. All are sold in jars or boxes to go or for mailing as gifts. Closed Sun.

Specialty Shops

The Book & Gift Gallery
    downtown at 1340 Bay St.   997-6205
A good selection of regional titles is the highlight in this compact bookstore-gift shop. A view through a back window to the Siuslaw River lends to the shop's charm.

★ **Lakeshore Myrtlewood Factory**
    4.5 mi. S at 83530 US 101   997-2753
An impressive assortment of myrtlewood utensils, furniture, and even jewelry is artistically displayed in a large roadside shop. As an added attraction, craftsmen can be seen working on the myrtlewood slabs in the factory connected to the salesroom.

Ragan Gallery
    19.5 mi. N on US 101
Paintings and pottery by local artists and craftsmen are showcased in this isolated roadside gallery by the sea. Open during summer only.

★ **The Toy Factory**
    6.1 mi. N at 88878 US 101   997-8604
They no longer design and create all of the toys displayed and sold here. Some were produced locally, while many of the unique playthings were gathered from all over the world to delight everyone with a fun-loving spirit.

Wind Drift Gallery
    downtown at 125 Maple St.   997-9182
For a good example of the evolution toward quality gift shops in Old Town, browse this gallery with its large assortment of Oregon-made candies, wood products, wall hangings, seashell jewelry, and other objects of art.

NIGHTLIFE

Peace and quiet reign after dark. Most of the "action " (such as it is) is concentrated in several watering holes in Old Town, where there is live music and dancing most weekends. A couple of plush newer lounges offer a choice of views oriented toward sunset on the ocean, or the lights of town across the river.

The Bridgewater Restaurant
   downtown at 1297 Bay St.   997-9405
Oregon wines by the glass, exotic drinks made from fresh fruits and juices, and finger foods are served to patrons comfortably ensconced on sofas in an oyster bar which occupies a portion of a restored historic building.

★ **Driftwood Shores Lounge**
   6 mi. NW at 88416 1st Av.   997-8263
The motor hotel's new lounge is a post-modern charmer, with pastel colors, blond wood trim, raised-relief carvings, etched mirrors, and a superb oceanfront view; plus occasional live music.

Fisherman's Wharf Cocktails
   downtown at 1347 Bay St.   997-2613
Local talent may provide live entertainment for dancing on weekends in a big funky tavern with four pool tables and a large island bar.

Jerry's Place
   5.5 mi. NW on Rhododendron Dr.   997-3815
This large roadside tavern on the way to the ocean has a shaped-up, woodcrafted interior. Pool tables and shuffleboard are in a spacious separate play area.

Pier Point Inn
   .6 mi. S at 85625 US 101   997-7191
Here's a comfortable place for conversation and drinks with a fine view of the river and Old Town.

RESTAURANTS

With a couple of exceptions, restaurants in the Florence area tend to serve conventional American-style meals in plain surroundings. Almost every one features local seafood—with more or less success. In two popular dining rooms, customers can enjoy captivating views of the town and river from tables by picture windows.

★ **Beachcombers Pub & Grub**
   downtown at 1355 Bay St.   997-6357
   B-L.   *Low*
Delectable homemade pies and giant fluffy biscuits with meat-rich country gravy are highlights of the best down-home fare in the area. This rustic wood-trimmed coffee shop opened in 1986 next to an Old Town tavern.

★ **The Bridgewater Restaurant**
   downtown at 1297 Bay St.   997-9405
   B-L-D.   *Moderate*
Seafoods and other dishes show a real flair, but some inconsistency,

in an appealingly restored historic building. Whitewashed clapboard in the spacious dining room is complemented by plants, bric-a-brac, and twirling fans. An oyster bar shares the same room and offers comfortable sofa seating. A charming garden patio is used for alfresco dining when weather permits. Wines by the glass and finger foods are featured, and there is also a wine and gift shop.

Charl's Pancake Haven
1.6 mi. N at 2575 US 101   *997-2490*
B-L-D. No D on Sun.   *Moderate*
Sourdough or buttermilk pancakes and omelets are featured on an all-American menu served amidst very plain coffee shop decor.

Driftwood Shores
6 mi. NW via Rhododendron Dr. at 88416 1st Av.   *997-8263*
B-L-D.   *Moderate*
Contemporary American dishes are served at all meals. The motor hotel's post-modern dining room (opened in late 1986) is the charmer, however. It's a multi-angled, multileveled tour de force where pastel hues, mirrors, polished woods, and picture windows contribute to each guest's enjoyment of a panoramic seascape from the beachfront location.

Fisherman's Wharf
downtown at 1341 Bay St.   *997-2613*
B-L-D (24 hours).   *Moderate*
Standard American food is served in a no-frills coffee shop that's open twenty-four hours a day.

Lam's Sand & Sea
.8 mi. N at 1179 US 101   *997-3813*
L-D.   *Moderate*
A wide assortment of Cantonese and American dishes is offered in a plain, comfortably furnished restaurant.

Morgan's Country Kitchen
1.7 mi. S at 85020 US 101   *997-6991*
B-L-D.   *Moderate*
Delicious pecan waffles are the highlight among homestyle American foods prepared from scratch in this very casual roadside cafe.

Mo's
downtown at 1436 Bay St.   *997-2185*
L-D.   *Low*
Huge crowds attest to the continuing popularity of the Mo's name on this recent addition to a burgeoning Oregon chain. The standardized seafood menu is xeroxed, but the food is good, the prices are cheap, and the view is special of the Florence bridge and Siuslaw River. The simply furnished interior, with picnic tables and benches in a cannery-like setting, is especially appealing to families.

Pier Point Inn
.6 mi. S at 85625 US 101   997-7191
B-L-D.   *Moderate*
The motor hotel's Red Snapper restaurant offers a conventional American menu with a seafood emphasis. The special feature is a window wall view of town from a dining room outfitted with glass-topped tables and otherwise comfortable furniture.

Seafood Grotto Restaurant
25 mi. S via US 101 at 8th/Broadway - Winchester Bay 271-4250
B-L-D.   *Low*
Local fresh salmon, crab and oysters are featured in season, accompanied by a salad bar. Clam chowder fans take note—the Grotto's version is so thick you can stand a spoon in it. The homemade pies and cinnamon rolls served in the casual dining rooms are very good.

Summer House Restaurant
.7 mi. N at 1015 US 101   997-7557
B-L-D.   *Moderate*
Some of the best breakfasts in Florence (conscientiously-prepared pancakes, waffles, and omelets from fresh ingredients) are served in a cheerful, comfortably furnished, plant-filled dining room.

Weber's Fish Market Restaurant
.5 mi. N at 802 US 101   997-8886
B-L-D.   *Moderate*
Routine seafoods are emphasized (there is an associated fish market next door) in this very plain family-oriented restaurant.

The Whistler Restaurant
.7 mi. N at 1073 US 101   997-2112
L-D.   *Moderate*
A modern seafood and steak menu is offered in a casual nautically-themed dining room outfitted with comfortable booths. A piano lounge adjoins.

★ **Windward Inn**
2.4 mi. N at 3757 US 101   997-8243
B-L-D.   *Moderate*
The entrees are, surprisingly, consistently good considering the breadth of the menu and size of the restaurant. But, everything about this place is carefully overseen, from the homemade desserts and breads to the fresh bouquets of flowers on each table and the selection of premium wines available by the bottle, half-bottle, and glass. For decor accents, one of the wood-paneled dining rooms has a large fireplace, another a skylight; all have fine forest views. Live classical music lends to the genteel air of Florence's most impressive roadside institution.

LODGING

Most accommodations in town are within walking distance of Old Town and the Siuslaw River, and a short drive from the ocean and dunes. Standard motels predominate (with only three notable exceptions). Bargain rooms are surprisingly scarce in summer. Many places reduce their rates by about 20% from fall through spring.

Americana Motel

2.5 mi. N at 3829 US 101   997-7115

This contemporary motel recently added a small indoor pool and whirlpool. Each nicely furnished unit has cable color TV.

regular room—   Q bed...$38

★ **Driftwood Shores**

6 mi. NW via Rhododendron Dr. at 88416 1st Av.   997-8263

Florence's only oceanfront accommodation is also its largest motor hotel. The four-story complex includes a stylish new ocean-view dining room and lounge, a large indoor pool, whirlpool, and saunas. Each comfortably furnished room has a phone, cable color TV, and a private patio or deck with an oceanfront view. For toll-free reservations in Oregon, call (800)422-5091; elsewhere (800)824-8774.

#330,#230,#130—3 BR suite, 2 baths, fireplace,

kitchen,   3 Q beds...$100

executive suite—large studio with kitchen,   2 Q beds...$60

regular room—some ocean view,   Q bed...$50

Florence Coast Motel

downtown at 155 US 101 (Box 187)   997-3221

This small older motel has a convenient location near Old Town. Each simply furnished unit has cable color TV.

regular room—   Q bed...$32

Gull Haven Lodge

19.1 mi. N at 94770 US 101 - Yachats 97498   547-3583

Perched on a grassy mountain slope by the highway high above a rugged shoreline is an old motel-style lodge with a lot of character, and a remarkable **bargain** unit.

"North Up"—2 BR, lg. living room with iron

fireplace & panoramic ocean views

from big corner windows, kitchen, T & 3 D beds...$45

"Shags Nest"—tiny studio cabin, hike to bath,

kitchenette, raised brick

fireplace, private coastline view

from floor/ceiling window,   D bed...$30

regular room—1 BR, fine ocean view,   2 D beds...$35

The Johnson House

downtown at Maple/1st Sts.   997-8000

A Victorian house has become a carefully converted bed-and-breakfast lodging—the first in Florence. Each of the rooms is decorated with some antiques, and all except one share baths. A full complimentary breakfast is served in the dining room.

private bath— D bed...$55
regular room—shared bath, D bed...$45

Le Chateau Motel
.7 mi. N at 1084 US 101 (Box 98) 997-3481
Several amenities lend appeal to this modern two-level motel—an outdoor pool, whirlpool, saunas, and a recreation room. Each room has a phone and cable color TV with movies.

regular room—spacious, wet bar, K bed...$42
regular room— Q bed...$38

Money Saver Motel
downtown at 170 US 101 997-7131
This modern motel has rooms with a phone and cable color TV with movies.

regular room— Q bed...$38

Ocean Breeze Motel
1.4 mi. S at 85165 US 101 997-2642
Here is a nicely refurbished older single-level motel that is a **bargain**. Each of the simply furnished rooms has cable color TV.

regular room— D or Q bed...$28

The Oregon House
18 mi. N at 94288 US 101 - Yachats 97498 547-3329
A small complex of buildings perched on a slope above the ocean is a tranquil getaway among coastal bed-and-breakfast facilities, and there is a **bargain** unit. Each nicely outfitted unit has a private bath. Breakfast is complimentary to guests in the main house. There is a glassed-in cliff tower for viewing the ocean, and a private trail to the beach below.

#1—large, 1 BR, fireplace, kitchen, pvt. deck
with fine ocean view, 2 T & Q beds...$66
B & B Ocean Blue Room—in main house,
private sunken tub,
breakfast, ocean view, K bed...$66
regular room #4—small, garden view, small
kitchen, Q bed...$30

Park Motel
1.6 mi. S at 85034 US 101 997-2634
One of the area's few **bargains** is this single-level motel. Each small, simply furnished room has a knotty-pine interior and cable color TV.

regular room— Q bed...$33
regular room— D bed...$30

★ **Pier Point Inn - Best Western**
.6 mi. S at 85625 US 101 997-7191
A choice location on the south shore of the Siuslaw River is the

most appealing feature of this modern motor hotel. Other amenities include two whirlpools, a ping pong table, and a sauna, plus a restaurant and lounge that share a fine bay view. Every well-furnished unit has a phone, cable color TV, and a private balcony. For toll-free reservations, call (800)528-1234.

#353,#351,#349—fine river and Old Town view

from	Q bed...$48
#348—fine river and Old Town view from	K bed...$53
regular room—	Q bed...$48

Silver Sands Motel

.9 mi. N at 1449 US 101 (Box 1516)   *997-3459*

A small outdoor pool with a slide, and privileges at an adjoining health spa with an indoor pool, whirlpool, saunas, and exercise room, are features of this modern two-story motel. Each unit has a phone and cable color TV.

regular room—   Q bed...$34

Villa West Motel

.6 mi. N at junction US 101/OR 126 (Box 1236)   *997-3457*

In this modern two-story motel, each room has a phone and cable color TV with movies.

regular room—   Q bed...$38

CAMPGROUNDS

Campgrounds are plentiful in the recreation wonderland surrounding Florence. Most are situated in forested areas near sand dunes and seashores. The best, Honeyman, has it all—a forested site with all facilities a short stroll from a warm freshwater lake backed by majestic dunes that extend to nearby ocean beaches.

Alder Dune Campground

7.7 mi. N on US 101

The Forest Service operates this facility. Tiny Alder Lake has several dunes sloping into the lake, and shaded picnic sites overlooking it. Fishing, swimming, and sunbathing are popular, along with hiking trails to beaches two miles away. Nicely spaced sites each have a picnic table and fire ring/grill. Sites are separated from each other by lush brush. Flush toilets, but no hookups and no hot water, are available.   base rate...$6

Cape Perpetua Campground

24.3 mi. N on US 101   *547-3289*

The Forest Service operates a heavily wooded campground along a clear stream just inland from the ocean. Well-marked trails provide access to Cape Perpetua (the Oregon coast's highest headland) and to tidepools, blowholes, and sandy coves nearby. Flush toilets, but no hot water, showers, or hookups are available. Each of the well-spaced, luxuriantly shaded sites has a picnic table and a fire ring/grill.   base rate...$6

★ **Honeyman State Park**
  2.5 mi. S at 84505 US 101   *997-3851*
This state-operated campground is one of the West's finest. Situated in a forest of tall pines, it adjoins a sparkling freshwater lake bordered on two sides by large clean sand dunes. The ocean and miles of broad beaches are a stroll beyond. There are many scenic hiking trails, and nearby are concessions for sand buggy rentals and sand bus trips. Each well-spaced site has a picnic table and fire ring—some have grills. Many sites are complemented by rhododendron bushes, and most have a feeling of privacy provided by lush vegetation. Firewood is provided. Well-maintained flush toilets and hot showers are provided, and hookups are available. There is a convenience store and cafe on the lake. Non-Oregonians add $2 surcharge to base rate.   base rate...$6

KOA - Florence Dunes
  3 mi. NW at 87115 Rhododendron Dr.   *997-6431*
This privately operated facility is located between town and the ocean beaches. Each site is separated by dense brush and includes a picnic table. Some have fire rings. Flush toilets, hot showers, and hookups are available. There is a separate tenting area.
                                                            base rate...$9

Rock Creek
  17 mi. N on US 101
Half a mile from the highway is a tiny public campground with a small number of creekside campsites in a lush forest/fern grotto setting. Each well-spaced site is in deep shade by the creek, and has a picnic table and fire ring/grill. Flush toilets, but no hot water, showers, or hookups are available. There is a trail down the creek one-half mile to a magnificent log-strewn beach.   base rate...$5

Siltcoos Lake Campground
  7 mi. S via US 101
Campsites are abundant in clusters along a one-and-one-half-mile paved road between the highway and the ocean. Hiking trails provide access to the ocean and to small freshwater lakes. Separate access is identified for ORV'ers interested in exploring the dunes. Flush toilets, but no showers or hookups, are available. Pine-shaded sites have picnic tables, and some (Lagoon and Waxmyrtle) have fire ring/grills.   base rate...$6

Sutton Creek Campground
  5.7 mi. N on US 101
Ocean beaches and dunes are approximately one mile west of this Forest Service campground. A well-marked trail leads to a Darlingtonia swamp where visitors can observe insect-eating plants in action. The campground is one and one-half miles from a large parking lot with a short trail to a wilderness dune overlook and hiking trails into a choice of beachfronting coastal dunes or large

pure-sand creekside dunes. Sutton Lake is a mile away inland with a boat launch and fishing sites. Each grassy site is shrubbery-screened, and includes a picnic table and fire ring/grill. Flush toilets, but no showers or hot water are available.   base rate...$6

★ **Washburne State Park**
   15.3 mi. N at 93111 US 101   547-3416
Oregon operates a campground here, with a small separated tenting area. Wheelbarrows are provided for heavily forested walk-in sites served by a building with flush toilets but no showers. Each tent site has a picnic table and fire ring. Regular sites are nicely spaced and tree-shaded, with a picnic table and fire ring. Hiking trails lead to a sandy ocean beach one-quarter mile away, and to adjoining mountain destinations. There are flush toilets, hot (solar) showers, and full hookups. Non-Oregonians add $2 surcharge to base rate.   base rate...$6

West Lake Area - Tyee Campground
   5.7 mi. S via US 101
Siuslaw National Forest operates a heavily forested small campground by a tiny lake across the highway from majestic sand dunes. Pit toilets, but no showers or hookups, are available. Each well-spaced tree-shaded site has a picnic table and fire ring/ grill.   base rate...$5

SPECIAL EVENT

★ **Rhododendron Festival**   *downtown*   *mid-May*
Nature's most flamboyant floral contribution to the Florence area has been celebrated annually since 1908 for three days during the peak blooming period. In addition to the rhododendron show, there is a parade; queen coronation and dance; Rhody Run, sail board races, and the annual Silver Trails Slug Race; plus arts and crafts displays; food vendors; and a carnival.

OTHER INFORMATION

Area Code: *503*
Zip Code: *97439*
Florence Area Chamber of Commerce
   downtown on US 101 at Maple St. (Box 712)   *997-3128*
Oregon Dunes National Recreation Area Office
   855 Highway Av. - Reedsport, OR 97467   *271-3611*

Gold Beach, Oregon

Gold Beach is the source for all kinds of freshwater and saltwater adventures. It is ideally located on the flat little delta at the mouth of the famed Rogue River. The Coast Range rises abruptly to the east. A fine sandy beach along the Pacific Ocean delimits the western boundary. To the north and south is a natural extravaganza of sea mounts, rocky promontories and sheltered coves, clear streams and verdant rain forests.

Gold Beach has the warmest climate of any of the coastal great towns in the Pacific Northwest. Freezes and snow are scarce. Still, at a latitude farther north than Chicago, visitors are usually surprised to see a date palm flourishing in a valley near town. Warm sunny weather is normal in summer, the prime season for both river anglers and deep sea fishermen. Others have come for exciting jet boat trips to whitewater stretches of the Rogue River. Those intent on getting-away-from-it-all can sunbathe on secluded beaches and swim in deep clear pools in the relatively warm river. Glorious scenery and thrilling rapids reward backpackers and river runners along the Rogue River Wilderness—a spectacular canyon that is off-limits to motor boats or vehicles. Along the coast, beachcombing, clamming, crabbing, and shore fishing are popular into fall, when rainstorms become almost continuous. Each winter, the fury of huge stormdriven waves pounding rugged shorelines attracts more visitors—who usually witness the spectacle from the comfort of a firelit oceanview room.

Gold in the dark sand at the mouth of the river first attracted miners to this site during the 1870s. The town even took its name from the phenomenon. But, it was the river that gave the remote settlement an air of permanence, starting with commercial fishing, canneries, and boatyards. In 1895, mail boats began to provide postal service to isolated up-river settlers. Freight was soon added, and it wasn't long before home-cooked meals were being served to river passengers who tagged along to Agness. Completion of the Oregon coast highway during the 1930s made the river and coast more accessible. Growth has continued to be slow but steady since.

Hydro-jet boats take record numbers of people on swift, thrilling whitewater trips into the beautiful Rogue River canyon these days. Salmon and steelhead fishing—the area's other passion—is buoyed by improving catches and major improvements to the harbor during the 1980s. Shops remain relatively scarce and ordinary, while restaurants have proliferated and now offer everything from hearty homemade fare to fresh local seafood in gourmet, ocean-view dinner houses. Nightlife is rudimentary and rustic, reflecting everyone's preoccupation with outdoor activities. During the past three years, lodgings have burgeoned. Gracious ocean-view and riverside resorts now provide alternatives to highway-fronting motels and rustic fishing lodges. Campgrounds have also been thoughtfully positioned in choice locations close to the ocean and river.

Elevation:

50 feet

Population (1980):

1,515

Population (1970):

1,554

Location:

290 miles Southwest of Portland

Gold Beach, Oregon
WEATHER PROFILE
Vokac Weather Rating

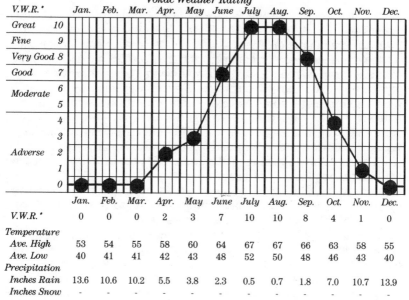

V.W.R. *		Jan.	Feb.	Mar.	Apr.	May	June	July	Aug.	Sep.	Oct.	Nov.	Dec.
Great	10												
Fine	9												
Very Good	8												
Good	7												
Moderate	6												
	5												
	4												
	3												
Adverse	2												
	1												
	0												

	Jan.	Feb.	Mar.	Apr.	May	June	July	Aug.	Sep.	Oct.	Nov.	Dec.
V.W.R. *	0	0	0	2	3	7	10	10	8	4	1	0
Temperature												
Ave. High	53	54	55	58	60	64	67	67	66	63	58	55
Ave. Low	40	41	41	42	43	48	52	50	48	46	43	40
Precipitation												
Inches Rain	13.6	10.6	10.2	5.5	3.8	2.3	0.5	0.7	1.8	7.0	10.7	13.9
Inches Snow	-	-	-	-	-	-	-	-	-	-	-	-

*V.W.R. = Vokac Weather Rating: probability of mild (warm & dry) weather on any given day.

Forecast

	V.W.R. *	Daytime	Evening	Precipitation
		Temperatures		
Jan.	0 Adverse	cool	chilly	continual downpours
Feb.	0 Adverse	cool	chilly	continual downpours
Mar.	0 Adverse	cool	chilly	continual downpours
Apr.	2 Adverse	cool	cool	frequent downpours
May	3 Adverse	cool	cool	frequent rainstorms
June	7 Good	cool	cool	infrequent rainstorms
July	10 Great	warm	cool	negligible
Aug.	10 Great	warm	cool	infrequent showers
Sep.	8 Very Good	warm	cool	infrequent rainstorms
Oct.	4 Adverse	cool	cool	occasional downpours
Nov.	1 Adverse	cool	cool	continual downpours
Dec.	0 Adverse	cool	chilly	continual downpours

Summary

Gold Beach occupies a spectacular site where the Rogue River breached the Coast Range and empties into the Pacific Ocean. Protected by mountains and tempered by the warming influence of the sea, the area benefits from a long growing season. Freezes are rare enough that even date palms flourish outdoors in sheltered sites near town— at a latitude as far north as Chicago! Snowfall is rare, but continual rainstorms make this one of the wettest places on the continent in **winter**. **Spring** remains cool and wet, but conditions improve quickly. After Memorial Day, there is a good chance of mild weather. **Summer** is ideal for exploring the river, ocean, and mountains around town. Warm sunny days are the rule, with only a slight chance of rain. In early **fall**, however, cool weather returns, accompanied by increasingly heavy rainstorms.

ATTRACTIONS & DIVERSIONS

★ **Arch Rock Viewpoint**
15 mi. S on US 101
A large natural arch has developed in a giant offshore rock due to wave action. From this highway viewpoint, many unusual wave-formed rock sculptures can be seen up close.

★ **Azalea State Park**
29 mi. S on US 101 - Brookings
Many mature native plants of several kinds of Western azaleas grow here. The park is especially beautiful in late spring, at peak bloom. You can enjoy the sight and fragrance while having a picnic at a table among the flowering bushes (many are over ten feet tall) or in a shady grove of cedars. A trail leads to a rock-lined observation structure at the high point in the gardens.

Boat Rentals
Jot's
1 mi. N at 94360 Wedderburn Loop   *247-6676*
Boats (with or without motors) and canoes can be rented at the resort's marina on the Rogue River by the hour or day.

★ ***Boat Rides***
Whitewater jet boat rides are Gold Beach's most exciting feature. Three companies offer a choice of 64-mile or 104-mile trips up the magnificent Rogue River canyon daily from May through October. The shorter trip (approximately six hours) explores a scenic section of the lower Rogue and includes a meal break. The longer excursion goes beyond to some thrilling whitewater. It's an all day (approximately eight hours) trip with a meal break at a wilderness lodge. Each company charges the same amount as the others do, leaves from near the bridge in town (their docks are well-marked), and provides meals at the same up-river lodges.

Court's	*Jot's Resort, P.O. Box "J"*	*247-6676*
Jerry's Rogue Jets	*P.O. Box 1011*	*247-4571*
Rogue River Mail Boat Trips	*P.O. Box 1165-G*	*247-7033*

★ **Cape Sebastian Viewpoint**
5.5 mi. S on US 101
A steep paved road winds up to the crest of a precipitous headland more than 700 feet above the sea. From the parking lot, visitors have a panoramic view of the coast northward to the mouth of the Rogue River and beyond. To the south is a "perfect" Northwestern scene—forested mountains tumbling down to broad sandy ocean beaches. Offshore, oddly shaped rocks and tiny islands are constantly battered by the pounding surf. Well-marked trails lead to other spectacular overlooks along the crest of the cape.

★ **Harris Beach State Park**
    27 mi. S on US 101 - Brookings   *469-2021*
Here's a fine introduction to what the Oregon coast has to offer—sandy beaches, a rugged coastline with offshore rocks, pine forests, and luxuriant undergrowth. Beachcombing, rock and surf fishing, and (for the hearty) surf swimming are popular activities. There are nature trails and picnic areas, and a campground with all facilities is in a luxuriant forest on a rise above the beach.

★ *Hiking*
Opportunities abound to explore coastal headlands and beaches and sylvan river valleys on foot. Best of all is the forty-mile Rogue River Trail, a well-marked pathway along the glorious canyon that is the heart of the designated Wild Rogue Wilderness. The river is nearly always in view, and frequent side paths provide access. Spring is the quietest time—the weather is mild and wildflowers are at peak bloom. Summer is the most popular season—days are often hot and the crystal-clear river is perfect for rafting, swimming, and fishing. As an unusual added feature, rustic riverside lodges are an easy hike apart along the entire trail. You can travel for days in the wilderness carrying only a light pack, and enjoy hot showers, clean beds, and hearty meals by reserving these places well in advance. For more information, contact:
    Illahe Lodge *37709 Agness-Illahe Rd. - Agness 97406*   *247-6111*
    Lodge at Half Moon Bar *410 N.W. E St. - Grants Pass 97526 476-4002*
    Paradise Bar Lodge *Box 456 - Gold Beach 97444*   *247-6022*
Horseback Riding
    Indian Creek Trail Rides, Inc.
    .5 mi. NE via US 101 on Jerry's Flat Rd.   *247-7704*
One hour (and longer) guided trail rides leave several times daily for horseback tours of scenic mountains above the Rogue River valley.

★ **Humbug Mountain State Park**
    21 mi. N on US 101   *332-6774*
The state has developed a superb park along a creek at the base of a mountain towering 1,756 feet above the sea—which borders the park on the west. Well-marked hiking trails lead to the top of Humbug Mountain (three miles); along a scenic (two-plus miles) stretch of no-longer-used coastal highway; and for miles along a picturesque beach. Swimming can be enjoyed by the hearty at the mouth of Brush Creek. Stream and ocean fishing are also popular, and excellent camping facilities (see separate listing) are available. A large myrtlewood tree is identified near the park entrance.

Library
    downtown at Colvin/Gauntlett Sts.   *247-7246*
The Curry Public Library is housed in a modern building outfitted with some comfortable armchairs. Nearby is a good selection of magazines and newspapers.

★ **Loeb State Park**
37 mi. S via US 101 & Northbank (Chetco River) Rd. - Brookings
One of the largest virgin stands of rare myrtlewood grows here,
and a redwood grove is nearby. The clear water of the Chetco
River is a delight for swimmers and fishermen on warm summer
days, and camping and picnic facilities have been provided.

★ **Lone Ranch Beach Picnic Area**
23 mi. S on US 101
Picturesque monoliths jutting into the sea frame a romantic little
cove with a broad sandy beach punctuated by rocky outcroppings
onshore and beyond where waves break endlessly around them.

★ **Prehistoric Gardens**
15 mi. N at 36848 US 101   *332-4463*
Here is an unusual tourist attraction that's surprisingly well done.
Life-sized technically correct replicas of prehistoric dinosaurs are
situated along meandering paths in a coastal rain forest luxuriant
with gigantic ferns and hanging moss. There's also a gift shop with
a prehistoric theme.

★ **Siskiyou National Forest**
starts 8 mi. E of town
Most of the southwestern corner of the state is included in this
vast forest. Nearly half of the designated National Wild and Scenic
River portion of the Rogue River, and Oregon Caves National
Monument, are the most renowned features. Less well-known, and
encompassing the rugged heart of the forest, is a botanical treasury
of rare and unusual plants—the Kalmiopsis Wilderness Area. Nearer
to the coast, a myrtlewood grove and the only redwood trees outside
of California are other highlights. Numerous paved and dirt roads,
and hundreds of miles of trails, provide access for river running,
fishing, swimming, hiking, backpacking, horseback riding, pack trips,
and camping. Detailed information and maps can be obtained at
the ranger's office in town at 1225 S. Ellensburg St.

★ *Sportfishing*
.4 mi. N at Gold Beach Marina
Many charter boats operate daily for river and ocean salmon and
steelhead fishing during the summer season. Guides are also readily
available at other times for river fishing trips. You can get more
information on who's available, and what's being caught, by calling:

Banshee Charters   *247-2112*
Jerry's Rogue Jets   *247-7601*
Jot's Resort   *247-6676*

SHOPPING

Gold Beach's business district is sprinkled through town along US
101 (Ellensburg St.). Almost all of the uniformly unassuming shops
address the everyday needs of residents and visitors.

111

Food Specialties

★ **Black Forest Kitchen**

9 mi. N via US 101 at 34161 Ophir Rd. - Ophir   247-2765

The owner of the Honey Bear Campground makes and sells more than a dozen kinds of authentic German sausages using natural casings, pure meat, and fresh spices. Samples are offered. Black Forest hams, sauerkraut and rye bread are some of the other delights produced in this culinary hideaway.

★ **Tobey's Bakery**

.7 mi. S at 965 S. Ellensburg St.   247-6418

Gold Beach has a modern full-line bakery that does nice work with unusual breads, donuts, pastries, cookies, cakes, and (especially) wild blackberry pies in season. All are served to go or with coffee at one of a few tables.

Specialty Shops

Kites and Gifts

downtown at 560 N. Ellensburg St.   247-7142

A good selection of kites and boomerangs is sold in this little shop, along with quality regional produce (smoked salmon fillets, jams and jellies) and some distinctive woodcrafted gifts like myrtlewood rolling pins and collapsible baskets.

Rogue Outdoor Store

downtown at 560 N. Ellensburg St.   247-7142

The area's largest sporting goods store sells everything you'll need for fishing, camping, hiking, and other outdoor recreation. They also rent all necessary fishing gear by the day, and will arrange drift boat fishing trips on the Rogue.

Rogue River Myrtlewood

downtown at 710 N. Ellensburg St.   247-2332

More than half of the first-rate assortment of myrtlewood items sold here is produced by the owners. A catalog identifies all of their kitchenware, home or office furnishings, toys, and collectibles that will be shipped anywhere.

NIGHTLIFE

After sunset, the loudest noises in Gold Beach usually come from the surf and a foghorn at the river's mouth.

Beach House Lounge

1.1 mi. S at 1350 S. Ellensburg St.   247-6626

Here's a cozy place to share a drink and conversation while watching a Pacific Ocean sunset.

Rogue Landing

1.1 mi. NE at 94749 Jerry's Flat Rd.   247-2711

Picture windows on two sides of this small lounge provide the best view in town of the river and bridge. In season, guests seated in padded armchair comfort watch shore fishermen land huge salmon along the Rogue a few feet from the lounge.

Rogue Room
  downtown at 321 N. Ellensburg St.   247-2421
There's live music on some weekends, food twenty-four hours a day in the next room, and legal gambling, pool, and electronic darts anytime amidst decor that is stark and dark.

RESTAURANTS

Restaurants are plentiful and plain. Most offer homestyle American dishes amid homespun decor. Seafood is a heavy favorite on menus, and two places do a nice job with fresh local varieties. More surprising are the first-rate Middle European and barbecue specialties prepared at two places near the river.

The Beach House
  1.1 mi. S at 1350 S. Ellensburg St.   247-6626
  B-L-D.   *Moderate*
The pastries and pies are homemade accompaniments to American standard seafoods and steaks. However, the real attraction is the ocean view—the best in town. A window wall frames a wild meadow and beyond, surf breaking on a dark sand beach. Contemporary decor, fabric-and-wood chairs, and pastel colors set the tone in a dining room where tables are outfitted with linen, candles, and fresh flowers. A cozy ocean-view lounge adjoins.

★ **Captain's Table**
  1.1 mi. S at 1295 S. Ellensburg St.   247-6308
  D only.   *Moderate*
A help-yourself fresh salad is brought to the table with four well-made dressings and tasty whole wheat rolls. All of the seafood dishes are either broiled or steamed—a nice change from the emphasis on frying in so many places. Tables are set with crisp white linens, and windows have a distant ocean view from the dining room or lounge.

Chowderhead Restaurant
  .7 mi. S at 910 S. Ellensburg St.   247-7174
  L-D.   *Moderate*
Seafoods predominate on a menu featuring cute names and descriptions of diverse preparations. A small soup and salad bar is complimentary with entrees in the casual family-oriented dining room.

★ **Ethyl's Fine Foods**
  downtown at 347 N. Ellensburg St.   247-7713
  B-L-D. No B on Sat. & Sun.   *Moderate*
Fruit, berry, and cream pies made here are splendid, and seasonal fruits from the area are used for delicious treats like wild blackberry cobbler. Generous portions of traditional all-American dishes are served, each reflecting a light, skilled hand in the kitchen. The shaped-up little cafe offers diners a choice of booth, table, or counter service.

The Golden Egg
.5 mi. S at 710 S. Ellensburg St.   247-7528
B-L-D.   *Moderate*
This popular breakfast spot features an appealing assortment of
well-made, generous omelets. The no-frills cafe in front offers a
choice of counter or booth service, while a large back room overlooks
the high school's football field and (in the far distance) the ocean.

Grant's Pancake and Omelette House
1 mi. NE at 94682 Jerry's Flat Rd.   247-7208
B-L.   *Moderate*
All kinds of pancakes, waffles, and choose-your-own-combination
omelets are served in generous quantities in a plain roadside cafe
with a window view of the lower Rogue River valley.

★ **Nor'wester Seafood Restaurant**
.3 mi. N at Port of Gold Beach   247-2333
D only.   *Moderate*
Fresh local seafood is emphasized in this upstairs dinner house—
broiled, baked, and sauteed, as well as grilled and deep-fried. Creamy
clam chowder and a choice of fresh spinach or tossed salad suggest
the quality of what's to come. The comfortably contemporary split-
level dining room includes a picture window view of the mouth
of the Rogue, a massive raised-relief wood mural of two whales,
and a free-standing fireplace that is much used in winter.

★ **Plum Pudding Restaurant**
28 mi. S at 1011 Chetco Av. on US 101 - Brookings   469-7506
B-L. Closed Sun.-Mon.   *Moderate*
A short list of skillfully made omelets and selected other breakfast
and luncheon specialties is served in a little roadside restaurant
outfitted with a lot of greens, and tables set with full linen.

Rod n' Reel Restaurant
1 mi. N at 94321 Wedderburn Loop   247-6823
B-L-D.   *Moderate*
Seafood, not surprisingly, is emphasized along with steaks in a
family-owned complex that has grown large in nearly forty years.
Tables are set with crisp linens, and diners have a choice of booths
or chairs in several dining areas. The main room has close-up
window views of a tiny man-made waterfall and rock garden. Nearby
is a small lounge, and an organist usually plays on weekends.

★ **Rogue Landing Restaurant**
1.1 mi. NE at 94749 Jerry's Flat Rd.   247-2711
D only.   *Moderate*
Dense, flavorful homemade breads, and strudels, baked stuffed
potatoes, and hearty beef soup reflect the heritage and skill of
the Czech chef/owner of this riverside roadhouse. Fresh seafoods,
beef, pork, and fowl are all given careful attention when he is in
attendance. Tables set with full linen, and comfortable wooden

armchairs grace a dining room which shares the area's best window wall view of the lower Rogue with an adjoining lounge.

Spada's
.8 mi. S at 1020 S. Ellensburg St.   247-7732
B-L-D.   Moderate

An ambitious assortment of Italian and American dishes, pizzas, and seafoods is served in casual, family-oriented dining rooms.

Sportsman's Grotto
downtown at 185 N. Ellensburg St.   247-2232
B-L-D.   Moderate

The clam chowder is very good. So are the bisques and fresh seafood entrees when they're prepared by the skilled chef/owner of this very casual new restaurant.

★ **This Old House**
1.1 mi. N at 94255 North Bank Rogue Hwy.   247-2141
L-D. Closed Sun.   Moderate

An oak pit barbecue is used in cooking beef, chicken, pork, and salmon. The results are outstanding, and the quantities are very generous in a new restaurant that also features delicious homemade pies. Old-fashioned wooden chairs and lace curtains contribute to the homey atmosphere.

LODGING

In the 1980s, Gold Beach finally transcended its original role as a casual overnight base for river fishermen. Several luxurious accommodations have opened recently on the southern outskirts of town to take full advantage of ocean views. Also, thanks to expansions and improvements, travelers can now opt for a plush room overlooking the Rogue. Most places reduce their prices by about 20% from fall through spring.

City Center Motel
downtown at 150 Harlow St.   247-6675

One of Gold Beach's scarce **bargain** lodgings is a single-level older motel set back from the highway. Each of the small rooms has a phone and cable color TV.
regular room—   D or Q bed...$30

Drift In Motel
downtown at 715 N. Ellensburg St. (Box 1115)   247-6020

This older single-level motel is a short stroll from the river and bridge. Each simply furnished unit has cable color TV.
regular room—   Q bed...$38
regular room—   D bed...$36

★ **Gold Beach Resort**
1.1 mi. S at 1330 S. Ellensburg St.   247-7066

The area's most elaborate beachfronting condo/motel was completed in late 1986. Amenities include private access to the dark sand beach, a tennis court, an indoor pool, a whirlpool, and a putting green. Each of the comfortably furnished condos and new motel rooms has a private balcony, phone, and cable color TV with movies. The condos also each have a wood-burning fireplace in the living room and a full kitchen.

#29—2 BR, upstairs, in-bath whirlpool, superb
surf view, T & D & Q beds...$95
#30—1 BR, downstairs, fine private ocean
views, Q bed...$85
#28—1 BR, downstairs, fine ocean views, K bed...$85
regular room—some have a fireplace, Q or K bed...$55

The Inn at Gold Beach
1.2 mi. S at 1435 S. Ellensburg St. *247-6606*
This nicely furnished one- and two-story motel is on a rise across the highway from a superb dark sand beach. Each room has a phone and cable color TV with movies.

regular room—some ocean view beyond
carport, Q bed...$45

★ **Inn of the Beachcomber - Best Western**
1.1 mi. S at 1250 S. Ellensburg St. *247-6691*
One of the first lodgings in the area to take advantage of the ocean view, this well-maintained motel also provides a paved path to the sandy beach, a large indoor pool, and a whirlpool. Each comfortably furnished unit has a phone and cable color TV with movies.

#239,#212—end rooms, private balcony,
fireplace, wet bar/refrigerator,
good ocean view from K bed...$80
ocean view room—surf beyond nearby roof top, 2 Q or K bed...$62
regular room—no ocean view, Q bed...$57

★ **Ireland's Rustic Lodge**
.9 mi. S at 1120 S. Ellensburg St. (Box 744) *247-7718*
The town's most attractively landscaped lodgings offer a choice of individual log cabins or modern (completed in 1986) motel rooms with knotty-pine interiors. Access is provided to a sandy ocean beach, which is a short stroll to the west. Each tastefully furnished room has cable color TV, and most have a wood-burning fireplace.

#24,#23—upstairs, vaulted ceiling, stone
fireplace, windows on two sides, pvt.
balc., pvt. ocean view from Q bed...$51
#22—kitchen, hooded free-standing fireplace,
private balcony with ocean view, Q bed...$66
#14 thru #17—older, raised stone fireplace,
private balcony with ocean view
from Q bed...$47
regular room—cabin, fireplace, no view, Q bed...$39

★ **Jot's Resort**
1 mi. N at 94360 Wedderburn Loop (Box J)   247-6676
The area's largest and most complete condominium/motor hotel
is on the north shore of the Rogue River. Amenities include an
outdoor pool; a whirlpool; restaurant and lounge; gift/tackle shop
and marina; plus (for a fee) bicycles or boat rentals, dock space,
fishing equipment, and reservations for river excursions and deep
sea fishing charters. Each modern, well-equipped unit has a private
balcony, phone, and cable color TV.
   one-bedroom—waterfront condo, kitchen,
                  L.R. with fireplace, river view,   Q bed...$85
   regular room—   2 T or Q bed...$65

Nimrod Motel
.6 mi. S at 775 S. Ellensburg St.   247-6635
This single-level motel offers modernized, simply furnished rooms.
Each has a phone and cable color TV with movies.
   regular room—   Q bed...$36
   regular room—   D bed...$34

Oregon Trail Lodge
downtown at 550 N. Ellensburg St.   247-6030
One of Gold Beach's oldest motels is a single-level **bargain**. Each
no-frills room has cable color TV with movies.
   regular room—   Q bed...$28
   regular room—   D bed...$25

Sand n' Sea Motel
.8 mi. S at 1040 S. Ellensburg St.   247-6658
Small and modern, this single-level motel offers rooms with a phone
and cable color TV.
   regular room—   Q bed...$39

Shore Cliff Inn
.9 mi. S at 1100 S. Ellensburg St. (Box 615)   247-7091
Completed in late 1986, this three-story motel was carefully
designed to take full advantage of ocean views. Access is provided
to the beach, which is a short stroll away, and there is an indoor
pool. Most of the large, attractively furnished rooms have a private
balcony. All have an ocean view, phone, and cable color TV with movies.
   #301—end room, private balcony, fine surf view
                  from   K bed...$56
   regular room—no balcony,   Q bed...$40

Sunset Inn
downtown at 585 N. Ellensburg St.   247-2762
This single-level older motel is a **bargain**. Each simply furnished
room has cable color TV.
   #48—large end unit, extra window with private
                  valley view,   Q bed...$28
   regular room—   Q bed...$28

★ **Tu Tu Tun**
   7 mi. NE at 96550 North Bank Rogue Hwy.   *247-6664*
Here is the most gracious lodge on the Rogue River. Amenities on the beautifully landscaped grounds include a long outdoor pool, a boat dock and ramp, and a pitch-and-putt course. The main lodge includes an engaging library, an intimate bar, and a casually elegant dining room with a superb view of the Rogue River canyon. Each of the inviting, contemporary guest rooms has a private bath and dressing area, a private balcony or patio overlooking the Rogue, and two extra-long double beds. Instead of phones or television, fresh flowers and current magazines enhance guests' enjoyment of the tranquil surroundings.
   "River Suite"—spacious 1 BR, kitchen, deck with
             wood-burning stove, great river views,2 D beds...$99
   regular room—fine river view,   2 D beds...$79
Western Village Motel
   .7 mi. S at 975 S. Ellensburg St.   *247-6611*
There are no amenities, but this modern single-level motel offers a phone and cable color TV with movies in each of the rooms.
   regular room—   Q bed...$40

CAMPGROUNDS

Gold Beach is located where the Northwest's greatest recreational river empties into the ocean. This fact, and some of the best coastal weather outside of California, has made the area a special destination for campers. An extraordinary assortment of public and private campgrounds has been provided. The best offer complete facilities and all kinds of water-related recreation in choice sites near ocean beaches or adjacent to the Rogue River.

★ **Arizona Beach Resort**
   15 mi. N on US 101 (Box 621)   *332-6491*
You can camp on the beach, in an adjoining meadow, or back in the woods by a tiny stream at this large private campground for both RV'ers and tenters. Beachcombing and hiking are popular, although listening to the sound of the surf and watching sunsets are the main events. Flush toilets, hot showers, and full hookups are available. The closely spaced sites lack privacy, but they're well maintained. Each has a rock ring fire pit, and a picnic table.
                                      base rate—beach...$10
                                      base rate—meadow...$ 8

★ **Harris Beach State Park**
   27 mi. S on US 101 - Brookings   *469-2021*
The best place to spend a night in Brookings is at the state-operated campground, above a scenic beach. Beachcombing, surf fishing, swimming, and sunbathing are popular. A bathhouse, and hiking and nature trails, have been provided. Flush toilets, hot showers, and full hookups are available. Each site is well spaced, manicured

(most are on grass), and includes a picnic table and fire grill. Campers can select sunny sites, or lush fern-lined sites in a dense forest. Non-Oregonians add $2 surcharge to base rate.

base rate...$6

★ **Humbug Mountain State Park**
   21 mi. N on US 101   *332-6774*
The state has developed an ideally located campground along a stream at the base of a towering coastal mountain. Hiking, fishing, beachcombing, and swimming (for the hearty) are popular. Flush toilets, hot showers, and hookups are available. Each closely spaced manicured site has a picnic table and fire ring. Some have shade, and are along a creek. Non-Oregonians add $2 surcharge to base rate.   base rate...$6

★ **Indian Creek Recreation Park**
   1 mi. NE via US 101 at 94680 Jerry's Flat Rd.   *247-7704*
A lush mixed forest covers the gentle slopes surrounding this large attractively landscaped private campground. The Rogue River is a short stroll north. A small creek runs through the property, which also includes a cafe and convenience store, plus the area's finest game room with ping pong, pool tables, electronic and card games, and table hockey, and a big stone fireplace surrounded by armchairs. Saunas, flush toilets, hot showers, and full hookups are available. A separate tenter area is further along the creek. Each closely spaced site has a picnic table and a fire ring/grill.   base rate...$8

★ **Quosatana Campground**
   15 mi. E at 99449 Agness Rd.   *247-6651*
The Siskiyou National Forest operates this campground in a beautiful sylvan setting by the Rogue River. Rocky beaches and sandy-bottomed swimming holes are nearby. There are boat ramps, fish cleaning stations, and flush toilets, but no showers, hot water, or hookups. Each widely spaced shaded site has a picnic table, fire ring, and grill. (Closed late October thru late April.)

base rate...$5

SPECIAL EVENT

Curry County Fair   *fairgrounds*   *August*
Oregon's largest flower show is a special feature of this celebration, along with a grand parade, tug-o-wars, live entertainment and dancing, colorful (and tasty) exhibits, and more.

OTHER INFORMATION

Area Code: *503*
Zip Code: *97444*
Gold Beach Chamber of Commerce
   .4 mi. S at 510 S. Ellensburg St.   *247-7526*
Siskiyou National Forest - Gold Beach Office
   1 mi. S at 1225 S. Ellensburg St.   *247-6651*

Grants Pass, Oregon

Grants Pass is the West's ultimate river town. It occupies the heart of a broad, mountain-rimmed valley midway along the fabulous Rogue River. This peerless recreational waterway assumes many forms during the relatively short run from its source near Crater Lake to the ocean. It is calm and clear as it glides past a lovely park by the heart of town. A few miles upstream, low dams have created several small, scenic lakes. Downstream, the river dashes wildly through breathtaking gorges, and it meanders in riffles deep within forested valleys surrounded by gentle mountains.

Noted for one of the mildest climates in the Northwest, Grants Pass is further enhanced by a profusion of broadleaf and pine trees and flowers. Rhododendron bushes twenty feet high flourish near some of the continent's most northerly inland palm trees. In winter, temperatures are relatively moderate and there is very little snowfall, but rainfall is almost continuous. Daytime temperatures are already warm by early spring. During the normally hot sunny days of summer, pretty little upstream lakes, peaceful stretches in town, and downstream "wild river" sections entice the year's largest crowds to delight in the wonderful diversity of water recreation available on the Rogue River. Nearby, a large national forest, a wilderness area, and several state and local parks provide additional outdoor recreation opportunities from spring through fall.

Tortuous mountain passes and unfriendly Indians discouraged

pioneers who came West over the Oregon Trail from settling in this area during the 1840s. However, with the first discovery of gold in Oregon in the neighboring Jacksonville area in 1851, hordes of soon-to-be-disappointed prospectors arrived. After the last major Indian battle in 1854, homesteaders began to move here to take advantage of the area's fertile soil and mild climate. The town was probably named after General U.S. Grant during the Civil War, when this area was being surveyed. With a diversified economy that included (and still includes) lumbering, dairying, and farming, growth has been steady since that time.

Residents' pride in their river remains the town's binding force. Sharing it with visitors has become a major industry in recent years. Guide and rental services now offer all kinds of vessels—jet boats, inflatable kayaks, and wind sailboards, plus old favorites like fishing boats and whitewater rafts—for experiencing the Rogue. One of the West's finest riverside parks is a short stroll from the heart of town. Downtown remains an unpretentious commercial center with a large number of conventional shops, bars, and restaurants. Plain, plentiful, and very reasonably priced accommodations are concentrated along business routes into town. The best lodgings, however, have delightful riverfront or lakeside locales. Nearby, some of the West's most picturesque campgrounds also feature idyllic sites along the river.

Elevation:

950 feet

Population (1980):

15,032

Population (1970):

12,455

Location:

240 miles South
of Portland

Grants Pass, Oregon
WEATHER PROFILE
Vokac Weather Rating

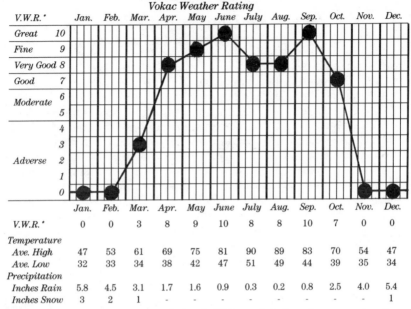

V.W.R.*	Jan.	Feb.	Mar.	Apr.	May	June	July	Aug.	Sep.	Oct.	Nov.	Dec.
V.W.R.*	0	0	3	8	9	10	8	8	10	7	0	0
Temperature												
Ave. High	47	53	61	69	75	81	90	89	83	70	54	47
Ave. Low	32	33	34	38	42	47	51	49	44	39	35	34
Precipitation												
Inches Rain	5.8	4.5	3.1	1.7	1.6	0.9	0.3	0.2	0.8	2.5	4.0	5.4
Inches Snow	3	2	1	-	-	-	-	-	-	-	-	1

V.W.R. = Vokac Weather Rating: probability of mild (warm & dry) weather on any given day.

Forecast

	V.W.R.*	Temperatures Daytime	Evening	Precipitation
Jan.	0 Adverse	chilly	chilly	continual rainstorms/snow flurries
Feb.	0 Adverse	cool	chilly	frequent rainstorms
Mar.	3 Adverse	cool	chilly	frequent rainstorms
Apr.	8 Very Good	warm	cool	occasional showers
May	9 Fine	warm	cool	occasional showers
June	10 Great	warm	cool	infrequent showers
July	8 Very Good	hot	warm	negligible
Aug.	8 Very Good	hot	warm	negligible
Sep.	10 Great	hot	cool	infrequent showers
Oct.	7 Good	warm	cool	occasional rainstorms
Nov.	0 Adverse	cool	chilly	frequent rainstorms
Dec.	0 Adverse	chilly	chilly	continual rainstorms

Summary

Grants Pass is located in the heart of the beautiful Rogue River Valley in a luxuriant pine-and-broadleaf forest framed by Coast Range mountains. The area enjoys one of the Northwest's mildest four season climates. **Winter** is cool and wet. More than half of the year's precipitation occurs during this season in continual rainstorms and rare snow flurries. **Spring** is delightful, with warm days, cool evenings, and occasional showers. From Easter through Memorial Day, outdoor activities are further enhanced by blossom-time, when nearby orchards and flowering shade trees lend fragrance and beauty to the setting. Hot, sunny days, warm evenings, and almost no chance of rain throughout **summer** are ideal conditions for enjoying the West's most usable river. In **fall**, comfortably warm days, cool evenings, and occasional rainstorms continue through Halloween, when brilliant foliage highlights the season.

ATTRACTIONS & DIVERSIONS

★ **Boat Rides**

An exciting and popular way to enjoy the spectacular Rogue River in summer is via jet boat. Trips involve some whitewater and range from one hour to five hours for the round trip to Hellgate Canyon. Some trips include a champagne brunch or country dinner by the river. For more information and reservations, contact:

Hellgate Excursions *.5 mi. S in Riverside Park*   *479-7204*
Jet Boat River Excursions *10 mi. E on OR 99*   *582-0800*
Rogue Whitewater Excursions *.4 mi. S at 953 SE 7th St.* *476-6401*

★ **Crater Lake National Park**

80 mi. NE via I-5 & OR 234 on OR 62

Oregon's only national park has as its centerpiece Crater Lake. The clear, brilliant blue waters of this magnificent mountain-rimmed lake are 1,932 feet deep—America's deepest. The renowned six-by-five-mile water body was formed when rain and snow filled what was left of volcanic Mount Mazama more than 6,000 years ago after violent eruptions collapsed the mountaintop. A breathtakingly beautiful thirty-two-mile rim drive around the lake doesn't open until approximately the 4th of July except in years of light snowfall. The main highway (OR 62) is kept open to Rim Village year-round, in spite of a normal snowfall of fifty feet each winter. Boat tours leave daily during the summer to Wizard Island, a symmetrical cinder cone that rises about 760 feet above the lake's surface. Scenic panoramas and, in summer, fields of wildflowers line spur roads and well-marked trails that extend from many points along the rim drive.

★ **Hellgate**

14.4 mi. NW on Galice Rd.

The Rogue River's phenomenal entrance into the Coast Range is a narrow passage with sheer rock walls more than 250 feet high. It is an especially popular section for river trips. Far above, a panoramic viewpoint has been provided by the road that parallels the river.

★ **Library**

downtown at 200 NW C St.   *474-5480*

The handsome Josephine County Library has an extensive display of periodicals, and upholstered reading chairs, in a large and cheerful room that also showcases a big globe. Closed Sat.-Sun.

★ **Oregon Caves National Monument**

49 mi. SW via US 199 on OR 46—Cave Jct.   *592-3400*

Visitors can explore many dramatic and beautiful chambers in the "Marble Halls of Oregon." Guide service is required and available year-round. For the strenuous cave tours, children under six are not permitted. Visitors should have a jacket since the average temperature is only 42°F, and non-slip walking shoes. There are hiking trails and picnic and camping facilities nearby in the lush mountain forest. The charming, rustic Chateau Hotel and restaurant are open in summer.

★ **Palm Tree**
   downtown at 7th/G Sts.

The diverse and luxuriant vegetation of the Rogue River Valley is perhaps best symbolized by a palm tree casually located by a downtown thoroughfare. Benches near the palm give visitors a chance to contemplate the fact that palm trees can and do grow year-round outdoors in the Northwest.

River Running

★ **Rogue River - downstream**
   west of town

In 1968, an eighty-four-mile segment of the Rogue River was designated as a "National Wild and Scenic River." The segment begins a few miles west of town at the junction of the Rogue and Applegate Rivers, and extends almost to the ocean. The stretch between Grave Creek and Illahe is the most remote. It has been classified as "Wild River" and is inaccessible except by a well-maintained and deservedly popular 39-mile hiking trail, or by man-powered boat. Gentler parts of the designated segment are classified as "Scenic" or "Recreational," and are accessible by the Galice Road which parallels the river for nearly thirty miles, and by jet boats which join rafts and other oar-powered craft on these stretches. An extraordinary diversity of river experiences is available. Scenic, whitewater, or fishing trips varying from a half day to nine days can be arranged in crafts ranging from jet boats to individual inflatable kayaks. Several rustic lodges and picturesque campgrounds are scattered along the river. Visitors bringing their own rafts can easily arrange to be left off and picked up at prearranged spots. Excellent maps, books, and complete lists of guide services can be obtained at the Chamber of Commerce. Some of the local guide services and their specialties are:

The Galice Resort (guided or rental rafts) *11744 Galice Rd.* *476-3818*
Orange Torpedo Boats (inflatable kayaks, rafts) *479-5061*
Osprey River Trips (inflatable kayaks, rafts) *479-4215*
Paul Brooks Trips (guided/rental rafts) *12221 Galice Rd.* *476-8051*
The Raft Shop (durt bags) *Gold Hill* *855-7238*
River Adventure Float Trips (rafts, McKenzie boats) *476-6493*
Rogue Canyon Guide Service (drift fishing, rafts) *479-9554*
Sundance (kayaks,rafts,drift fishing) *14894 Galice Rd.* *479-8508*
White Water Cowboys (guides or rentals) *209 Galice Rd.* *479-0132*
Wilderness Water Ways (rafts,inf.kayaks) *12260 Galice Rd.* *479-2021*

★ **Rogue River - upstream**
   east of town

Several small scenic reservoirs have been created behind dams upstream from town. The smooth waters are popular for speed boating and waterskiing as well as for most watercraft. Picturesque areas for picnicking, sunbathing, swimming, and fishing abound. Riverside campgrounds, lodges, and motels are also numerous along the Rogue River Highway (OR 99) which parallels the river east of town.

★ **Riverside Park**
.5 mi. S on E. Park St.
Well-maintained lawns sloping down to the Rogue River delight sunbathers, and swimmers enjoy calm, clear pools just offshore. Above, noble trees provide shade for picnic tables. Imaginative play equipment (like a large wooden maze), formal flower gardens, and playfields are other attractions of this outstanding riverfront park.

★ **Rogue River Hiking Trail**
starts 23 mi. NE on Galice Rd. at Grave Creek
The "Wild River" segment of the Rogue River is paralleled by a scenic hiking trail along the entire north bank. The forty-mile-long trail begins at Grave Creek on the Galice Road and ends at Illahe. It is closed to motorized vehicles, horses, and pack animals. Hiking the entire distance normally takes about five days.

★ **Siskiyou National Forest**
S & W of town   *479-5301*
This vast forest includes most of the southwestern corner of the state. The only redwood trees outside of California are an unusual feature. The Kalmiopsis Wilderness Area, at the rugged heart of the forest, is a botanist's paradise of rare and unusual plants. Nearly half of the designated National Wild and Scenic River portion of the Rogue River is in the forest, as is Oregon Caves National Monument. A good system of paved and dirt roads and hundreds of miles of trails provide access for river running, swimming, fishing, hiking, backpacking, horseback riding, pack trips, and camping. Information and maps may be obtained at the Forest Supervisor's Office in town.

Winery

★ **Siskiyou Vineyards**
33 mi. SW via US 199 at 6220 Oregon Caves Hwy. - Cave Jct. 592-3727
One of Oregon's youngest premium wineries is flourishing in the Illinois River valley. There is a picnic area, and the tasting room is open 11-5 daily.

SHOPPING

Grants Pass has a lively downtown oriented primarily toward meeting the conventional needs of residents and outdoor recreation enthusiasts. Attractively landscaped buildings and parking lots and an abundance of shade trees enhance the area. Parking meters became a thing of the past in 1986.

Food Specialties

★ The Cake Shop
8.8 mi. NW at 215 Galice Rd.   *476-7087*
In addition to beautifully decorated cakes, this roadside bakery offers outstanding breads (like sheepherder, earth, and sourdough), plus old-fashioned cinnamon rolls and other delicious treats on weekends. Closed Mon.-Thurs.

The Donut & Pie Shop
.6 mi. S on US 199 at 131 SE Redwood Hwy.   *476-8623*
A full range of donuts, plus assorted berry and cream pies, are made here and served with coffee at indoor (or patio) picnic tables, or to go. Closed Sun.

Grants Pass Pharmacy
downtown at 414 SW 6th St.   *476-4262*
In the center of an updated, long-established pharmacy is an island ice cream bar where a variety of flavors and styles is served to go or at some tables overlooking the main street.

★ The Ice Cream Factory
downtown at 203 SE H St.   *476-1462*
New owners continue to make many flavors of chemical-free, natural ingredient ice cream here. In addition to all kinds of delicious cold creations, there are also some tasty pastry desserts served in a cheerful little parlor, or to go.

★ Mexia's
39 mi. N on I-5 (near exit 95) - 2 mi. S of Canyonville
The original owner is still serving delicious two-crust fresh fruit and berry pies in the same roadside cottage that he opened for business back in 1927.

Rogue Gold Dairy
downtown at 234 SW 5th St.   *476-7786*
Locally made cheeses are sold in this small retail outlet, along with assorted teas and spices.

Specialty Shops

Blind George's News Stand
downtown at 117 SW G St.   *476-3463*
Here is an unusually extensive assortment of newspapers, magazines, and paperback books—including many about the Northwest.

The Book Stop
downtown at 211 SE 6th St.   *479-1587*
This inviting store features books about southern Oregon and the Rogue River in a good selection of well-organized books. There is an easy chair for browsers.

Myrtlewood Products, Inc.
downtown at SW 6th/D Sts.   *479-6664*
Artistic and functional pieces from Oregon's most-sought hardwood

tree are displayed in this small shop. Closed Sun.

Riverside Gift Shop
.4 mi. S at 980 SW 6th St.   474-2918
Made-in-Oregon products ranging from foods to one-of-a-kind
handcrafted objects of art are featured in an attractive shop that
opened in 1986.

The Train Gallery
2 mi. SW via US 199 at 1951 Redwood Av.   476-1951
Downstairs, one of the largest model railroad exhibits in the Northwest
is evolving. There is a casual art gallery upstairs. Closed Sun.

NIGHTLIFE

Many casual bars, lounges, and roadside taverns are scattered in and
around town. Several offer live music and dancing. Three overlook the
Rogue River.

Casa del Rio
2.1 mi. SE at 1936 Rogue River Hwy.   479-4318
Live music for dancing happens on weekends in a big, casual cantina
next to a Mexican restaurant. The deck overlooking the Rogue River is
a fine place to enjoy a Margarita on a hot summer day.

Herb's La Casita Lounge
.6 mi. SE at 515 SE Rogue River Hwy.   476-1313
Live music and dancing are featured most nights in the plain, popular
Kashmir Room lounge behind a 24-hour coffee shop/restaurant.

Merlin Mining Company
8.5 mi. W at 330 Merlin Rd.   476-5403
Live music and dancing are offered on weekends in an updated
Western saloon.

Pastime Tavern
downtown at 121 SW G St.   479-0332
Even the notable hardwood back bar is treated casually in this frayed
relic from the turn of the century. Pool, ping pong, and darts provide
the action in an authentic old-time workingman's bar.

R-Haus
2.7 mi. SE at 2140 Rogue River Hwy.   476-4287
The antique-filled Liberty Lounge overlooking the Rogue is a tranquil
spot for a quiet conversation above a restaurant.

★ **Riverside Inn**
.4 mi. S at 971 SE 6th St.   476-2488
There's music for listening or dancing most nights in the motor hotel's
classy, contemporary lounge. Patrons can relax in padded velour
armchairs and enjoy a picture window view of the river and town park.
Refreshments are also served on a sunny riverside deck.

Woodshed Lounge
1.4 mi. SW on US 199 at 690 Redwood Hwy.   479-0012
Live music and dancing are offered several nights each week in a large,
rustic Western-style saloon and restaurant complex.

RESTAURANTS

In recent years, several very good restaurants have opened which feature Italian, Japanese—and even Thai cuisine. However, most of the local dining rooms still offer hearty American fare and conventional Western decor. The wholesome, plentiful food and casual surroundings are well suited to the town's preoccupation with robust outdoor activity focused on the river. Prices at most of the recommended restaurants are among the lowest anywhere in the West.

★ **The Bistro**
.9 mi. N at 1214 NW 6th St. 479-3412
L-D. No L on Sat. & Sun. Low
Among the many pizza parlors in Grants Pass, the Bistro has the right stuff for deep-dish Chicago-style pizzas. The furnishings are a comfortable alternative to the usual pizza-chain decor, with walls covered with old movie star posters, and a choice of booths or chairs.

The Brewery
downtown at 509 SW G St. 479-9850
L-D. No L on Sat. Closed Sun. Moderate
Contemporary American dishes are served in comfortably furnished dining rooms in a skillfully converted brewery. An inviting bar adjoins.

Casa del Rio
2.1 mi. SE at 1936 Rogue River Hwy. 479-4318
L-D. Low
The accustomed array of Mexican dishes is served in a rustic wood dining room, or on a patio when weather permits, overlooking the Rogue River. A view cantina adjoins.

Erik's
.8 mi. E at 1067 Redwood Spur 479-4471
L-D. No L on Sat. Moderate
This large, showy restaurant features a comprehensive assortment of contemporary American specialties (teriyaki beef, broiled mahi mahi, grilled pork chops, elaborate salad bar, etc.) amidst appealing wood-and-plants decor.

Galice Restaurant and Store
21 mi. W at 11744 Galice Rd. 476-3818
B-L-D. No D on Mon.-Thurs. Low
Giant homemade cinnamon rolls are a specialty among hearty American dishes served in a rustic cafe with a big fireplace, or on an inviting deck where occasional steak cookouts accompany a great view of some of the best riffles of the Rogue. The place is perfectly geared for river-users.

Granny's Kitchen
downtown at 117 NE F St. 476-7185
B-L-D. Moderate
Since 1985, glass cases near the entrance have tempted patrons with

toothsome displays of two dozen cream, meringue, fruit, and berry pies. But among the all-American foods served here, it is the cinnamon roll that is unforgettable—a humongous loaf filled with raisins and apple slices and topped with a warm glaze. Well-padded booths fill the capacious rooms in the big, modern coffee shop.

★ **Hamilton House Restaurant**
1.5 mi. E at 344 NE Terry Lane   479-3938
D only. Closed Mon.   *Moderate*
Carefully prepared American entrees always include seasonally fresh fish as well as assorted steaks, chops, and poultry. Complete family-style meals are accompanied by a salad bar highlighted by fresh fruits and pastas. In this out-of-the-way restaurant, a local favorite, the pleasant dining rooms both have garden views.

Jean's Kitchen & Pie Shop
downtown at 117 SW H St.   476-0837
B-L. Closed Sun.   *Low*
The homemade cream and berry pies, and biscuits, are good reasons to try this pleasant split-level coffee shop/deli.

★ **Little Italy Ristorante**
downtown at 201 SW G St.   479-1066
L-D. Closed Sun.   *Moderate*
Authentic Italian dishes are described on a remarkably long menu. The homemade soups and desserts are especially fine accompaniments to the several kinds of veal and the wealth of other entrees available in a skillfully converted historic building where candlelit tables are set with full linen.

Matsukaze Restaurant
1.3 mi. N at 1675 NE 7th St.   479-2961
L-D. No L on Sat. Closed Sun.   *Moderate*
Here is a surprising new addition to the local dining scene. Authentic Japanese tempura, teriyaki, and other specialty dishes are carefully prepared and properly served to diners at fabric booths, tables and chairs, or low tables with foot-wells. The understated contemporary decor is a peaceful contrast to the building's shopping center facade.

Merlin Mining Co.
8.5 mi. NW at 330 Merlin Rd.   476-5403
L-D. Closed Mon.   *Moderate*
Prime rib, steaks, and seafood are served in a Western-style dining room. An adjoining lounge offers live entertainment on weekends.

Mrs. G's Restaurant
1.4 mi. N at 1802 NW 6th St.   476-8513
B-L-D.   *Low*
The area's best open-24-hours-daily coffee shop offers fast food, fair prices, and friendly service in a plush, plant-filled setting.

Nature's Best
    downtown at 422-A SW 5th St.   476-0440
    B-L.   *Low*
Tasty whole grain pancakes, assorted fertile-egg omelets, and natural-ingredient pastries are featured. Grants Pass' organic coffee shop opened in 1986 in a spacious, simply furnished room in a converted cottage.

★ **Paradise Ranch Inn**
    7.5 mi. NW via I-5 (Merlin exit) at 7000 Monument Dr.   479-4333
    B-D.   *Expensive*
Seasonally fresh local produce is used in the skilled preparation of classical dishes like chicken Florentine and regional specialties like grilled lamb chops. Entrees are accompanied by breads and desserts made here. The ranch's romantic, casually elegant dining room provides a panoramic view of manicured lawns and a small lake backed by the evergreen Coast Range.

★ **Pongsri's**
    1.2 mi. N at 1571 NE 6th St.   479-1345
    L-D. Closed Mon.   *Low*
The spicy Thai and flavorful Chinese creations featured here are as authentic as they are delectable. In fact, the food is so good and reasonably priced that the plain little out-of-the-way dining room has already been expanded to reduce the waiting lines that became common soon after the restaurant opened in 1985.

Powderhorn Cafe
    downtown at 321 NE 6th St.   479-9403
    B-L. Closed Sun.   *Low*
Dishes are prepared fresh from scratch by the chef/owner, and his omelets and homemade biscuits are true examples of American-style home cooking. The no-frills cafe opened in early 1986, and is developing a loyal local following.

R-Haus
    2.7 mi. SE at 2140 Rogue River Hwy.   476-4287
    D only.   *Moderate*
Italian dishes, steaks, and seafoods are featured in abundant meals served in casual dining rooms. Early diners by the windows get a view of the Rogue River, as do patrons of the upstairs lounge.

Riverside Inn Restaurant
    .4 mi. S at 971 SE 6th St.   476-2488
    B-L-D.   *Moderate*
American dishes are served in a plush contemporary dining room with splendid picture window views of the Rogue River and the town park on the other bank.

Shepp's Sportsman Inn
    2.4 mi. SE at 1883 Rogue River Hwy.   479-2832
    B-L-D.   *Moderate*
Steak and family-style hearty American meals are served in a casual

dining room. The adjoining lounge features live music and dancing on weekends.

Wagon Wheel Restaurant
 1.4 mi. N at 111 NE Hillcrest Dr.   *479-0823*
 B-L-D.   *Low*
From homemade cinnamon rolls and biscuits with breakfast, to pot roast or chicken with dumplings for dinner, the Wagon Wheel offers hearty portions of traditional American dishes. Fabric-backed booths are given some privacy by high wooden dividers in a large dining room with a lot of Old West flourishes.

★ **We-Ask-U Inn Cafe**
 6 mi. E at 5560 Rogue River Hwy.   *479-1485*
 B-L.   *Low*
The sign on the door says "If you can't take a joke . . . don't open this door." Do it anyway, or you'll miss some of the finest victuals in southern Oregon. Everything the new (since 1986) owners cook—from crepe-style omelets through jalapeno/cheddar corn muffins and huge fluffy biscuits to seasonally fresh fruit and berry pies—is delicious! Frilly curtains and a lot of healthy green plants soften the fishing shack rusticity of this rickety roadside cafe.

★ **Wolf Creek Tavern**
 20 mi. N on I-5   *866-2474*
 L-D.   *Low*
American fare is served family-style in a large, wonderfully authentic 1850s stagecoach stop that has been painstakingly restored and furnished in period pieces. It is on the National Historic Register. Upstairs, eight antique-filled rooms provide novel overnight accommodations at a bargain price. A firelit barroom/lobby and exquisitely detailed parlor adjoin the nostalgic dining rooms.

★ **Yankee Pot Roast**
 .4 mi. N at 720 NW 6th St.   *476-0551*
 D only.   *Low*
Here is the Rogue Valley's most consistent source of tasty, down-home all-American cooking. It is served in abundance by waitresses costumed in granny gowns that blend smoothly amidst old-time decor in several cozy dining rooms of a recycled historic house.

LODGING

There are plenty of places to stay in and around town. The best have riverfront views. A remarkable number of bargain motels are located on 6th and 7th Streets between downtown and Interstate 5. Many of the recommended accommodations offer 10% and greater rate reductions apart from summer.

Colonial Inn
 1.5 mi. N at 1889 NE 6th St.   *479-8301*
An outdoor pool is the feature of this modern two-level motel. Each

well-furnished room has a phone and cable color TV.

regular room— Q bed...$40

★ **Del Rogue Motel**

3 mi. E at 2600 Rogue River Hwy. 479-2111

This beautifully landscaped little motel has a delightfully tree-shaded location by the river. Each well-furnished unit has cable color TV and a private screened porch. A kitchen may be added for $7.

#D,#C,#A—fine river views from upstairs, Q bed...$37

regular room— Q bed...$37

Egyptian Motel

.4 mi. N at 728 NW 6th St. 476-6601

There is a large landscaped outdoor pool in this **bargain** single-level motel. Each small, simply furnished room has a cable color TV.

regular room— Q bed...$28

regular room— D bed...$22

Fireside Motel

.5 mi. N at 839 NE 6th St. 474-5558

An outdoor pool is a feature of this small, older **bargain** motel. Each simply furnished room has cable color TV with movies.

regular room— 2 D or Q bed...$24

Golden Inn Motel

1.6 mi. N at 1950 NW Vine St. 479-6611

One of the area's newer **bargain** motels has a large outdoor pool. Each tastefully furnished room has a phone and cable color TV with movies.

regular room— Q bed...$24

★ **Half Moon Bar Lodge**

27 mi. W on the Rogue River 476-4002

The small lodge has no access road. It can only be reached by boat, plane, or on foot. The rate includes gourmet home-cooked meals prepared from their own garden-fresh produce and served to (at most) twenty guests sharing the Rogue River wilderness. Rates include three family-style meals plus Oregon wines at dinner. (Additional nights are 20% less.) Business office: 410 NW E St. in Grants Pass.

regular room— D bed...$150

Hawks Inn Motel

1.1 mi. N at 1464 NW 6th St. 479-4057

This smaller, older single-level **bargain** motel has an outdoor pool with a slide. Each of the refurbished, simply furnished rooms has a color TV.

regular room— Q bed...$28

regular room— D bed...$22

★ **Morrison's Lodge**

17 mi. NW at 8500 Galice Rd. - Merlin 97532 476-3825

A bend in the Rogue River provides a choice site for a very popular ranch-style lodge and cabins complex. There's boating, fishing for

132

salmon and steelhead, swimming, gold panning, and rockhounding in the river; an outdoor pool with a view deck and two tennis courts; plus a restaurant. Each spacious unit has a private bath, fireplace, and a riverview deck.

"lodge"—American plan (breakfast & dinner),   2 T or D bed...$110
"housekeeping cottage"—2 BR, kitchen,   2 T or D bed...$75

Motel 6
1.4 mi. N at 1800 NE 7th St.   *476-9096*
The nationwide **bargain** chain is represented here by a large modern motel with an outdoor pool. Each no-frills room has TV.

regular room—   D bed...$25

★ **Paradise Ranch Inn**
7.5 mi. NW via I-5 (Merlin exit) at 7000-D Monument Dr. 479-4333
One of the Northwest's most complete resorts is in a delightful ranch setting overlooking the Coast Range. Manicured grounds include a large outdoor pool and whirlpool, two lighted tennis courts, a small lake for (catch and release) fishing and boating, hiking and biking trails, a recreation center and a gourmet restaurant, plus a new 18-hole golf course. Each of the spacious, luxuriously appointed units has a private bath and (if requested) color TV.

"House in the Woods"—(4 units), shared kitchen,
lounge, whirlpool, private
forest views,   Q bed...$96

regular room—   2 D or Q bed...$74

Redwood Motel
.8 mi. N at 815 NE 6th St.   *476-0878*
A large landscaped outdoor pool is the focal point. In this older, single-level motel, each nicely maintained unit has a phone and cable color TV with movies.

regular room—   Q bed...$34

Regal Lodge
1 mi. N at 1400 NW 6th St.   *479-3305*
A small outdoor pool is a feature of this modern **bargain** motel. Each room has a phone and cable color TV.

regular room—   D or Q bed...$26

★ **Riverside Inn - Best Western**
.4 mi. S at 971 SE 6th St.   *476-6873*
A choice riverfront location across from the town park is the site for the area's largest motor hotel. Facilities include two outdoor pools (the large one overlooks the river), two whirlpools, plus (for a fee) jet boat rides. The stylish dining room and a deck have fine river views, and there is a comfortable riverview lounge with entertainment. Each spacious, well-furnished room has a phone and cable color TV. For toll-free reservations in Oregon, call (800)331-4567; elsewhere (800)334-4567.

#367,#267—newer, quiet end, private balcony
    with river rapids view,   2 Q beds...$73
#365,#363,#360,#359—top floor, private
    balcony, fine river view,   K bed...$70
#204,#206,#208,#210—top floor, great pool/
    river/park view,   K bed...$64
#200—very large, double private balcony, fine
    private river/park view,   K bed...$80
    regular room—no river view,   Q bed...$54

Rodeway Inn

1.7 mi. E by (exit 55) I-5 at 111 NE Agness Av.   *476-1117*

This large newer motor hotel has an outdoor pool and whirlpool, plus a restaurant and lounge. Each spacious, well-furnished room has a phone and cable color TV. For toll-free reservations, call (800)228-2000.

    "Executive Room"—spacious, in-room whirlpool,   K bed...$70
    regular room—   Q bed...$45

Royal Vue Motor Inn

1.5 mi. N at 110 NE Morgan Lane   *479-5381*

Hard by I-5 is one of the valley's most complete motor hotels. Amenities include a large outdoor pool, plus (indoors) a whirlpool, and (his and hers) saunas and steam baths. A restaurant and lounge are also on the property. Each well-outfitted room has a private patio or deck, and cable color TV with movies. For toll-free reservations in Oregon, call (800)452-1452; elsewhere (800)547-7555.

    deluxe room—refrigerator/wet bar,   K bed...$53
    regular room—   Q bed...$44

Shilo Inn

1.5 mi. N at 1880 NW 6th St.   *479-8391*

The local representative of a major Western lodging chain is a modern two-level motel with an outdoor pool and whirlpool. Inside are a sauna and a steam room. Each comfortably furnished room has a phone and cable color TV with movies. For toll-free reservations, call (800)222-2244.

    regular room—   Q bed...$46

Travelodge

downtown at 748 SE 7th St.   *476-7793*

There is a small outdoor pool by this modern two-story motel. Each simply furnished room has a phone and cable color TV. For toll-free reservations, call (800)255-3050.

    regular room—   Q bed...$36

Uptown Motel

.9 mi. N at 1253 NE 6th St.   *479-2952*

In this small, single-level **bargain** motel, each room has cable color

TV with movies.
  regular room—   Q bed...$26
  regular room—   D bed...$24

The Washington Inn
  .5 mi. N at 1002 NW Washington Blvd.   476-1131

A large Victorian house on the National Historic Register was recently skillfully converted into a well-landscaped bed-and-breakfast inn in a tranquil residential area near downtown. Bicycles are complimentary to guests, as is a Continental breakfast.

  "Linda's Love Nest"—upstairs, spacious, private
                        bath and balcony,
                        fireplace,   Q bed...$65
  regular room—shared bath,   Q bed...$55

CAMPGROUNDS

The West's greatest recreational river and an unusually long season of warm weather make this a special destination for campers. Numerous public and private campgrounds offer complete facilities and all kinds of water recreation. The best are remarkably scenic, complete, and well-situated by the river.

Circle W Campground
  9 mi. SE at 8110 Rogue River Hwy.   582-1686

This small, private campground on the Rogue River offers waterskiing, swimming, and fishing. Flush toilets, hot showers, and hookups are available. Each closely spaced site has a picnic table. There are two fine shady sites on grass by the river.   base rate...$9

★ **Indian Mary**
  16 mi. NW: 3.4 mi. N on I-5 & 12.6 mi. NW on Galice Rd. 474-5285

Josephine County has provided an outstanding campground on a beautifully landscaped site among pines and hardwoods by the Rogue River. Features include river swimming, boating (plus a boat ramp), fishing, and marked nature trails. Flush toilets, hot showers, and hookups are available. Each shaded, well-spaced site has a picnic table and fire grill.   base rate...$7

Riverfront Trailer Park
  7.6 mi. SE at 7060 Rogue River Hwy.   582-0985

This private facility by the Rogue River features swimming, boating, waterskiing, fishing, and a (fee) boat launch. Flush toilets, hot showers, and hookups are available. All sites are shaded and each has a picnic table. Two tent sites are beautifully positioned by the river.   base rate...$10

★ **Schroeder Campground**
  3.5 mi. W via US 199 & Willow Lane   474-5285

Josephine County has provided a well-landscaped campground and park by the Rogue River. Features include boating (and ramp), fishing and swimming in the river, plus tennis courts and large lawn areas. Flush toilets, hot showers, and hookups are available. Each hardwood and pine-shaded site has a picnic table and fire grill/ring.

base rate...$7

SPECIAL EVENT

★ **Boatnik Festival**　　*downtown and Riverside Park*　　*late May*
Boat races highlight an extended Memorial Day weekend celebration of the Rogue River. The fun-filled "boatnik" run ends at the beautiful riverside park near downtown, and the thrilling whitewater race to Hellgate Canyon both starts and ends there. Festivities begin with a downtown parade. A carnival, concessions, craft displays, a beer garden, and live entertainment are featured in the park.

OTHER INFORMATION

Area Code:　　*503*
Zip Code:　　*97526*
Grants Pass Chamber of Commerce
　1 mi. N at 1439 NE 6th St.　　　　　　　　*476-7717*
Siskiyou National Forest - Supervisor's Office
　1.5 mi. N at 200 NE Greenfield Rd.　　　　*479-5301*

Lincoln City, Oregon

Lincoln City is the ocean-view capital of the Pacific Northwest. More local dining rooms and lodgings feature picture window panoramas of seascapes than anywhere in the region. Lincoln City sprawls for more than seven miles along gentle bluffs above broad sandy beaches by the Pacific Ocean. To the south lies the tranquil estuary of the Siletz River, while pine-forested foothills of the Coast Range dominate the east view. Midway through town, the "D" River flows for a few hundred feet between Devils Lake (a large freshwater lake along the town's northeastern boundary) and the ocean. The tiny river is the world's shortest.

A temperate climate prevails year-round. Hot spells or freezes are rare. All of the year's warm sunny weather usually occurs in summer, when the beaches are ideal for beachcombing, clamming, shore fishing, and kite flying. Even swimming and surfing are enjoyed by a hearty few. Bicycling, hiking, and golf are also popular. While snow is scarce, there are almost continuous rainstorms from fall through spring. Gigantic windwhipped surf pounding against beaches and bluffs attracts increasing numbers of storm-watchers each year to witness one of nature's grandest spectacles—usually from the comfort of oceanfront view rooms.

Unlike most Oregon towns, the local economy was never based on fishing, lumber, or minerals. Instead, residents here have always been preoccupied with fulfilling the needs of vacationers. Tourism was given a major boost by the completion of the Oregon Coast Highway (U.S. 101) during the 1930s. In 1965, five villages (Oceanlake, Delake, Nelscott, Taft, and Cutler City) sprinkled along the lovely beach merged to better coordinate their ability to serve visitors. The amalgamation worked, starting with the acquisition of an impressive bronze statue of Abraham Lincoln for Kirtsis Park. A handsome recreation center with an Olympic-sized indoor pool, several beach accesses, and major park improvements followed.

Today, Lincoln City is one of the largest and most popular vacation destinations on the West coast. Thanks to new public facilities by the scenic ocean beach and the freshwater lake at either end, the "D" River area is becoming the heart of town with a nucleus of parks, shops, restaurants, and first-rate lodgings. Studios, galleries, and gift shops featuring regional arts and crafts, and specialty food stores offering local seafood and gourmet produce, are spread along the main highway. Nightlife is relaxed and often in comfortable settings where entertainers have to compete with memorable sunsets and floodlit surf. Chefs have the same challenge. A few are up to it with skillfully prepared renditions of fresh seafoods and other local specialties. The choice of ocean-view lodgings is the area's most remarkable feature, ranging from cozy cottages perched on bluffs above the surf to resort hotels with panoramic views by the beach or in nearby hills with golf courses, tennis courts, and other amenities. While there are no ocean-view campgrounds, one by the lake in town is a short stroll from an ocean beach.

Elevation:

80 feet

Population (1980):

5,469

Population (1970):

4,198

Location:

90 miles Southwest of Portland

WEATHER PROFILE
Vokac Weather Rating

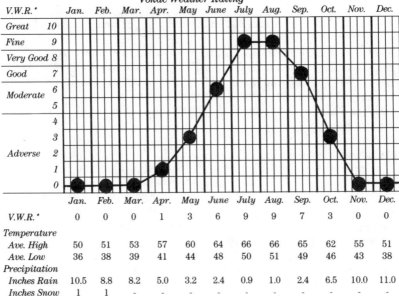

V.W.R. *		Jan.	Feb.	Mar.	Apr.	May	June	July	Aug.	Sep.	Oct.	Nov.	Dec.
V.W.R. *		0	0	0	1	3	6	9	9	7	3	0	0
Temperature													
Ave. High		50	51	53	57	60	64	66	66	65	62	55	51
Ave. Low		36	38	39	41	44	48	50	51	49	46	43	38
Precipitation													
Inches Rain		10.5	8.8	8.2	5.0	3.2	2.4	0.9	1.0	2.4	6.5	10.0	11.0
Inches Snow		1	1	-	-	-	-	-	-	-	-	-	-

*V.W.R. = Vokac Weather Rating: probability of mild (warm & dry) weather on any given day.

Forecast

	V.W.R. *	Temperatures Daytime	Evening	Precipitation
Jan.	0 Adverse	cool	chilly	continual downpours
Feb.	0 Adverse	cool	chilly	continual rainstorms
Mar.	0 Adverse	cool	chilly	continual rainstorms
Apr.	1 Adverse	cool	chilly	continual rainstorms
May	3 Adverse	cool	cool	frequent showers
June	6 Moderate	cool	cool	occasional showers
July	9 Fine	warm	cool	infrequent showers
Aug.	9 Fine	warm	cool	infrequent showers
Sep.	7 Good	warm	cool	occasional showers
Oct.	3 Adverse	cool	cool	frequent rainstorms
Nov.	0 Adverse	cool	chilly	continual rainstorms
Dec.	0 Adverse	cool	chilly	continual downpours

Summary

Lincoln City is a seaside community that is nearly surrounded by the Pacific Ocean, a freshwater lake, and a river estuary. The distinctive maritime influence assures a temperate climate and a very long growing season. While freezes and snowfalls are rare, it does rain—a lot. **Winter** is uniformly cool and very wet. Continual downpours preclude most outdoor recreation. **Spring** remains cool and wet with gradually increasing temperatures and diminishing rainfall. Fine weather for enjoying the surrounding seashore, lake, forests, and mountains finally arrives in mid-**summer**. For two very special months, long warm days and cool evenings prevail, and they are only infrequently marred by showers. Starting again in early **fall**, however, temperatures cool rapidly and rainstorms become increasingly frequent.

ATTRACTIONS & DIVERSIONS

★ *Bicycling*

There are many miles of picturesque highways and byways on the relatively flat terrain in and around town. While the place identified below only sold handcrafted kites until recently, their fledgling bicycle rental business will also hopefully take off in 1987.

Flying Things   *.7 mi. N at 1528 N. US 101*   994-4808

★ **Depoe Bay**

13 mi. S on US 101   765-2889

An appealing village has grown up around a tiny rock-bound harbor that may be the world's smallest. A sea wall promenade and bridge are the best places for watching sportfishing and pleasure boats negotiate the harrowingly narrow, rock-lined channel between the harbor and the sea. On the north side, the state has provided a lookout tower and gift shop, and grassy picnic areas below a sidewalk promenade. Just west of the promenade are "spouting horns"—natural rock formations throwing geyserlike sprays of surf high in the air. Various sightseeing and deep sea fishing trips depart from the harbor daily. Several restaurants offer picture window views of the exciting coastline.

Devils Lake State Park

1.5 mi. E on E. Devils Lake Rd.   994-2002

This popular park adjoins part of a two-mile-long freshwater lake, separated from the ocean by the 440-foot-long "D" River, the shortest river in the world. Swimming is popular at Sand Point Park (on the eastern shore) because the lake is relatively warm in summer. Boating, wind surfing, and fishing will get better as restoration to remove over-dense aquatic vegetation progresses. Paddleboats can be rented at:

Blue Heron Landing *4 mi. N at 4006 W. Devils Lake Rd. 994-4708*

★ **"D" River Beach Wayside Park**

downtown at US 101/1st St. S.E.

Oregon's most popular wayside park was recently developed where the world's shortest river flows into the ocean. The usually sunny beachfront park provides access to miles of sandy beaches to the north and south.

★ **Fogarty Creek State Park**

10.5 mi. S on US 101 - Depoe Bay

A small, crystal-clear stream tumbles across a broad sandy beach before emptying into a sheltered cove. The state has provided dressing rooms and picnic facilities. It is an idyllic site for picnicking, sunbathing, swimming, beachcombing, and surf fishing.

Golf

Devils Lake Golf and Racquet Club

4 mi. N on US 101   994-8442

The area's first golf course started becoming an 18-hole layout with a superb new clubhouse in 1986. The much-improved and expanded facility—in a gentle valley near the ocean—is open to the public and includes a pro shop, club and cart rentals, a driving range, plus a restaurant and lounge.

★ **Salishan Golf Course**
6.7 mi. S on US 101 - Gleneden Beach   764-2471
The famed resort's magnificent 18-hole championship golf course provides panoramic ocean views and lush fairways in picturesque sylvan frames. It is open to the public and includes a pro shop, club and cart rentals, a driving range, and a fine view restaurant and lounge.

Horseback Riding
★ **Neskowin Stable**
10 mi. N on US 101 - Neskowin   392-3277
Guided horseback rides on a sandy ocean beach can be reserved from mid-May through September. Closed Oct.-Apr.

Library
2.5 mi. S at 4333 S.W. Coast   996-2277
The Driftwood Library is small and well organized. As a special feature, the magazine area adjoins comfortable seats by a picture window view of the distant coast. Closed Sun.

★ *Sportfishing*
13 mi. S on US 101 at mouth of harbor - Depoe Bay
Salmon fishing is one of the major attractions of the Oregon coast. Depoe Bay is home port to several fishing charters—all located in the world's smallest natural harbor. Salmon trolling and other deep sea fishing, and whale watching excursions, are featured by:

Deep Sea Trollers Co.	*Box 513*	765-2248
Depoe Bay Sportfishing & Charter	*Box 388*	765-2222
Tradewinds	*Box 123*	765-2345

Warm Water Feature
Lincoln City Swimming Pool
1 mi. N at 2150 N.E. Oar Av.   994-5208
Visitors are welcome to swim in the city's Olympic-sized pool in the modern community center during designated hours.

★ *Wineries (Tasting Rooms)*
Honeywood Winery
downtown at 30 S.E. US 101   994-2755
Downstairs in Oceans West Gallery is a large gift shop with a sales and tasting bar for Honeywood Winery of Salem—the oldest producing winery in the state (1933). Berry and fruit wines are the specialty. Tastes of each are offered, along with Gallico varietal wines, from 9-5 daily.

Oregon Wine Tasting Room at Lawrence Gallery
39 mi. NE on OR 18   843-3787
Sharing a handsome building with the first-rate Lawrence Gallery and Augustine's Restaurant is an inviting tasting and sales room

for Amity Vineyards. This small winery is located in the nearby foothills at the western edge of Oregon's major wine producing district. Estate-bottled premium varietals are generously available for tasting from 12-5 daily.

Shipwreck Cellars Oak Knoll Winery
2.1 mi. S at 3521 S.W. US 101   996-3221
A very attractive roadside building overlooking the ocean is a tasting and sales room for Oak Knoll Winery of Hillsboro. Fruit and varietal wines are offered for tasting from 11-5 daily.

SHOPPING

Lincoln City's business district ebbs and flows for miles to the north and south of D River/US 101—identified as the nominal "heart of town." There is no strollable downtown. Instead, notable gourmet shops, arts and crafts galleries, etc. are sprinkled along the main highway.

Food Specialties

Barnacle Bill's Seafood Market
1 mi. N at 22nd St./US 101   994-3022
This open-air fish stand features smoked, fresh, and canned salmon and other fish, plus walkaway shrimp, crab, and oyster cocktails.

Colonial Bakery
.7 mi. N at 1734 N.E. US 101   994-5919
This large bakery tries to do it all—donuts, pastries, pies, cakes, breads, and even fruitcakes, with more or less success. Everything is available to go or to eat in the well-worn industrial-sized showroom for the main store of a chain.

★ **Neptune's Reserve**
13 mi. S on US 101 - Depoe Bay   765-2286
One of the Northwest's finest fish markets is in a large roadside store (you can't miss the eight-foot-tall chain-sawed wood sculpted fish out front). Fresh, frozen, maple-smoked, and hand-packed canned seafoods in enticing displays are sold to go or through catalog mail order or gift packs. They provide samples on request.

Premier Market
.4 mi. N at 825 N.W. US 101   994-3025
This grocery store specializes in a variety of tasty home-smoked ham, beef, and fish.

★ **Read's Homemade Candies**
.4 mi. N at 1009 N.W. US 101   994-2966
Sixteen flavors of saltwater taffy are made on the premises, along with a variety of chocolates and other candies (like seafoam). In addition to retail sales, they mail gift packages anywhere.

Salty Von's Seafood Market
.4 mi. N at 1114 N.E. US 101   994-2070
A variety of smoked salmon, plus other local seafoods like whole crab, can be purchased at this small seafood market.

Specialty Shops

★ **Alder House II**
6.5 mi. S: 5.8 mi. S on US 101 & .7 mi. E on Immonen Rd. 996-2483
In an alder glade a short distance from Siletz Bay is a rustic, geodesic glass blowers studio/gallery. Assorted first-rate functional and artistic glass pieces are produced here, and displayed for sale.

Café Roma
.6 mi. N at 1437 N.W. US 101   994-6616
This cheerful shop features books of regional interest in a back room. Up front is a specialty coffee bar with tasty muffins, pastries, and desserts to enjoy at tables.

★ **Catch the Wind**
downtown at 266 S.E. US 101   994-9500
A large, colorful array of kites is displayed in this cheerful and popular representative of an Oregon chain that has taken off in recent years.

★ **Marketplace Shopping Center**
6.6 mi. S on US 101 - Gleneden Beach
One of the West coast's finest specialty shopping experiences awaits in a natural-wood-toned complex set back from the highway by a golf course. Highlights include **Allegory Bookstore** (with a fine collection of Northwestern books); **Hot Pots** (gourmet cookware, and free classes in an exhibition kitchen each Saturday); **Coast Roast Coffee Co.** (coffees, teas, and Italian sodas, plus delicious scones, tea cakes, and cinnamon rolls baked here); **Sweet Delights** (homemade fudge); **Crane & Co.** (a gourmet food market featuring Northwest wines and provisions); and **Lawrence Gallery** (museum-quality contemporary art of all kinds).

★ **Mossy Creek Pottery**
6.2 mi. S: 5.8 mi. S on US 101 & .4 mi. E on Immonen Rd. 996-2415
A large, beautifully organized selection of all kinds of pottery and ceramics by local craftsmen is displayed in a charming roadside cottage in the woods.

Seagull Factory
downtown at 1020 S.E. 3rd St.   994-2660
Cement sea gulls and other weather-resistant birds are produced and sold here. You can watch the various stages of creation.

Swede's Myrtlewood Etc.
.7 mi. N at 1747 N.W. US 101   994-5970
A surprising diversity of myrtlewood objects, ranging from functional and unusual (like a myrtlewood "bacon button") through collectible trinkets, is cheerfully displayed in this two-level emporium.

The Wood Works
downtown on US 101   996-2484
Cedarwood that has been handcrafted into whimsical planters and statues is casually exhibited in a transformed greenhouse/aviary.

NIGHTLIFE

There are plenty of casual taverns and a few places with occasional live entertainment sprinkled along US 101. But, the best after-dark activity is generally in the oceanfront hotels, where comfortably furnished lounges feature live music for dancing, plus picture window views of the surf—at sunset and flood-lit afterward.

★ **The Inn at Spanish Head**
2.4 mi. S at 4009 S.W. US 101   *996-2161*
This small comfortable lounge features picture window views of the beach and ocean, armchair comfort, live entertainment most nights, and a small dance floor.

★ **Lighthouse Brew Pub**
2.2 mi. N at 4157 N. US 101   *994-7238*
The Oregon coast's premier "boutique brewery" opened in Lincoln City in 1986. You can watch the equipment in operation, and enjoy complimentary tastes of their brews, in addition to a fine selection of other beers like Labatt's and Henry's on tap. Backgammon, chess, checkers, etc. are loaned to players in the balcony seating area, and light foods like pizza bread and burgers are served.

★ **Salishan Lodge**
6.6 mi. S on US 101 - Gleneden Beach   *764-2371*
The resort's Attic Lounge offers live entertainment for dancing or listening, plus a choice of plush seating in a stylish upstairs room. The subdued decor is accented by panoramic views of Siletz Bay, and by a massive fireplace.

★ **Shilo Inn**
2 mi. N at 1501 N.W. 40th St.   *994-5255*
The oceanfront view is splendid through picture windows, and live piano music or disco provides dancing or listening pleasure. A gas fireplace with adjoining seating lends warmth to the comfortably outfitted room.

RESTAURANTS

Along this portion of the Oregon coast, restaurants are abundant. Seafood predominates, and in the hands of the area's most talented chefs, fresh local varieties achieve memorable distinction. As an added incentive for eating out, the Lincoln City area has more dining rooms with ocean or bay views than any other town in the Northwest.

★ **The Bay House**
3.6 mi. S at 5911 S.W. US 101   *996-3222*
D only. Sun. brunch.   *Expensive*
Classic Continental stylings of the freshest available fish and produce are served in a casually elegant dining room with a picture window view of adjoining Siletz Bay.

Captain John's
1 mi. N at 2130 N.E. US 101   994-2270
B-L-D.   *Moderate*
Standard American fare is served in generous quantities in a large modern coffee shop with a choice of padded counter stools, booths, or tables and chairs.

★ **Chez Jeannette**
7 mi. S at 7150 Old US 101 - Gleneden Beach   764-3434
D only.   *Expensive*
Contemporary adaptations of classic Continental specialties reflect the discipline and spirit of the chef. The gourmet cuisine is served in a hideaway cottage at candlelit tables adorned with full linen napery and flowers. Classical music, picture window views of the surrounding forest, and two fireplaces contribute to the romantic mood.

Dory Cove
3 mi. N at 5819 Logan Rd. (at Road's End)   994-5180
L-D.   *Moderate*
This first-rate family-oriented fishhouse features an impressive variety of seafoods in all-American renditions like beer-battered fish and chips and broiled salmon filets, plus assorted burgers and other landlubber favorites. Homemade cream pies provide an accompaniment. The large, casual-and-usually-crowded dining room has an old-fashioned seaside fishhouse feeling, and a partial view of the ocean.

Hershey's Place
3.1 mi. S at 815 S.W. 51st St.   996-9966
B-L-D.   *Moderate*
Generous servings of homestyle American dishes—epitomized by gigantic cinnamon rolls with raisins and walnuts—are served in a modern, comfortably furnished split-level dining room with view windows on two sides overlooking Siletz Bay and the ocean.

The Inn at Spanish Head
2.8 mi. S at 4009 S.W. US 101   996-2161
B-L-D. Sun. brunch.   *Moderate*
Local seafoods, including seasonal specialties like petite Yaquina Bay oysters, are featured on a contemporary menu. Diners enjoy a wonderful surf view from picture windows on two sides of the hotel's large oceanfront restaurant.

Irene's Coffee Shop
downtown at 30 S.E. US 101   996-3888
B-L-D.   *Moderate*
Generous portions can't mask the hit-or-miss quality of the plastic-wrapped homemade pastries and other light fare from pizza to seafood in this highway-fronting deli/diner. A distant view of the ocean is the highlight in a very plain coffee shop.

★ **Kyllo's**

1.4 mi. N at 2733 N.W. US 101   *994-3179*
L-D.   *Moderate*

All-American dishes with an emphasis on fresh regional seafoods are given conscientious attention. Casual, cheerful surroundings are enhanced by plants and flowers throughout cozy dining areas and window views of a flower garden by the highway.

Lil Sambo's Restaurant

1.6 mi. N at 3262 N.E. US 101   *994-3626*
B-L-D.   *Moderate*

Here's a 1950s throwback for hungry families, nostalgia buffs, and early risers. No finesse—just big portions of omelets and biscuits, pancakes, and other American standards for breakfast plus all-you-can-eat dinners. There are purple plastic booths, and the "themed" menu and trinket displays haven't changed much in thirty years.

Marketplace Restaurant

6.6 mi. S on US 101 - Gleneden Beach   *764-3681*
L-D.   *Moderate*

An updated American menu including mesquite-broiled local seafoods is offered in a comfortable, contemporary dining room. Picture windows frame Siletz Bay in the distance.

★ **Mister Critter's Pizza Company**

13 mi. S on US 101 - Depoe Bay   *765-2277*
L-D.   *Low*

Even if the pizza wasn't good (it is), the location makes this contemporary pizza parlor a must. The split-level dining room is perched on a cliff and outfitted with booths. Window walls on three sides provide a breathtaking view of a surf-lashed cove and headlands.

Mo's

3.1 mi. S at 860 S.W. 51st St.   *996-2535*
L-D.   *Low*

Seafood is offered in the local representative of a Newport-based chowder house chain. The real feature is a waterfront view of Siletz Bay from two sides of the large, very casual dining room.

North Point Restaurant

13 mi. S on US 101 - Depoe Bay   *765-2645*
B-L.   *Moderate*

Specialties like clam fritters and homemade desserts enliven a menu of American standards. But, the real reason for being here is to enjoy the panoramic overview of surf breaking in a rocky cove from one of five cliffside tables.

★ **Otis Cafe**

5.6 mi. NE on OR 18 at Otis Junction - Otis   *994-2813*
B-L-D. No D Mon.-Wed.   *Low*

Here is the area's most delightful surprise. When the chef/owner is in attendance, the inexpensive homemade meals are tributes to American-style cuisine—highlighted by all sorts of homemade pies, breads, cinnamon rolls, and even their own mustard. Wood booths, windows on three sides, and a counter lend to the homespun charm of the tiny roadside cafe.

Pier 101

downtown at 415 S.W. US 101   994-8840
L-D.   *Moderate*

Seafood dishes are served in a family-oriented, wood-trimmed dining room with nautical decor. A lounge adjoins.

The Pines

3.1 mi. S at 5065 S.E. US 101   996-3333
B-L.   *Low*

You might guess that a place that says it has "the best breakfast in town" doesn't. The only thing fresh here is the eggs used for well-made omelets and a few other dishes served in the painfully plain other half of a "locals" tavern.

★ **Salishan Lodge**

6.6 mi. S on US 101 - Gleneden Beach   764-2371
D only.   *Very Expensive*

Continental cuisine is formally presented nightly in the large, well-regarded Dining Room. All three dining levels in this showplace of contemporary opulence overlook the resort's artful landscaping and, in the far distance, the ocean.

Sea Hag

13 mi. S on US 101 - Depoe Bay   765-7901
B-L-D.   *Moderate*

The homestyle American food offered here, including fresh-daily cinnamon rolls, is plain and plentiful. The simply furnished long-popular dining room offers a choice of booths or tables amidst nautical decor.

Shilo Inn Restaurant

2 mi. N at 1501 N.W. 40th St.   994-5255
B-L-D.   *Moderate*

An updated Continental menu features seafood accompanied by a stunning window wall view of a picturesque section of the Oregon coast. Full linen and fresh flowers enhance the table settings at dinner in the motor hotel's large and stylish dining room.

Spouting Horn

13 mi. S on US 101 - Depoe Bay   765-2261
B-L-D.   *Moderate*

Old-fashioned seafood dishes are offered in a comfortably furnished restaurant that has been in operation for about half a century. The crowd-pleaser is the recently-added upstairs room with a spectacular window wall view of tiny Depoe Bay and the inlet bridge. A cozy bar shares the scene.

LODGING

More noteworthy lodgings overlook the ocean in the Lincoln City area than in any other town in the Northwest. Numerous excellent accommodations have choice beachfront locations, and an even larger number of surprisingly inexpensive motels are inland along US 101 through town. Many offer 25% and greater rate reductions apart from summer.

Anchor Motel

2.6 mi. S at 4417 S.W. US 101　　　　　　　　　　*996-3810*

This refurbished older motel is a **bargain**. Each simply furnished room has cable color TV.

regular room—　　　　　　　　　　　　　　　Q bed...$25

★ **Baywest**

3.1 mi. S at 1116 S.W. 51st St.　　　　　　　　　*996-3549*

This new condominium-style motel fronts on Siletz Bay. Amenities include a whirlpool and a sauna. In addition to stylish contemporary decor and furnishings, each unit has a phone and cable color TV. The one- and two-bedroom units have a kitchen, fireplace, and balcony.

#301—1 BR, top floor, kitchen, tiny fireplace,
　　　floor-to-ceiling window view of bay
　　　beyond private balcony,　　　　　　　　　Q bed...$55

regular room—no view,　　　　　　　　　　　Q bed...$35

Beachfront Motel

1.7 mi. N at 3313 N.W. Inlet Av.　　　　　　　　*994-2324*

A broad ocean beach adjoins this tiny modern motel. Each well-furnished unit has kitchen facilities and a color TV.

#5—1 BR, kitchen, free-standing fireplace,
　　private oceanside balcony,　　　　　　2 T & Q beds...$55

#3—studio, kitchen, Franklin fireplace, private
　　ocean view,　　　　　　　　　　　　　Q bed...$42

regular room—studio, kitchenette, fine ocean
　　　　　view,　　　　　　　　　　　　2 T & Q beds...$38

Beachwood Motel

1.6 mi. N at 2855 N.W. Inlet Av.　　　　　　　　*994-8901*

This older motel is on a bluff by the beach. Each simply furnished, well-worn unit has cable color TV, and there are **bargain** rooms.

#303,#302,#301—spacious, fireplace, top floor,
　　　　　　　oceanfront view, private
　　　　　　　balcony,　　　　　　　　　Q bed...$55

regular room—no view,　　　　　　　　　　D bed...$30

Bel-Aire Motel

1.6 mi. N at 2945 N.W. US 101　　　　　　　　　*994-2984*

Some of the **bargain** rooms in this nicely maintained older motel have a distant ocean view. Each spacious room has a cable color TV.

regular room—　　　　　　　　　　　　　　Q bed...$22

Captain Cook's Motel
    1.4 mi. N at 2626 N.E. US 101   *994-2522*
This small, single-level motel is a **bargain**. Each nicely maintained, older room has a cable color TV.
    regular room—   Q bed...$24

★ **Cavalier Condominiums**
    8.6 mi. S on US 101 (Box 59-A) - Gleneden Beach 97388 764-2352
If you're looking for a large, modern home-away-from-home, this three-level complex is an answer. In addition to an isolated oceanfront location with a private stairway down a bluff to the beach, the complex includes a large indoor pool, sauna, and recreation room. Each spacious, well-appointed unit has an ocean view, a carport, kitchen, fireplace, balcony, phone, and cable color TV.
    #49,#40—2 BR, top, end, extra side windows &
             floor/ceiling door/windows & deck
             all have superb ocean view,   2 Q beds...$85
    regular room—2 BR,   2 Q beds...$85

★ **Channel House**
    13 mi. S on US 101 (Box 56) - Depoe Bay 97341   *765-2140*
Perched on the rocks above the harrowing channel between Depoe Bay and the ocean is a superb little contemporary inn above an ocean-view dinner house. Each beautifully furnished unit has a cable color TV with movies. A Continental breakfast is included.
    #3—oceanfront suite, kitchen, 2 fireplaces,
             wood deck with private whirlpool &
             awesome marine view,   Q bed...$120
    #5—top floor oceanfront suite, kitchen, 2
             fireplaces, in-bath whirlpool, large deck,
             awesome marine view,   Q bed...$120
    #4—memorable ocean and bay view,   Q bed...$55
    regular room #2—partial ocean view,   D bed...$35

City Center Motel
    .4 mi. N at 1014 N.E. US 101   *994-2612*
This single-level motel by the highway is a **bargain**. Each simply furnished small room has cable color TV with movies.
    regular room—   Q bed...$23

Coho Inn
    .7 mi. N at 1635 N.W. Harbor Av.   *994-3684*
All rooms are oceanfronting in this modern, blufftop motel. Each unit has a phone and cable color TV.
    suite—1 BR, request 3rd (top) floor, kitchen,
             (pressed log) fireplace, private ocean-
             view balcony,   2 T & Q beds...$56
    regular room—ocean view,   2 D or Q bed...$36

★ **Cozy Cove**
    downtown at 515 N.W. Inlet Av.   *994-2950*
One of Oregon's most sybaritic lodgings is a contemporary complex

adjoining the beach in the heart of town. Amenities include a private beach access, large outdoor pool, whirlpool, and sauna. Each of the attractively furnished units has cable color TV.

#303,#308,#309,#315,#316—raised fireplace, remote-controlled TV, private floor/ ceiling glass-doored balcony, raised in-room whirlpool with fine ocean view,		Q bed...$70
deluxe view—as above, but no whirlpool,		Q bed...$55
regular room—courtyard view,		Q bed...$32

"D" Sands Motel

downtown at 171 S.W. US 101   994-5244

An indoor pool and whirlpool, plus an oceanfront location, are features of this modern motel. Each unit has a private balcony with an ocean view, kitchenette, phone, and cable color TV with movies.

3rd floor south building—1 BR, gas fireplace,	2 T & Q beds...$64
regular room—studio, gas fireplace (in south building),	2 T & Murphy Q beds...$54

Edgecliff Motel Apartments

2.2 mi. S at 3733 S.W. US 101   996-2055

This small single-level older motel is perched on the rim of a hill, and most of the units have an unobstructed ocean view. There is a private beach access. Each simply furnished room has a cable color TV.

#8—large, end, wood-burning fireplace, private balcony, ocean-view windows on 2 sides,	Q bed...$38
#11—semi-private balcony, fine ocean view from	Q bed...$35
regular room—some ocean view,	Q bed...$35

Ester Lee

2.3 mi. S at 3803 S.W. US 101   996-3606

An older motel has recently added some impressive apartment-style units to its blufftop location high over the beach. Each of these nicely furnished spacious units includes a wood-burning fireplace, an ocean view, and cable color TV.

#211,#202—top floor, private ocean view on 2 sides, kitchenette, fireplace in front of	Q bed...$57
#212,#201—top floor, 1 BR, private ocean view on 2 sides, kitchenette, fireplace in living room,	Q bed...$59
regular room—	Q bed...$49

Holiday Surf Lodge

12 mi. S on US 101 (Box 9) - Depoe Bay 97341   765-2134

Travelers have a choice of A-frame cabins, cottages, or modern lodge rooms in this oceanside motel, or the complete facilities of the adjoining RV park. Amenities include a new recreation building with an indoor pool, whirlpool, sauna, and game room. Each well-equipped unit has an ocean view and cable color TV. For toll-free reservations in Oregon, call (800)452-2108.

oceanfront A-frame—1 BR, fireplace in L.R.,
           kitchen, private deck, fine
           ocean view,   2 T & Q beds...$60
oceanfront lodge room—fine ocean view,   K bed...$48
regular room—no view,   Q bed...$32

★ **The Inn at Spanish Head**
2.4 mi. S at 4009 S.W. US 101   *996-2161*

One of Lincoln City's largest hotels is an oceanfronting ten-level convention-oriented facility with a large outdoor pool by the beach, whirlpool, saunas, and a game room, plus an ocean-view restaurant and lounge. Each conventionally furnished unit has a phone and cable color TV. For toll-free reservations in Oregon, call (800)452-8127; elsewhere (800)547-5235.

#120—beach level, kitchenette, floor/ceiling
      window view from   K bed...$68
#141—2nd floor, private balcony with floor/
      ceiling window view from   K bed...$68
#106—beach level, kitchenette, floor/ceiling
      view of coast, semi-private patio,   K bed...$62
#114—beach level, kitchenette, semi-private
      patio, coast view,   K bed...$62
regular room—coast view,   Q or K bed...$62

★ **Lincoln Sands Inn - Best Western**
downtown at 535 N.W. Inlet Av.   *994-4227*

One of the area's newer resort condos is located on the beach. Amenities include an outdoor pool and whirlpool. Each beautifully decorated unit is exceptionally well-equipped with a fine ocean view, a private patio or balcony, kitchen, two baths, two phones, and two cable color TVs with movies. For toll-free reservations in Oregon call (800)452-5727.

regular room—1 BR, request 3rd (top) floor for
      best ocean view,   Q bed...$60

★ **McCoy's Hideaway Motel**
.6 mi. S at 810 S.W. 10th St.   *994-8874*

High on a bluff above a broad sandy beach is a tiny, meticulously maintained cottage colony that captures the charm of an earlier time. Each of the spotless, well-furnished units has a kitchen, living room with a fireplace and an ocean view, plus cable color TV with movies.

#2—2 BR, L.R. with wood-burning fireplace,
      private ocean view,   D & Q beds...$55

#10,#6—1 BR, L.R. with wood-burning
      fireplace, private ocean view,   Q bed...$45
regular room—1 BR, electric fireplace, ocean
      view,   D bed...$40

Nidden Hof Motel

downtown at 136 N.E. US 101   994-8155

The D River adjoins this modern **bargain** motel, and the ocean is only a block away. Each nicely furnished unit has cable color TV and a phone. For toll-free reservations in Oregon, call (800)29-COAST.

#317—private balcony with river/ocean view,
      small raised fireplace,   K bed...$42
#323—small raised fireplace, river/ocean view,   Q bed...$45
regular room—some river or ocean view,   Q bed...$29

★ **Nordic Motel**

1 mi. N at 2133 N.W. Inlet Av.   994-8145

An indoor pool and saunas complement this modern blufftop motel with a private access to the broad sandy beach. Each unit has a phone and cable color TV.

#309,#310—studio, kitchenette, raised
      fireplace, fine ocean view from   Q bed...$54
#318—studio, raised fireplace, balcony, fine
      view from   Q bed...$48
regular room—ocean view,   Q bed...$42

Oceanside Motel

1.7 mi. N at 3264 N.W. Jetty   994-6155

An old motel less than a block from the beach has been updated, and is a **bargain**. Each nicely furnished room has cable color TV.

regular room—   Q bed...$25

Ocean Terrace Motel

2.5 mi. S at 4229 S.W. Beach Av.   996-3623

A newer three-level condo/motel occupies a choice site adjoining a broad sandy beach. Amenities include a large indoor pool with whirlpool jets, saunas, and a game room with ping pong and pool. Each spacious, well-furnished one-bedroom unit includes a kitchen, living room with a floor/ceiling sliding glass door view of the surf, and cable color TV with movies.

#30—1 BR, top, end, semi-private balcony,
      great ocean view,   Q bed...$60
regular room—non-oceanfront,   Q bed...$40

Red Carpet Inn

1.5 mi. N at 2645 N.W. Inlet Av.   994-2134

This two-level motel, situated on a low bluff adjacent to the beach, has a private beach access and an indoor pool. Each attractively furnished unit has an ocean view, cable color TV, and a phone.

suite—1 BR, kitchen, fireplace,   Q bed...$55
regular room—   Q bed...$42

Sailor Jack Motel
.4 mi. N at 1035 N.W. Harbor Av.   *994-3696*
The surf in front of this three-story apartment is flood-lit at night, and there is easy beach access. Apart from a sauna, amenities are in the well-equipped units, which each have an ocean view, phone, and cable color TV.

#49,#47,#48—refrigerator, raised hooded
                     fireplace, fine ocean view from
                     large windows,   K bed...$53
regular room—ocean view,   Q bed...$42

★ **Salishan Lodge**
6.6 mi. S on US 101 - Gleneden Beach 97388   *764-2371*
Exquisite sensitivity was applied in synthesizing luxurious leisure facilities with a natural Oregon landscape. The result is Salishan, a large, world famous resort where contemporary low profile buildings are sequestered into many acres of manicured grounds. Amenities include a big indoor pool, whirlpool, saunas, fitness center, putting green, playground, nature trails, and (for a fee) a championship 18-hole golf course and four tennis courts (three indoors), plus lavish dining and lounge facilities, and a stylish complex of specialty shops. The nearest ocean beach is a half-mile away. Each beautifully decorated, spacious room has a phone, cable color TV, a fieldstone fireplace, a covered carport, and a balcony with a view of either the nearby golf course or distant bay and ocean. For toll-free reservations in Oregon, call (800)452-2300; elsewhere (800)547-6500.

"Chieftain House North"—(several) refrigerator,
                     best bay views,   K bed...$136
regular room—   2 D or K bed...$104

Sandcastle Motel
2 mi. S at 3417 S.W. Anchor Av.   *996-3613*
A broad sandy beach adjoins this modern motel. Each spacious, nicely furnished one-bedroom unit has a full kitchen, a living room with a floor/ceiling window ocean view, and cable color TV.
regular room—1 BR,   Q bed...$46

Sea Echo Motel
1.9 mi. N at 3510 N.E. US 101   *994-2575*
On the brow of a hill above the highway is a single-level **bargain** motel. Each simply furnished unit has a cable color TV with movies.
regular room—   Q bed...$25

Sea Gull Motel
.7 mi. N at 1511 N.W. Harbor Av.   *994-2948*
In this older, three-level motel, every unit fronts on a bluff high above the beach. Each large, simply furnished unit has cable color TV. For toll-free reservations in Oregon, call (800)29-COAST; elsewhere in the Northwest, call (800)98-COAST.
regular room—ocean view from   Q bed...$38

153

Sea Gypsy
downtown at 145 N.W. Inlet Av.   *994-5266*
Bargain rooms are a feature of this modern three-level motel which
is well situated by a beach in the heart of town. An indoor pool
and sauna are amenities. Each well-furnished room has a phone
and cable color TV with movies. For toll-free reservations in Oregon,
call (800)452-6929; elsewhere (800)341-2142.

ocean-view unit—(request 3rd floor),		
	kitchenette, fine ocean view,	Q bed...$48
regular room—no view,		Q bed...$30

★ **Shilo Inn**
2 mi. N at 1501 N.W. 40th St   *994-3655*
Lincoln City's largest and most complete beachfront hotel sprawls
along a sandy, picturesque shoreline. The recently remodeled
complex includes an ocean-view dining room and lounge, a gift
shop, meeting facilities, a large indoor pool, whirlpool, saunas, and
a game room. Each attractively furnished unit has a phone and
satellite color TV with movies. For toll-free reservations, call
(800)222-2244.

top floor—3rd floor, remote-controlled TV,		
	refrigerator, best full ocean view,	K bed...$79
ground floor—direct access to beach, public		
	patio, ocean view,	K bed...$79
regular room—tree view,		Q bed...$49

Siletz Bay Inn
3.1 mi. S at 861 S.W. 51st St.   *996-3996*
There are some **bargain** rooms in this nicely maintained older motel
across a street from Siletz Bay. Each of the units has cable color
TV with movies. For toll-free reservations in Oregon, call (800)843-4940.

#27,#26—upstairs, large, in-room whirlpool,		
	ocean view,	Q bed...$85
#25,#24—ground level, large, in-room		
	whirlpool, no view,	Q bed...$75
regular room—small, no view,		D or Q bed...$25

Southshore Motel
downtown at 1070 S.E. 1st St./US 101   *994-7559*
The newest downtown motel is a **bargain** that borders a creek
across the highway from a beachfront park. Guests can reserve
an indoor whirlpool. Each room is spacious, decorated in appealing
contemporary colors and fabrics, and includes a private balcony
with an ocean or lake view, plus a phone and cable color TV.

"Honeymoon Suite"—very large, refrigerator/		
	wet bar, fireplace, in-bath	
	whirlpool & skylight,	K bed...$59
#341,#343,#339—fireplace, some ocean view,		K bed...$45
#328,#330,#332,#334,#336—tranquil lake/		
	mountain view,	K bed...$29

regular room—lake/mountain view,   K bed...$29

★ **Surfrider**

10.3 mi. S on US 101 (Box 219) - Depoe Bay 97341   764-2311

High on a bluff overlooking the ocean just north of Fogarty Creek State Park is a handsome contemporary motel with a large indoor pool, whirlpool, sauna, and a ping pong room, plus an ocean-view restaurant and a plush ocean-view lounge with live entertainment for dancing most nights. Each nicely furnished, spacious unit has a phone and cable color TV with movies.

#69,#64—end units, semi-private balcony,
raised fireplace, in-bath whirlpool,
splendid ocean view from   K bed...$64

#40,#47—semi-private balcony, raised
fireplace, large sunken tub, splendid
ocean view from   K bed...$56

#12,#23—fireplace, private deck, fine ocean
view,   Q bed...$52

#50,#57—1 BR, semi-private balcony, fireplace,
kitchen, great ocean view,   Q bed...$56

#51,#56—semi-private balcony, fireplace, ocean
view,   Q bed...$52

regular room—ocean view,   2 D or Q bed...$46

★ **Surftides Beach Resort**

1.6 mi. N at 2945 N.W. Jetty Av. (Box 406)   994-2191

Lincoln City's oldest oceanside resort hotel includes a gift shop, conference facilities, ocean-view restaurant and lounge, an indoor pool, whirlpool, sauna, and indoor tennis. Each spacious unit has cable color TV and a phone. For toll-free reservations in Oregon, call (800)452-2159.

#1010 thru #1013—large, private balcony,
fireplace, beach/ocean
view from   K bed...$68

regular room—   Q bed...$39

Surftides Plaza Condominium

1.6 mi. N at 1415 N.W. 31st St.   994-8121

This modern three-story condo, behind oceanfronting buildings, has an indoor pool and whirlpool. Each unit has a complete kitchen, a private balcony, gas log fireplace, and color TV.

third floor—1 BR, top, best ocean views,   Q bed...$54

regular room—studio, some ocean view,
hideabed   Q bed...$44

Westshore Oceanfront Motel

1.9 mi. S at 3127 S.W. Anchor Av.   996-2001

A private stairway links this blufftop motel directly with the broad sandy beach. Each nicely furnished unit has a complete kitchen and cable color TV.

third floor—1 BR, top floor, raised wood-
burning fireplace, private ocean
view,   2 Q beds...$47
regular room—1 BR, ocean-view patio,   2 Q beds...$42

CAMPGROUNDS

Campers have a choice of riverfront or lakeside sites in public or private campgrounds with complete facilities in and near town.

Coyote Rock R.V. Park
7 mi. S via US 101 on OR 229 (Box 299)   996-3436
Along the shoreline of the Siletz River in a heavily wooded canyon two miles inland from the ocean is a large privately-operated RV/ tent campground. There is a boat ramp, boat rental, and tackle shop. Salmon fishing is especially popular during the summer season. Flush toilets, hot showers, and full hookups are available. Each closely spaced site has a picnic table. Tent sites are in grassy areas. Many sites border the river.   base rate...$9

★ **Devils Lake State Park**
.6 mi. NE at 1450 N.E. 6th Dr.   994-2002
The state has provided a campground on a quiet freshwater lake separated from an ocean beach by the 440-foot-long D River, "the shortest river in the world." There is a boat dock on the lake, and a designated swimming area is nearby. Miles of broad sandy ocean beaches begin a short stroll to the west. Flush toilets, hot showers, and full hookups are available, as are separated tent sites. Non-Oregonians add $2 surcharge to base rate.   base rate...$8

KOA - Lincoln City
5 mi. NE on E. Devils Lake Rd. (Rt. 2, Box 255)-Otis 994-2961
This privately operated facility is a short walk from Devils Lake. Flush toilets, hot showers, and hookups are available. Each closely spaced grassy site has a picnic table, and some are tree-shaded.   base rate...$11

SPECIAL EVENT

★ **International Kite Festival** *early May and last weekend in Sept.*
Kites become the center of attention twice each year in Lincoln City. Kite-flying skill demonstrations, and contests to select the most beautiful, innovative, and amusing kites are featured on a broad sandy beach in the heart of town—where the world's shortest river meets the sea.

OTHER INFORMATION

Area Code: *503*
Zip Code: *97367*
Lincoln City Chamber of Commerce
2 mi. N at 3939 N.W. US 101 (Box 787)   994-3070
(In Oregon, call toll-free (800) 452-2151)

Newport, Oregon

Newport is the keystone to the pleasures of the Pacific Northwest coast. The town covers a scenic peninsula where the Yaquina River flows into the Pacific Ocean. For a century, people have been attracted to this favored site bordered by broad sandy ocean beaches and a calm harbor sheltered by bluffs near the river's mouth. Over the years, the best features around town have been enhanced by an assortment of beachfronting state parks and harborside marinas.

Beachcombing, clamming, crabbing, shore and sportfishing, sailing (and even swimming for a hearty few) are popular leisure activities during the normally sunny days of summer. Golf, tennis, and bicycling are enjoyed in town, and the colorful bayfront district is the most exhilarating maritime attraction on the Northwest coast. Nearby, gentle forested slopes of the Coast Range beckon hikers and backpackers. Temperatures year-round are surprisingly moderate. Freezes are unusual in town, and no snow is recorded during some years. However, there are almost continuous rainstorms from fall through spring. The spectacle of wildly stormy coast is attracting increasing numbers of visitors annually.

Maritime activities have always been the compelling attraction of Newport. Named after the resort in Rhode Island, the town was established in 1866 and incorporated in 1882. By the early twentieth century, it was a rustic coastal tourist destination for Willamette Valley residents who lived in tents in what is now the Nye Beach neighborhood. The splendid Yaquina Bay bridge was completed during the Great Depression. It was a final link on the national highway that opened the entire magnificent Oregon coast to travelers. Tourism continues as a major segment of the local economy—along with commercial fishing and forest products industries.

Today, most of the area's conventional businesses are scattered along the main highway on the blufftop through town. Below, along the river in the shadow of the bridge, is a compact district known as Bay Front, or Old Town. This historic enclave is the real heart of Newport. Unfortunately, since the mid-1980s, Old Town has been bombarded with tourist traps, T-shirt and trinket parlors, and a garish convenience store. Nevertheless, a captivating hodgepodge of shops, restaurants, and bars still enlivens refurbished Victorian buildings amidst a mosaic of unpretentious canneries and other maritime businesses. In keeping with Newport's role as the self-proclaimed Dungeness crab capital of the world, canneries, seafood markets, cafes, and restaurants in Old Town do an outstanding job of showcasing this gourmet crustacean. A plush bayside resort hotel is a short stroll from Old Town. As alternatives, reasonably priced highway-fronting motels are plentiful. So are luxurious accommodations with splendid oceanfront views along secluded coves and broad ocean beaches on the west side of town. One of the most scenic and complete campgrounds along the Pacific Northwest coast is also nearby.

Elevation:

130 feet

Population (1980):

7,519

Population (1970):

5,188

Location:

110 miles Southwest of Portland

WEATHER PROFILE
Vokac Weather Rating

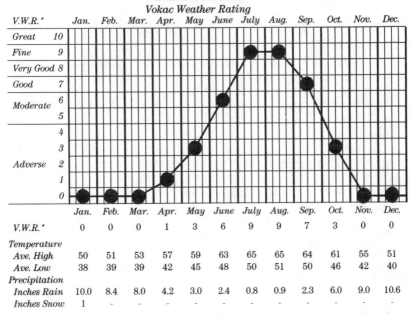

V.W.R.*		Jan.	Feb.	Mar.	Apr.	May	June	July	Aug.	Sep.	Oct.	Nov.	Dec.
V.W.R.*		0	0	0	1	3	6	9	9	7	3	0	0
Temperature													
Ave. High		50	51	53	57	59	63	65	65	64	61	55	51
Ave. Low		38	39	39	42	45	48	50	51	50	46	42	40
Precipitation													
Inches Rain		10.0	8.4	8.0	4.2	3.0	2.4	0.8	0.9	2.3	6.0	9.0	10.6
Inches Snow		1	-	-	-	-	-	-	-	-	-	-	-

*V.W.R. = Vokac Weather Rating: probability of mild (warm & dry) weather on any given day.

Forecast

	V.W.R.*		Temperatures		Precipitation
			Daytime	Evening	
Jan.	0	Adverse	cool	chilly	continual downpours
Feb.	0	Adverse	cool	chilly	continual rainstorms
Mar.	0	Adverse	cool	chilly	continual rainstorms
Apr.	1	Adverse	cool	chilly	continual rainstorms
May	3	Adverse	cool	cool	frequent showers
June	6	Moderate	cool	cool	occasional showers
July	9	Fine	warm	cool	infrequent showers
Aug.	9	Fine	warm	cool	infrequent showers
Sep.	7	Good	cool	cool	occasional showers
Oct.	3	Adverse	cool	cool	frequent rainstorms
Nov.	0	Adverse	cool	chilly	continual rainstorms
Dec.	0	Adverse	cool	chilly	continual downpours

Summary

Newport occupies a handsome peninsula above the Oregon coast's finest beach-and-harbor. While enjoying one of the longest growing seasons in the West outside of California because of the ocean's moderating influence, the area endures one of the nation's heaviest annual rainfalls. **Winter** is uniformly cool and very wet. Since freezing temperatures are unusual, snowfall is rare, but continual heavy rainstorms preclude most outdoor recreation. **Spring** remains unpleasantly cool and wet with slightly higher temperatures and diminishing rainstorms lasting through Memorial Day. **Summer** is the special season. Relatively warm days, cool evenings, and surprisingly infrequent showers provide suitable conditions for comfortably enjoying all of the features of this coastal wonderland. **Fall** weather deteriorates rapidly, with brisk days and evenings, and increasingly frequent rainstorms before Halloween.

ATTRACTIONS & DIVERSIONS

★ **Boat Rentals**

There are several places on Yaquina Bay where boats and gear may be rented by the hour or day. Among the most convenient are:

Embarcadero Marina. *7 mi. E of Old Town at 1000 SE Bay Blvd.* 265-5435

Riverbend Moorage *4.5 mi. E at 5262 Yaquina Bay Rd.* 265-9243

★ **Devil's Punch Bowl State Park**

8 mi. N on US 101

A huge bowl-shaped rock formation fills from below with a roar at high tide. Scenic picnic sites, a long spectacular curve of clean sandy beach, swimming (for the hearty), tidepools, and ocean-carved caves are other features of this delightful day use park.

Flying

Sunrise Aviation

3 mi. S via US 101 at Newport Airport 867-7597

Scenic flights along the coast, and beyond for whale watching, are offered on a walk-in basis. Charter service and rentals are also available.

Golf

Agate Beach Golf Course

2.4 mi. N at 4100 Golf Course Dr. 265-7331

Located on a relatively flat bluff inland from the coast, this 9-hole seaview course is open to the public. Facilities include a pro shop, club and cart rental, a driving range, and a cafe.

★ **Hatfield Marine Science Center**

1.8 mi. S on Marine Science Rd. 867-3011

Oregon State University operates this large coastal research center on Yaquina Bay. The public is invited to view marine fish and invertebrates in tanks that simulate their natural environments. There is a handling pool where visitors can pick up and examine starfish and other intertidal creatures. Material in the center's bookstore and numerous exhibits explain coastal geology, tides, and harbor life. During the summer, marine workshops, field trips, lectures, and films are offered to the public in the Seatauqua program. Nearby on Yaquina Bay is the Salmon Ocean Ranch, where visitors may view salmon in holding tanks.

★ **Library**

downtown at 35 NW Nye St. 265-2153

The Newport Public Library is an exciting new addition to the town's cultural facilities. In addition to a large well-displayed book, magazine, and newspaper collection, the stylish building offers padded armchairs in front of an artistic, tile-faced fireplace. Closed Sun.

Lincoln County Historical Museum

downtown at 545 SW 9th St. 265-7509

Two buildings, the Burrows House (1895) and a log cabin, display

Newport area memorabilia and relics from Victorian and later times. Closed Mon.

★ **Ona Beach State Park**
  8.3 mi. S on US 101
  A bathhouse and boat ramp contribute to this day use park's attraction for swimming and fishing. There are many scenic picnic sites on a grassy lawn with shade trees overlooking the mouth of a creek and a sandy ocean beach.

★ **Oregon Oyster Farm**
  8 mi. E at 6878 Yaquina Bay Rd.   *265-5078*
  Yaquina Bay is generally regarded as one of the best environments in the Northwest for growing oysters. Near the head of the bay, the Wachsmuth family has been cultivating the tasty mollusks for generations. A substantial part of their annual harvest still goes to Dan and Louis Oyster Bar in Portland, as it has for many decades. Oysters are grown in all shapes and sizes on plastic trays and strung on wires above the bay's mud. But, the specialty is the incomparable Kumamoto—a miniature Japanese variety with an exquisite flavor and texture. Visitors are welcome to watch the harvest and shucking, and samples may be offered apart from summer when warming bay water renders the oysters unpalatable.

★ *Rock Hunting*
  beaches north and south of town
  Tide-polished gem stones, agates, petrified wood, and coral may be found on the sand wherever streams cross coastal beaches.

★ **Siuslaw National Forest**
  NE and SE of town   *547-3289*
  This is the only coastal national forest in the Northwest. Cape Perpetua Visitor Center (27 mi. S on US 101) offers a movie and exhibits about the Oregon coast. Ten miles of scenic hiking trails branch out from the center into lush rain forests, driftwood-strewn beaches, and rock-bound tidepool formations. The view from the top of Cape Perpetua is magnificent. Accessible by car, the cape is the highest point on the Oregon coast. Nearby are some fascinating rock and sea attractions—the Devil's Churn and Cook's Chasm. Inland, luxuriant forests blanket Coast Range mountains that reach elevations over 4,000 feet above sea level.

★ **South Beach Marina**
  1.8 mi. S via US 101 on Oceanography Rd.   *867-3800*
  One of the Northwest's largest and most complete marina facilities is near the outlet of Yaquina Bay. In addition to a huge moorage and complete marine services, there is a public fishing pier with fine bay views, a bait and tackle store, floating restaurant, deep sea charters, a picnic area with barbecues, and a crab cooking facility.

South Beach State Park
2 mi. S on US 101
Expansive low dunes and a broad sandy beach lie between a campground and picnic facilities, and the ocean. Fishing and beachcombing are popular.

★ *Sportfishing*
Salmon fishing is one of the major attractions off the Oregon coast in summer. Newport is home port to several sportfishing charters located along the Old Town waterfront. Salmon trolling, tuna and deep sea fishing, and whale watching excursions are featured by:

Cape Perpetua Charters *Old Town at 839 SW Bay Blvd.* 265-7777
Newport Sportfishing. *7 mi. E of Old Town at 1000 SE Bay Bl.* 265-7558
Rich's Tradewinds *Old Town at 653 SW Bay Blvd.* 265-2101
Sea Gull Charters *Old Town at 343 SW Bay Blvd.* 265-7441
South Beach Charters *1.8 mi. S on Oceanography Rd.* 867-7200

★ **Undersea Gardens**
Old Town at 267 SW Bay Blvd. 265-7541
Marine creatures can be viewed in their natural habitat from a room surrounded by underwater viewing windows. There are also scuba diving shows. An upstairs gift shop offers appropriate mementoes.

Warm Water Feature
Newport Swimming Pool
1.2 mi. NE at 1212 Fogarty St. 265-7770
Lap, recreational, and family swimming sessions are open to the public year-round in a large, heated indoor pool.

★ **Yachats**
23 mi. S on US 101 547-3530
Yachats' motto is "the gem of the Oregon coast," and the location lives up to it. The tiny village has an idyllic site where lush forested slopes tumble into a churning sea adjacent to the sandy mouth of Yachats Creek. Carefully tended flower gardens and a grassy state park on the ocean side lend to the scenic appearance of the village. The area has become the permanent home of a growing number of artists and craftsmen, and several local galleries display their paintings, ceramics, and wood works. Beachcombing, tidepool viewing, rockhounding, and shore fishing are popular activities.

★ **Yaquina Bay State Park**
.6 mi. SW on US 101 at N end of bridge
Dozens of scenic picnic sites are positioned on a well-landscaped blufftop with panoramic views of sandy ocean beaches and the mouth of Yaquina Bay. Sunbathing, beachcombing, fishing, and swimming (for the hearty) are also popular. The park's focal point is historic Yaquina Bay Lighthouse (1871). This combined lighthouse/residence has been restored and refurnished in period style and is open to the public Thursday through Monday.

SHOPPING

Intriguing shops are clustered in several locations in town. Downtown offers a small, growing cluster of newer shops near the civic buildings along US 101 on the bluff. It lies between two contemporary specialty shopping complexes that prove that new suburban shopping centers are not inevitably boring. Below the bluff about half a mile south of downtown is one of the West's liveliest and most distinctive shopping and strolling districts—Old Town—along the colorful Yaquina Bay waterfront.

Food Specialties

Arrow Food Market
downtown at 425 SW US 101   265-2132
In addition to groceries, this place features magazines, paperback books, and a gourmet deli that serves a wide assortment of sandwiches, and wine or beer from extensive collections, in a surprisingly pleasant hideaway dining area.

Aunt Belinda's
Old Town at 663 SW Bay Blvd.   265-9540
Tillamook ice cream is featured in a variety of flavors and styles along with all kinds of snacks in this small carryout shop.

Berries & Cream
Old Town at 640 SW Bay Blvd.   265-4610
Delicious ice cream (BJ's of Florence) in many styles and flavors is served in a too-bright, antiseptic parlor, or to go.

★ Bridge Bakery
.4 mi. SW at 1006 SW US 101   265-8067
This popular full-line bakery offers a variety of notable pastries, donuts, cookies, pies, and breads to go, or with coffee at a few tables. Closed Sun.

★ The Cape House
.5 mi. SW at 1164 SW US 101   265-5491
Gourmet specialty foods—jams, coffee beans, Burr House flours, etc.—deli delights, and culinary accessories have been given an especially appealing display in a shop in the Bay Bridge Mall.

★ Fish Peddler's Market
Old Town at 617 SW Bay Blvd.   265-7057
From the viewing area of the Depot Bay Fish Company, visitors can watch the processing of fish, crab, and shrimp. In the retail market, seafood is sold fresh, frozen, smoked, or canned, and in special gift packs.

★ Gino's Seafood & Deli
Old Town at 808 SW Bay Blvd.   265-2424
This large, clean fish market features fresh, smoked, and canned seafoods, plus a good assortment of cheeses and other food items.

★ **Jack's Sea Food Inc.**
  Old Town at 456 SW Bay Blvd.   265-5442
A large assortment of all types (fresh-packed, alder-smoked, barbecued, etc.) of canned seafoods is attractively displayed. They will also custom smoke your fish. "Sea Pak gift boxes" can also be purchased, ready for mailing.

JC's Ice Cream Parlor
  downtown at 19 N. US 101/US 20   265-3040
All natural ingredients and an unusually high cream content are featured in a variety of fine ice cream flavors and styles served to go or in a modern parlor.

★ **Swafford's Oregon Specialties**
  1.1 mi. N at 1630 N. US 101   265-3044
Oregon specialties—wine, seafoods, wild berry preserves, filberts, etc.—are beautifully displayed along with local crafts. Many gift pack varieties will be shipped anywhere from this tantalizing contemporary shop in Sea Towne Shopping Center. In an adjoining dining area, fine pastries, desserts, and light fare are served for lunch. Closed Sun.

West Candies Mfg.
  .8 mi. N at 1329 N. US 101   265-7317
Saltwater taffy, homemade chocolates, and cranberry candies are among the distinctive candies made and sold in this long-established candy store. Custom packed boxes will be shipped anywhere.

White's Corner Donuts
  downtown on US 101 at 715-A SW Hurbert St.   265-7231
A variety of good donuts, muffins, and pastries, plus sandwiches, are served with coffee in a pleasant shop, or to go. Closed Sun.

Specialty Shops

Bay Bridge Mall
  .5 mi. SW on US 101 at Minnie St.
Just north of the bridge and Yaquina Bay Park, a small shopping center has showcased some good specialty shops in buildings with appealing contemporary architecture and decor.

The Book End
  1.1 mi. N at 1670 N. US 101   265-6252
One of the largest magazine selections on the Oregon coast, plus a good display of books about the Northwest, are highlights in a pleasant shop in Sea Towne Mall.

★ **Canyon Way Bookstore & Restaurant**
  downtown at 1216 SW Canyon Way   265-8319
A large and eclectic assortment of books, arts, and crafts fills several rooms adjoining a well-outfitted bakery/deli carryout shop, and an unusually distinctive restaurant featuring gourmet lunches and dinners.

Land's End Gifts
   1.1 mi. N at 1610 N. US 101   *265-7526*
Arts and crafts, candies, and nautical items—many with a Northwestern flair—are invitingly displayed in this contemporary shop in Sea Towne Mall.

★ **The Myrtlewood Chalet**
   Old Town at 333 SW Bay Blvd.   *265-6979*
A fascinating assortment of myrtlewood items is given a large, well-organized display in a factory outlet that also has a fine bay view.

★ **Oceanic Arts Center**
   Old Town at 444 SW Bay Blvd.   *265-5963*
First-rate wall hangings, wood crafts, woven materials, hand-blown glass, and jewelry by talented local and Northwestern artists and craftsmen are displayed and sold in an impressive new gallery.

★ **Sea Gulch**
   10 mi. S on US 101 - Seal Rock   *563-2727*
The world's largest collection of chain-sawed wood sculptures is given humorous displays, and many are for sale in this unusual roadside business. Visitors can watch the motorized artists at work most days.

★ **Sea Towne Mall**
   1.1 mi. N at US 101/16th St.
A classy cluster of specialty shops lends vitality to nautically-themed structures (built in simple "salt box" architectural style) and colorful gardens in Newport's most handsome shopping center.

★ **The Wood Gallery**
   Old Town at 818 SW Bay Blvd.   *265-6843*
Superb selections of carved driftwood and other unique wood creations, pottery, and jewelry are showcased in a captivating gallery. The recently expanded display area also features wine tasting (12-5:30 daily) of selected premium wines produced in Oregon by Alpine Vineyards.

NIGHTLIFE

One of the West's most refreshing "action" centers is the wonderful jumble of adult diversions that come alive after dark along historic Old Town's Bay Boulevard. Scruffy bars and legal gambling dens are interspersed with big whitewashed canneries, cozy cafes and contemporary restaurants, gift shops and galleries, and sleek lounges with spectacular bay views and live entertainment in a vibrant potpourri of businesses that suggests what Fisherman's Wharf in San Francisco may have been like in the "old days."

★ **The Adobe Lounge**
   22 mi. S at 1555 N. US 101 - Yachats   *547-3141*
Wood-toned architecture and decor in this superb two-level oceanfront lounge is complemented by padded armchairs at tables set along window walls. The seascape is stunning.

Barge Inn
Old Town at 358 SW Bay Blvd.   *265-8051*
The "home of winos, dingbats and riffraff" is a frayed tavern that is a
local favorite with pool, shuffleboard, and premium beer on tap.

★ **Captain Kidd's**
downtown at 706 SW Hurbert St.   *265-5114*
Pool, ping pong, darts, foosball, shuffleboard, legal gambling, and
electronic games contribute to the popularity among locals of a funky
tavern outfitted with wooden armchairs near a hooded gas fireplace.

Embarcadero Hotel Lounge
.7 mi. E of Old Town at 1000 SE Bay Blvd.   *265-8521*
Live entertainment is offered in a plush, contemporary lounge with a
(gas) firelit nook equipped with overstuffed armchairs and sofas.

4J's Lounge
.4 mi. SW at 614 SW Elizabeth St.   *265-2562*
It'd be just another dark and cozy lounge with live music for dancing on
weekends, except that patrons have a panoramic view of the nearby
beach and surf.

★ **The Inn at Otter Crest**
9 mi. N on US 101 - Otter Rock   *765-2111*
While live music for dancing is furnished most nights in the resort's
plush modern lounge, the spectacular window wall view of the Oregon
coast is the main attraction.

Neptune's Wharf
Old Town at 325 SW Bay Blvd.   *265-5316*
Fine bay and bridge views are features in a large casual lounge above a
bayfront restaurant.

★ **Newport Hilton**
2 mi. N at 3019 N. US 101   *265-5341*
Casey's provides live entertainment for dancing most nights. The hotel's
polished, contemporary lounge also has a fireplace and a panoramic
view of Agate Beach.

★ **Pip Tide**
Old Town at 836 SW Bay Blvd.   *265-3138*
Live music and dancing are offered every night in a large and popular
lounge, while upstairs, Yaquina Fats Game Room features gambling
(legal poker, etc.). The complex also has a firelit dining room and a
coffee shop serving complete meals twenty-four hours daily.

★ **Smuggler's Cove**
Old Town at 333 SE Bay Blvd.   *265-4614*
A hard-driving disco beat is accompanied by big screen video, plus
multicolored and blinking lights in the Dungeon—a rock-walled cellar
with a large dance floor. An adjoining room offers legal gambling,
pool, darts, and electronic games. There's also a multilevel lounge with
a panoramic view of Yaquina Bay, and a connected view terrace.

★ **Whale Cove Inn**
  11 mi. N on US 101 - Depoe Bay   765-2255
Local artists occasionally provide live music in a cozy lounge with a big
sofa in front of a slick-rock fireplace. A window wall provides one of the
most romantic seascape views on the Oregon coast.

RESTAURANTS

Seafood is appropriately emphasized, since fishing is a major local
industry. Readily available local fresh fish and extraordinary shellfish
like Yaquina Bay oysters and Dungeness crab reinforce Newport's
status as the gourmet center of the coastal Northwest. Several dining
rooms feature enchanting views of the ocean or bay.

The Adobe Restaurant
  22 mi. S at 1555 N. US 101 - Yachats   547-3141
  B-D.   *Moderate*
The seafoods and salad bar are conventional, but the spectacular
oceanfront view from the well-spaced comfortably furnished tables in
the large semicircular room compensates. A delightful oceanview
lounge adjoins.

Betty and Ike's
  downtown on US 101 at 104 SW 2nd St.   265-6901
  B-L. Closed Sun.   *Low*
The American standards are fresh and honest (they use Tillamook
cheddar and make their own pies). It's all priced to make you smile in
this shaped-up little coffee shop with padded booths.

★ **Bridge Company**
  .5 mi. SW at 1164 SW US 101   265-9551
  B-L-D.   *Moderate*
Homestyle meals including homemade desserts are featured on a
contemporary American menu. There is also a salad bar backed by a
memorable mural of the Yaquina Bay Bridge in this handsome, high-
tech dining room in the Bay Bridge Mall.

★ **Canyon Way Bookstore & Restaurant**
  downtown at 1216 SW Canyon Way   265-8319
  L-D.   *Moderate*
Delicious and unusual international specialties (beef Wellington,
shepherd's pie, seafood in mustard sauce, etc.) and fine homemade
baked goods and desserts are served in several dining areas and in a
garden patio. Fine coffees and teas, premium wines, and tap beers are
also available. An outstanding bookstore adjoins.

★ **Champagne Patio**
  1.1 mi. N at 1630 N. US 101   265-3044
  L only. Closed Sun.-Mon.   *Moderate*
Carefully prepared soups, salads, sandwiches, and delectable fresh-
baked bread and rich desserts are served in a small, nicely furnished

dining room. Northwest wines selected from the outstanding Oregon specialty foods store in the next room will be poured for a low corkage fee.

The Chowder Bowl
.4 mi. NW at 728 NW Beach Dr.   265-7477
L-D.   *Moderate*

Clam chowder is the well-regarded highlight among short order seafoods served in a casual little dining room where fresh flowers usually brighten each hardwood table. A recently added outlet in Old Town also sells gelato.

Embarcadero Resort Hotel
.7 mi. E of Old Town at 1000 SE Bay Blvd.   265-8521
B-L-D.   *Moderate*

Dungeness crab and salmon are among local specialties given serious attention at The Moorage. The Friday seafood buffet is a genuine extravaganza in this large handsome dining room on picturesque Yaquina Bay.

★ The Experience
19 mi. SE via US 101 at 3750 OR 34 - Waldport   563-4555
D only. Closed Tues. (and Mon. in winter)   *Moderate*

The main course is exclusively seafood for the gourmet dinners served here, and it may be such seasonal super-treats as tiny Yaquina Bay oysters or halibut cheeks. Everything from soup to desserts like cashew-kumquat pie is skillfully homemade. The comfortable little dining room has a fine forest view and an unusual world map mural wall. By reservation only.

4J's Restaurant
.4 mi. SW at 614 SW Elizabeth St.   265-2562
B-L-D.   *Low*

Stop by any time for any meal on an extensive American menu—from pancakes to steaks and seafood. The large, plain dining room has a window wall with an oceanfront view.

Galley Ho
.8 mi. N at 1255 N. US 101   265-5104
B-L-D.   *Moderate*

Decent omelets with biscuits and gravy are breakfast specialties, and seafoods and a salad bar with an all-you-can-drink beer or wine policy set the tone for dinner. Diners at padded booths or tables and chairs have some greens and a large aquarium to look at. Live music for dancing is available most nights in an adjoining lounge.

The Inn at Otter Crest
9 mi. N via US 101 - Otter Rock   765-2060
B-L-D.   *Moderate*

At the Flying Dutchman Restaurant, conventional Continental dishes are accompanied by homemade breads and pastries. Meals give patrons an excuse to linger over a magnificent panoramic view of the Oregon coast from the large, plush dining room. An adjoining view lounge features live music and dancing.

★ La Serre
23 mi. S on US 101 at 2nd/Beach Sts. - Yachats   547-3420
B-L-D.   *Moderate*

Freshness, quality ingredients, and a creative spirit with herbs and sauces are the hallmarks of this restaurant. Some of the most satisfyingly innovative dishes on the Oregon coast are served in a capacious skylit atrium dining room. A jungle of healthy green plants surrounds hardwood armchairs by tables set with fresh flowers and old-time oil lamps. A tranquil new firelit lounge adjoins.

Lightship Restaurant
1.8 mi. S via US 101 at S. Beach Marina Dock A   867-8077
L-D.   *Moderate*

Assorted seafoods like gravy-thick clam chowder and deep-fried oysters are served at vinyl-clad tables set with simulated flowers in the hold of the lightship "Swiftsure" which now serves as a family-oriented floating restaurant.

Mo's
Old Town at 622 SW Bay Blvd.   265-2979
L-D.   *Low*

The clam chowder is notorious, and homestyle cooking lends distinction to fresh fish dishes and pies. This noisy little no-frills fish shack was the first of a redoubtable restaurant empire started by an Indian named Mohava Niemi.

★ Mo's Annex
Old Town at 657 SW Bay Blvd.   265-7512
L-D.   *Low*

Fresh fish stews join the touted clam chowder as specialties in an extremely popular restaurant across the street from the original cafe. Mo's Annex balances congested, picnic table decor in a bayside dining room with delightful views of waterfront activity, and a fine collection of Oregon wines.

Neptune's Wharf
Old Town at 325 SW Bay Blvd.   265-5316
L-D.   *Moderate*

Fresh sauteed seafood and a house bouillabaisse are featured in this contemporary, casually elegant dining room with a delightful view of Yaquina Bay.

Newport Hilton
2 mi. N at 3019 N. US 101   265-9411
B-L-D. Sun. brunch.   *Moderate*

At Casey's Bar and Grill, salmon is cooked over alder wood on the front lawn. But, the seafood specialties take a back seat to the panoramic view of Agate Beach from the large, luxuriously furnished dining room.

★ Pie and Kite Shop

23 mi. S on US 101 - Yachats   *547-3360*
L only.   *Moderate*

Tasty soups and light fare are served in a warm and cozy little dining area, but the real attraction is the delectable pies made here.

Pip Tide

Old Town at 836 SW Bay Blvd.   *265-7796*
B-L-D.   *Low*

Basic American dishes are served twenty-four hours daily here. The bright and cheerful coffee shop has a cannery/bay view. A firelit dining room adjoins.

Smuggler's Cove

Old Town at 333 SE Bay Blvd.   *265-4614*
L-D. Sun. brunch.   *Moderate*

A new chef and management are trying to make something of the big dining and drinking establishment on a slope above Old Town. Seafood is emphasized. A few tables have Yaquina Bay views. The multilevel bar has a better view, as do alfresco diners on the terrace (when weather permits).

Vic's on the Wharf

Old Town at 839 SW Bay Blvd.   *265-8907*
B-L-D. Closed Tues.   *Low*

Vic's biscuits and gravy are some of the finest in the Northwest. These and other very good homestyle fare are served in an unassuming little bayside cafe with a delightful view of the waterfront. For dinner, a limited menu offers exclusively seafood entrees—with local specialties featured.

Welton's Towne House

3.2 mi. N at 5251 N. US 101   *265-7263*
B-L-D.   *Expensive*

A conventional menu of seafoods is offered in a recently reopened hilltop restaurant. The large dining room is nicely outfitted in full linens and contemporary place settings. A window wall ocean view on two sides and a large copper-hooded gas fireplace are features. An ocean view lounge adjoins.

Whale Cove Inn

11 mi. N on US 101 - Depoe Bay   *765-2255*
B-L-D.   *Moderate*

A customary American menu with a seafood emphasis offers an extraordinary specialty—a cinnamon roll of truly epic proportions. The simply furnished dining room features a window wall view of picturesque Whale Cove including an impressive whale tale sculpture on a lawn below the dining room. Binoculars are provided at the windowside tables.

★ **Whale's Tale**

Old Town at 452 SW Bay Blvd.   265-8660
B-L-D. Closed Jan.   *Moderate*

Breakfasts are especially notable, including specialties like poppyseed pancakes from stone-ground flour, and oyster omelets. Local artwork enlivens the handcrafted wood-toned interior, and there is occasional live entertainment in the evening.

Yaquina Marina Restaurant

4.5 mi. E on Yaquina Bay Rd.   265-2941
B-L-D. Closed Mon.-Tues.   *Low*

Simply prepared fried and grilled American dishes, including a few local seafoods, are served in a cheerful cafe with a Franklin fireplace and booths by picture windows overlooking upper Yaquina Bay.

LODGING

Several extraordinary accommodations overlook the ocean or the bay. Numerous motels, ranging from old and modest to posh and contemporary, are inland along US 101 through town. Many offer 25% and greater rate reductions apart from summer.

★ **The Adobe**

22 mi. S at 1555 N. US 101 (Box 219) - Yachats 97498   547-3141

A rocky basalt coastline borders the spacious lawns of this modern motel. Features include an indoor whirlpool and a sauna, an ocean view restaurant, and an enchanting ocean view lounge. Each nicely appointed unit has a refrigerator, phone, and cable color TV with movies.

"original adobe rooms"—carport, fireplace, good
         ocean view,   K bed...$53

"new south units"—fireplace, (ask for upstairs west
         side), excellent ocean view,   K bed ...$53

regular room—hillside view,   Q bed...$38

The Anchorage

4.1 mi. N on US 101 - Star Rt. N (Box 364)   265-5463

This older cottage colony is on a bluff above an ocean beach. Each unit offers privacy in a well-forested location, a wood-burning fireplace, and a full kitchen, plus cable color TV.

cottage #4—1 BR, remote, private, fine ocean
         view,   D & Q beds...$47

cottage #3—2 BR, private, near bluff, fine ocean
         view,   2 Q beds...$50

regular room—limited ocean view,   Q bed...$44

City Center Motel

downtown at 538 SW US 101   265-7381

In this small, older **bargain** motel, each simply furnished room has a cable color TV.

regular room—movie channel on TV,   Q bed...$28
regular room—small, no movie channel,   Q bed...$25

Driftwood Village Motel
4.7 mi. N on US 101 - Star Rt. N (Box 380)   *265-5738*
At the top of a hill, high above a sandy beach, is a small single-level older motel. Each unit has a fine ocean view and sliding glass doors to a private deck, plus a wood-burning fireplace and cable color TV.
"Viewpoint"—1 BR, kitchen, fireplace, carport,
        deck, superb ocean view on two
        sides,   2 T & K beds...$55
regular room—ocean view,   D bed...$43

Dunes Ocean Front Motel
.4 mi. SW at 536 SW Elizabeth St.   *265-7701*
A large indoor pool and a whirlpool are features of this big modern three-level motel sprawled along a broad sandy beach. Each room has an ocean view beyond a parking lot, a phone and cable color TV.
#133,#148—fine ocean views,   Q bed...$49
regular room—   Q bed...$45

★ **Embarcadero Resort Hotel**
.7 mi. E of Old Town at 1000 SE Bay Blvd.   *265-8521*
Newport's largest condominium motor hotel fronts on Yaquina Bay. Nicely landscaped grounds include several contemporary wood-toned buildings, a large indoor pool with a bay view, whirlpool, sauna, fishing and crabbing piers, outdoor barbecue and crab cooking facilities, a marina with rental boats, plus a view restaurant and lounge. Each spacious well-furnished unit has a phone, cable color TV, and a private balcony. For toll-free reservations, call: in Oregon (800)452-8567; elsewhere (800)547-4779.
Building C—1 BR bayside suite, kitchen, fireplace
        in LR, fine bay/bridge view,   Q bed...$85
Buildings D,E,F,G—as above, but bay view only
        (no bridge),   Q bed...$85
regular room—   2 T or Q bed...$54

★ **The Inn at Otter Crest**
9 mi. N on US 101 (Box 50) - Otter Rock 97369   *765-2111*
Majestically located in a pine forest high above the ocean, this large contemporary condominium hotel offers a private sandy cove, a large outdoor pool with splendid views, a whirlpool, saunas, a putting green, hiking trails, a funicular, a recreation room, (fee) indoor and outdoor tennis courts, plus a spectacularly located restaurant, and a lounge with live entertainment and dancing. Each well-furnished unit has a refrigerator, a deck, a phone, and cable color TV with movies.
#133,#405 "loft suites"—fireplace, kitchen,
        stunning views, loft with   K bed...$95
regular room—   2 Q beds...$65

★ **Little Creek Cove**
   2.3 mi. N via US 101 at 3651 NW Ocean View Dr.   265-8587
   A secluded beachfront cove has been transformed with perfectly-scaled naturalistic buildings and landscaping into an enchanting little condominium motel. Each beautifully furnished unit has a phone, cable color TV with movies, fireplace, kitchen, and a private deck.
      #29—1 BR, magnificent ocean/beach views,   K bed...$67
      #3—studio, magnificent ocean view,   Murphy Q bed...$57
      regular room—studio, some ocean view,   Murphy Q bed...$57

★ **Moolack Shores Motel**
   4.9 mi. N on US 101   265-2326
   This contemporary single-level motel is in a secluded spot at the edge of a bluff above the beach. Each room is artistically decorated in a different theme, and has cable color TV.
      #10A—corner, kitchenette, ocean view windows,
         view deck,   D & Q beds...$52
      #4,#5A,#9—Franklin (pressed log) fireplace,
         kitchenette, ocean view,   Q bed...$52
      regular room—small, (pressed log) fireplace,
         refrigerator, some ocean view,   Q bed...$46

★ **Newport Hilton**
   2 mi. N at 3019 N. US 101   265-9411
   Overlooking picturesque Agate Beach is a large, modern six-story hotel with a big outdoor pool and a whirlpool, plus a view restaurant, and a view lounge with entertainment. Each well-furnished room has a phone and cable color TV. For toll-free reservations, call (800) 445-8667.
      #630,#620,#612,#610,#602—balcony, outstanding
         private ocean view,   K bed...$70
      regular room—faces a hillside,   2 D or K bed...$45

Newport Motor Inn
   1 mi. N at 1311 N. US 101   265-8516
   Each room in this modern **bargain** motel has a phone and cable color TV with movies.
      regular room—   Q bed...$29

Park Motel
   .3 mi. SW via US 101 at 1106 SW 9th St.   265-2234
   This is a modern, single-level **bargain** motel. Each simply furnished room has a phone and cable color TV with movies.
      regular room—   Q bed...$28

Penny Saver Inn
   .6 mi. N at 710 N. US 101   265-6631
   One of the area's newer motels features a phone and cable color TV with movies in each room.
      regular room—   Q bed...$32

Sands Motor Lodge
.3 mi. N at 206 N. US 101   *265-5321*
A sauna is featured in a **bargain** motel where each plainly furnished
room has a phone and cable color TV.

regular room—newer, TV with movies,   Q bed...$30
regular room—older,   D bed...$28

★ **Schooner Landing**
3.8 mi. N on US 101 at 1 Schooner Dr.(Box 703)   *265-4501*
One of Newport's newest and finest lodgings is a cluster of condo/
time-share townhouses on a wooded coastal bluff. Amenities include
private hiking paths to the beach, a long indoor swimming pool,
whirlpool, sauna, racquetball court, and a game room. Each of the
attractively furnished Cape Cod-style units has a full kitchen with
microwave, a wood-burning fireplace, deck, in-bath whirlpool, phone,
stereo, and cable color TV. For toll-free reservations in Oregon, call
(800)468-8811; elsewhere (800)592-2208.

#306—2 BR, private, coastal/forest view,   2 Q beds...$150
#307—1 BR, upstairs, private, coastal/forest
       view,   Q bed...$105
regular room—1 BR, forest view,   Q bed...$105

Seven Seas Motel
.3 mi. SW at 861 SW US 101   *265-2277*
This modern motel is by the highway in a convenient location. Each
plain room has a phone and cable color TV.

regular room—   Q bed...$32

★ **Shamrock Lodgettes**
23 mi. S on US 101 (Box 346) - Yachats 97498   *547-3312*
At the mouth of the Yachats River immediately south of Yachats is an
inviting complex of log cabin-style lodgings in a park-like setting. A
whirlpool and sauna are available as is a licensed massage therapist
(by appointment). A sandy beach overlooking town lies just beyond a
public road. Each unit includes a cable color TV with movies.

#16 thru #19—spacious, kitchenette, fireplace,
               in-bath whirlpool, ocean view,   K bed...$60
regular room—fireplace, refrigerator, private
               deck, river view,   K bed...$45

★ **Starfish Point**
3 mi. N on US 101 at 140 NW 48th St.   *265-3751*
High on the rim of a scenic bluff overlooking the ocean is one of the
Oregon coast's finest examples of the latest in post-modern
Northwestern architecture. Each of the units in this tiny condo cluster
has two bedrooms and baths, an unusual octagonal study, private deck,
whirlpool, Jenn-aire range in the full kitchen, stereo, wood-burning
fireplace, and cable color TV, plus expansive ocean views.

"Sandpiper"—2 BR, 2 decks, 2 octagonal studies
    with ocean view, large whirlpool
    with ocean view,   D & Q beds...$110
"Seagull"—2 BR, loft/deck, whirlpool in bath, fine
ocean view,   D & Q beds...$98
regular room—   D & Q beds...$98
Summer Wind Motel   265-5722
.6 mi. N at 728 N. US 101   *265-5722*
This small, single-level older motel is a **bargain**. Each of the simply furnished rooms has a cable color TV.
regular room—   Q bed...$24
Surf 'n Sand
4.6 mi. N on US 101 - Star Rt. N (Box 390)   *265-2215*
In this tiny oceanfront motel, each unit is nicely furnished and has cable color TV.
  #16,#17—fine ocean view from 2 sides,
        free-standing fireplace, refrigerator,   K bed...$44
  #11,#15—fine corner window ocean views,
        free-standing fireplace, kitchen,   Q bed...$44
regular room—some ocean view,   Q bed...$36
Waves Motel
.4 mi. NW at 820 NW Coast St.   *265-4661*
New in 1985, this three-level motel is set back from an ocean bluff. Each spacious, nicely furnished room has a phone and cable color TV. The top floor rooms have a fair ocean view.
regular room—   2 Q beds...$44
West Wind Motel
.3 mi. SW at 747 SW US 101   *265-5388*
An indoor pool and a whirlpool are features of this small, single-level **bargain** motel. Each of the frayed, simply furnished rooms has a phone and cable color TV.
regular room—   Q bed...$28
Whale Cove Inn
11 mi. N on US 101 (Star Rt. South Box 1X) - Depoe Bay 97341 765-2255
In 1986, new owners took over one of Oregon's most spectacularly located historic lodgings. They're doing good things in the restaurant and lounge, and they've upgraded some of the accommodations. Each nicely furnished room has cable color TV and a memorable view of beautiful Whale Cove and the ocean.
  #69—raised, mirrored in-room whirlpool with
      superb private cove view, remote control TV, K bed...$85
  #2—spacious, grand seascape view from   K bed...$42
  #4—spacious, outstanding cove view from   Q bed...$42
regular room—no view,   Q bed...$32

The Whaler Motel
.3 mi. W at 155 SW Elizabeth St.   *265-9261*
One of Newport's newest seaside motels is a three-story complex across a street from the ocean. Each attractively furnished room has a phone and cable color TV. For toll-free reservations in Oregon, call (800)433-4360; elsewhere (800)433-9444.

#79,#59—corner windows, ocean view,	2 Q beds...$56
#77—(pressed log) fireplace, good ocean view,	2 Q beds...$61
#41,#40—(pressed log) fireplace, good ocean view,	Q bed...$53
regular room—	Q bed...$43

Willers Motel
.3 mi. S at 754 SW US 101   *265-2241*
In this older **bargain** motel, each of the simply furnished rooms has a phone and cable color TV.

regular room—	Q bed...$30

★ **The Windjammer - Best Western**
.4 mi. SW at 744 SW Elizabeth St.   *265-8853*
This attractive motel is on a bluff above the ocean. The whole property is being refurbished, and new facilities are in the works on the south side. Each nicely furnished unit has an oceanfront view, a phone, and cable color TV. For toll-free reservations, call (800)528-1234.

#224—raised brick fireplace, raised in-room whirlpool, fine ocean view,	Q bed...$85
#444—raised brick fireplace, great corner window with ocean views,	Q bed...$60
#435—fireplace, kitchen, huge ocean view window, loft,	2 Q beds...$70
regular room—ocean view,	Q bed...$45

CAMPGROUNDS

Several campgrounds are scattered along the coast near town. The best is a nearly perfect combination of an easy drive to town, complete facilities, and a scenic sheltered location a short stroll from a picturesque sandy beach.

★ **Beverly Beach State Park**
6.7 mi. N on US 101   *265-9278*
The state operates this big facility located in a lush forest along a little stream near a fine sandy ocean beach. Features include saltwater or freshwater swimming and fishing in the ocean or Spencer Creek, beachcombing, and marked nature trails. Flush toilets, hot showers, and hookups are available. Each of the well-spaced, tree-shaded sites has a picnic table and a fire ring/grill. A scenic day use picnic area adjoins. Non-Oregonians add $2 surcharge to base rate.   base rate...$7

South Beach State Park
2 mi. S on US 101   *867-4715*
This large state operated facility is in scrub pines across some low

dunes from a long ocean beach. Beachcombing and fishing are within walking distance. Flush toilets, hot showers, and hookups are available. Each site has a picnic table and fire ring/grill. Non-Oregonians add $2 surcharge to base rate.   base rate...$7

SPECIAL EVENTS

★ **Seafood and Wine Festival** *. 7 mi. NE at Fairgrounds late February*
In only a few years, this weekend festival has become one of the largest of its kind on the West Coast. Oregon wines and seafoods are featured, with music and arts and crafts as sidelights.

Loyalty Days and Sea Fair Festival *around town first weekend in May*
A parade, sailing regatta, military ship tours, art and seafood booths, a chicken barbecue, and live entertainment are popular highlights of this long-established four-day celebration.

OTHER INFORMATION

Area Code: *503*
Zip Code: *97365*
Greater Newport Chamber of Commerce
 downtown at 555 SW US 101   *265-8801*

Seaside, Oregon

Seaside is the premier coastal playground of the Pacific Northwest. It was the region's first town to wholeheartedly espouse a tourist-serving destiny. For more than a century, vacationers have been attracted to the broad sandy beach that links the ocean with a massive forested headland at one of the most dramatic sites on the Northwest coast.

Long warm days and relatively little rain attract capacity crowds during summer, the year's only busy season. Popular activities include beachcombing, moped and three-wheeled "brike" riding, and automobile driving on miles of hard beach sand. Bicycle paths, hiking trails, and campgrounds are available in nearby state parks. While the ocean water is always relatively cold, it is used for swimming and surfing by hearty visitors in summer. Attractive facilities for golf, tennis, and indoor swimming have been provided in town. One of the few old-fashioned commercial "fun zones" remaining in the western United States is downtown. The most noteworthy man-made attraction, however, is a scenic two-mile-long concrete promenade bordering the beach. For many decades, this has been the place to stroll, ride a bicycle, people-watch, or enjoy a sunset. From fall through spring, almost continuous rainfall curtails the area's usability for most outdoor recreation. However, increasing numbers of visitors arrive each winter to stand in awe (or watch from an ocean-view room) as gigantic storm-lashed surf pounds the beaches.

Seaside, Oregon

Seaside is the western end of the Lewis and Clark Trail. Members of that famous expedition boiled water to obtain salt here in the winter of 1806. Settlement didn't really start until the 1870s, however, when travelers began to journey here because of the site's handsome coastal location. The promenade, amusement facilities, and elaborate accommodations were soon constructed, establishing Seaside as the first major coastal resort in the Northwest. Completion of the Oregon coast highway (US 101) during the 1930s, and a bridge across the mouth of the Columbia River in 1966 made the area more easily accessible. Later, a civic center and convention facilities were added to further enhance the town's ability to handle large numbers of visitors.

Seaside is undergoing a renaissance. Several major improvements were recently completed in the heart of town. A well-landscaped pedestrian-and-auto mall on the main street is attracting distinctive new specialty shops and restaurants, and the remaining amusement concessions are being upgraded. Several atmospheric bars on the revitalized little thoroughfare offer live entertainment. A new multistoried landmark hotel anchors the promenade at the main street turnaround by the beach. Many other contemporary lodgings are also concentrated downtown and along the beach. Several feature oceanfront views and plush amenities within an easy stroll of the heart of town. Oregon's largest public campground is next to the ocean a short drive to the north.

Elevation:

10 feet

Population (1980):

5,193

Population (1970):

4,402

Location:

80 miles Northwest of Portland

179

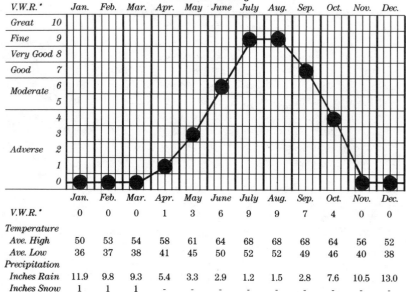

Seaside, Oregon
WEATHER PROFILE
Vokac Weather Rating

V.W.R.*	Jan.	Feb.	Mar.	Apr.	May	June	July	Aug.	Sep.	Oct.	Nov.	Dec.
V.W.R.*	0	0	0	1	3	6	9	9	7	4	0	0
Temperature												
Ave. High	50	53	54	58	61	64	68	68	68	64	56	52
Ave. Low	36	37	38	41	45	50	52	52	49	46	40	38
Precipitation												
Inches Rain	11.9	9.8	9.3	5.4	3.3	2.9	1.2	1.5	2.8	7.6	10.5	13.0
Inches Snow	1	1	1	-	-	-	-	-	-	-	-	-

*V.W.R. = Vokac Weather Rating: probability of mild (warm & dry) weather on any given day.

Forecast

		V.W.R.*	Daytime	Evening	Precipitation
			Temperatures		
Jan.	0	Adverse	cool	chilly	continual downpours
Feb.	0	Adverse	cool	chilly	continual rainstorms
Mar.	0	Adverse	cool	chilly	continual rainstorms
Apr.	1	Adverse	cool	chilly	continual rainstorms
May	3	Adverse	cool	cool	continual showers
June	6	Moderate	cool	cool	frequent showers
July	9	Fine	warm	cool	infrequent showers
Aug.	9	Fine	warm	cool	infrequent showers
Sep.	7	Good	warm	cool	frequent rainstorms
Oct.	4	Adverse	cool	cool	frequent downpours
Nov.	0	Adverse	cool	chilly	continual downpours
Dec.	0	Adverse	cool	chilly	continual downpours

Summary

Backed by low evergreen mountains, Seaside extends northward from a massive headland along a magnificent broad sandy beach. Because of the ocean's moderating influence, the area enjoys one of the longest growing seasons in the West outside of California, while it endures one of the nation's heaviest annual rainfalls. **Winter** days are uniformly cool, and continual rainstorms preclude most kinds of outdoor recreation. **Spring** remains unpleasantly cool and wet, with only gradually increasing temperatures and diminishing rainfall through June. For two delightful months in mid-**summer**, fine weather prevails. Warm days, cool evenings, and surprisingly infrequent showers make it easy to comfortably enjoy the splendid beach and nearby highlands. **Fall** weather deteriorates rapidly into brisk days, and increasingly frequent heavy rainstorms.

180

ATTRACTIONS & DIVERSIONS

★ **Astoria**

17 mi. N on US 101   *325-6311*

The oldest permanent American settlement in the Northwest dates back to the erection of Fort Astoria in 1811. Historic events that occurred in the region are depicted in spiral murals that wind up the outside of the Astoria Column—a 125-foot tower on Coxcomb Hill topped by an observation deck more than 700 feet above the Columbia River. Many examples of Victorian architecture remain, most notably the refurbished Flavel Mansion which now serves as the local historical society's museum. The Maritime Museum, the most comprehensive of its kind in the Northwest, is housed in a strikingly modern building on the waterfront at the foot of 17th Street. Near the west end of town, a graceful toll bridge more than four miles long spans the Columbia River. This final link in US 101 (a transcontinental highway from Canada to Mexico) was completed in 1966.

★ *Beach Drive*

starts 3 mi. N at Marion & 10th - Gearhart

The expansive, hard sand beach from Gearhart north for ten miles to Fort Stevens State Park is open to automobile traffic when the tide is low. It is an exhilarating scenic drive and an unusual experience.

★ *Bicycling*

There is a lot of flat coastal terrain in the Seaside area that can be toured on miles of paved separated bikeways including a nearly two-mile-long concrete promenade for leisurely rides, as well as scenic highways and byways. All kinds of bicycles, brikes (zany new three- wheelers), and roller skates are rented downtown by the hour at:

Funcycle Rentals   *Columbia St./Av. A*
Ocean Air Tricycles   *Columbia St./Av. A*
Old Spa   *Columbia St./Av. A*
Prom Bike Shop   *325 S. Holladay Dr.*   *738-8251*

★ **Fort Clatsop National Monument**

17 mi. N: 12 mi. N on US 101 & 5 mi. E on marked hwy.   *861-2471*

A full-scale reconstructed log fort is on the site of the Lewis and Clark expedition's headquarters during the winter of 1805. An adjacent visitor center houses a museum and audio-visual programs, and has a good selection of books and maps for sale. Living history demonstrations of frontier skills and tasks are presented by rangers in period costumes during summer. Short trails lead to the camp's freshwater spring and to a canoe landing with a replica of a dugout canoe of that period.

★ **Fort Stevens State Park**
 17 mi. N via US 101 861-2000
The park features remnants of military installations that protected the mouth of the Columbia River from the Civil War through the end of World War II. This is the only military post in the lower forty-eight states to have been fired on by foreign sources since 1812. (A Japanese submarine fired its five-inch gun on the fort in 1942.) There is an interpretive center in the War Games Building and self-guided trails to batteries, guardhouses, and earthworks. Wreckage of the "Peter Iredale," a schooner that went aground here in 1906, may be seen on the beach. Camping and picnicking facilities are plentiful. In addition, there are more than five miles of scenic hiking trails, six miles of bike paths, and two swimming areas with sandy beaches on Coffenbury Lake, which is also popular for boating and fishing.

★ *Fun Zone*
 downtown on Broadway
Skill games, electronic amusements, and rides are still featured in a cluster of commercial entertainment places on the main street between the river and the beach, as they have been for decades.

Golf
 Gearhart Golf Course
 2.5 mi. N on N. Marion Av. - Gearhart 738-8331
This 18-hole golf course is the oldest in the Pacific Northwest. Open to the public, it features long challenging straightaways. Facilities include a pro shop, club and cart rentals, a restaurant, and a lounge.

Horseback Riding
 Circle Creek Trail Rides
 1 mi. S on US 101 738-9263
Guided rides along inland streams and mountain trails are offered.
 Gearhart Stables
 4 mi. N via US 101 - Gearhart 738-7709
Horses are ridden on the nearby hard sand beach, but only in conjunction with guided trail rides.

Library
 downtown at 60 N. Roosevelt 738-6742
The Seaside Public Library is a comfortable, modern facility decorated with fresh flowers and plants. Features include a current newspapers/magazines area with padded armchairs, plus scheduled film showings.

★ *Moped Rentals*
Mopeds can be rented by the hour or longer for relatively effortless tours of the scenic countryside at:
 Arco Gas Station *downtown at 231 S. Holladay Dr.* 738-7015
 Trucke's Oasis *.9 mi. S on S. Holladay Dr.*

★ The Promenade

N & S from downtown

Built in 1920, this concrete walkway borders the beach for nearly two miles. It is a delightful place to stroll, skate, or ride a bicycle with sand and surf views on one side and impressive beach homes on the other. Near the midpoint, "the Turnaround" at the west end of Broadway is the designated "End of the Lewis and Clark Trail." Near the south end of the Promenade (on Lewis and Clark Way) a reconstructed Salt Cairn marks the place where expedition members boiled sea water to obtain salt during the winter of 1805.

Saddle Mountain State Park

14 mi. E via US 26

A three-mile trail leads to the top of 3,283-foot Saddle Mountain, one of the higher peaks in the Coast Range. From the summit, there is an outstanding view on clear days. Unusual alpine wildflowers are tucked amid rocky crags along the way. Picnicking and primitive camping facilities are also available.

Seaside Aquarium

downtown at 200 N. Prom   *738-6211*

Marine life from the North Pacific is displayed in this venerable aquatic exhibit, and you can feed the trained seals seen and heard from the Promenade. Open daily in summer. Closed Mon.-Tues. in winter.

★ Seaside Beach

W of downtown

Bordering the west side of town is a broad beach of hard-packed sand backed by low sand dunes extending to the Promenade. Lifeguard services are provided in summer. While the surf looks inviting, the water is inevitably cold, so sunbathing and beachcombing are the most popular activities. Surfing is not permitted within Seaside's city limits. However, one of the most popular "breaks" along the entire Northwest coast is adjacent to town on the south side near Sunset Boulevard.

★ Sitka Spruce

8 mi. SE : 2 mi. SE of jct. US 101 on US 26

The world's largest Sitka spruce (216 feet tall, 53 feet in circumference) is the highlight of a small privately owned park a short distance from the highway near the Necanicum River. Lush undergrowth has been thinned nearby so that informal picnic and camp sites could be added to give visitors more opportunities to enjoy the presence of the stupendous monarch of the forest.

★ *Sportfishing*

16 mi. N off US 101 - Hammond

Numerous charter boat services feature salmon fishing over the nearby Columbia River Bar. Each provides bait and tackle and arranges for freezing or canning your catch. The nearest to the ocean are:

Corkey's   *1180 Pacific Dr. - Hammond*   *861-2668*
Fort Stevens Salmon Charters *918 Pacific Dr. - Hammond* *861-1211*
Surf Charters   *890 Pacific Dr. - Hammond*   *861-2208*
Tiki Salmon Charters   *897 Pacific Dr. - Hammond*   *861-1201*

★ **Tillamook Head**
2.2 mi. SW via Sunset Blvd.
The area's most impressive landmark is a massive quarter-mile-high cape jutting into the sea between Seaside and Cannon Beach. Tillamook Head Trail, which is six miles each way, rewards energetic hikers with memorable coastal panoramas while attaining a height of nearly 1,200 feet above sea level. The trailhead begins at a parking lot at the end of Sunset Rd.

Warm Water Feature
Sunset Pool
.3 mi. E at 1140 Broadway   *738-3311*
This large indoor heated pool is open to the public most days.

SHOPPING

Seaside's compact business district is concentrated along Broadway on both sides of the Necanicum River. This main business thoroughfare was recently converted to an attractively landscaped, one-way-drive mall where old-fashioned arcades and amusements are still intermixed with a flourishing assortment of specialty shops, restaurants, and lounges.

Food Specialties
★ **Bell Buoy Crab Co.**
.9 mi. S at 1800 S. Holladay Dr.   *738-6354*
Delicious fresh or canned Dungeness crab, and fresh or smoked salmon, are specialties in an impressive line of seasonally available fresh, smoked, and canned seafoods. Custom smoking or canning can also be arranged. Various seafood cocktails are displayed to go.

★ **Boardwalk Bakery**
downtown at 85 Broadway   *738-6140*
Here is a recent spur of the Cannon Beach Bakery. The raspberry butterfly and cinnamon rolls are notable among the skillfully produced pastries, and "haystack" is the most popular bread. Everything is served to go, or with coffee at three tables amidst the contemporary decor. Closed Tues.-Wed.

Fenton's Garden Center
7 mi. N on US 101   *738-7332*
A tempting array of locally grown fruits, vegetables, and flowers are featured here in season. Oregon gifts are also sold.

Harrison's Bakery
 downtown at 608 Broadway   738-5331
This full-line takeout bakery offers a good selection of coffee cakes and
Danish pastries, plus breads (including salt-rising bread) and cookies.
Closed Tues.

★ **Josephson's Specialty Seafood**
 downtown at 87 Broadway   738-5716
Gourmet seafoods and other provisions of Oregon are the highlights in
this classy recent addition to Seaside. (The original outlet is in Astoria.)
Fresh-smoked salmon and oysters, canned salmon and crab, cooked
whole Dungeness crabs, and Oregon preserves are sold to go, or in gift
packs. Pre-packaged, carry-away seafood cocktails and other snacks
are also served.

★ **Kristina's Health Foods & Bakery**
 .7 mi. S at 1445 S. Holladay Dr.   738-9211
An impressive array of European specialty breads, pastries (such as
Kolachky), and rolls are featured. The large, well-organized health-
oriented store also includes many bins with trail mixes, etc.

★ **Leonard's**
 downtown at 111 Broadway
All kinds of saltwater taffy are pulled before your eyes. Gift packs will be
mailed anywhere. Popcorn samples are also offered at this spiffy,
trinketless carryout.

Ocean Fresh Crab & Seafood Market
 .6 mi. S at US 101/Av. M   738-7226
This clean and cheerful new roadside fish market has tempting
displays of all that is locally fresh from the sea, including walkaway
shrimp or crab cocktails plus assorted fresh and smoked salmon and
shellfish.

★ **Phillips Candies**
 downtown at 217 Broadway   738-5402
Saltwater taffy made here has been the specialty since before the turn
of the century. Gift packages will be mailed anywhere.

★ **Portland Fudge Company**
 downtown at 102 Broadway
You can watch them make creamy smooth fudges here; samples are
offered. Caramel apples are also sold at this clean contemporary
carryout.

Specialty Shops

Columbia Books
 downtown at 10 N. Columbia St.   738-8176
Books of regional interest are featured in the well-displayed collection
in this small store.

North Coast Myrtlewood Outlet
 .9 mi. S at 1827 S. Holladay St.   738-6673
All kinds of artistic and functional pieces crafted from Oregon's prized

hardwood are showcased in several rooms of a converted cottage.

Oregon Only
2.2 mi. N at 3211 N. US 101   738-3396
Arts, crafts, food products, and baked goods—all produced in Oregon—are displayed and sold in a large, casual roadside store that also includes artisans' workshops.

Turnaround Books
downtown at 111 Broadway, Suite 3   738-3211
There is a notable travel and local interest section among the new and used books, plus classical background music and a juice bar.

The Weary Fox
downtown at 111 Broadway, Suite 11   738-3363
Quality arts and crafts in a variety of media are attractively displayed. The gallery recently moved into larger quarters on the mall.

NIGHTLIFE

After dark, the concentration of bars and lounges on downtown Broadway caters to adult crowds with comfortable, casual furnishings, live music, and dancing. Meanwhile, a similarly notable assortment of amusement parlors on the same street beckon to anyone with an interest in old-fashioned (or electronically updated) games of skill or chance.

The Bounty
downtown at 504 Broadway   738-7342
Live music for dancing is furnished on weekends in a cozy fireside lounge with comfortable sofas and armchairs. Seafood is featured in the adjoining grill.

The Bridge Tender
downtown at 554 Broadway   738-8002
Pool tables and a view of the river are some of the attractions in this popular, casual tavern.

El Toucan
downtown at 334 Broadway   738-8417
Live entertainment and dancing happen most nights in a cantina in the back of a conventional Mexican-style restaurant.

The Frontier Club
downtown at 405 Broadway   738-3712
After the dinner hours, this casual place usually provides live music for dancing.

RESTAURANTS

Most area restaurants offer conventional American fare in family-oriented surroundings. A few exceptions serve fresh seafoods and other Northwestern regional specialties in distinctive surroundings. Even fewer have ocean views.

Alpine Gardens European Restaurant
   downtown at 412 Broadway   *738-8530*
   L-D. Closed Tues.   *Moderate*
European dishes (wienerschnitzel, chicken paprika, cabbage rolls, etc.) and seafoods are served in a very casual little dining room enhanced by many plants.

★ **Black Forest Inn**
   3.2 mi. N on US 101 - Gearhart   *738-8995*
   B-L-D. Closed Mon.-Tues.   *Moderate*
European specialties are tastily translated into American dishes— including a tantalizing showcase of delicious homemade pies—in a little roadside dining room where diners are seated in armchair comfort amidst casual Old World decor.

Bounty Bar and Grill
   downtown at 504 Broadway   *738-7342*
   L-D.   *Moderate*
Local seafoods like salmon and Dungeness crab are featured (in season) on a conventional American menu. Beyond the pleasant, contemporary dining room is a fireside lounge.

The Channel Club
   downtown at 521 Broadway   *738-8618*
   D only. Closed Sun.-Mon.   *Moderate*
Conventional American-style steaks and seafoods are accompanied by a salad bar in a new, simply furnished dining room.

Crab Broiler
   4.4 mi. S at jct. US 101 & US 26   *738-5313*
   L-D. Sun. brunch.   *Moderate*
A full range of American dishes includes seasonally fresh seafoods and homemade baked goods. Since 1938, the restaurant has grown into several expansive dining rooms surrounded by tranquil Japanese-style gardens. A fireside lounge, a gift shop, and a wine shop emphasizing Oregon wines are also included in a large and well-known roadside landmark.

★ **Dooger's Seafood & Grill**
   downtown at 505 Broadway   *738-3773*
   L-D.   *Moderate*
The tastiest clam chowder in the area and regional seafoods lightly breaded to order or sauteed are the best bets among the conscientiously prepared American-style entrees. From-scratch accompaniments range from homemade blue cheese dressing to peanut butter pie. The recently enlarged, pleasant dining room is an area favorite.

Lighthouse Restaurant
   1 mi. S at 220 Av. U   *738-7471*
   L-D. Sun. brunch. Closed Wed.   *Low*
Carefully prepared all-American dishes are served in a cheerful,

homespun dining room with lots of plants and windows. It's out of the way, but worth finding for good food at very reasonable prices.

Lumpy's Fishworks

downtown at 104 Broadway   738-7176
B-L-D.   *Moderate*

Breakfast and seafood specialties are highlights in a casually attractive restaurant.

Norma's

downtown at 20 N. Columbia St.   738-6170
L-D. Closed Nov.-Feb.   *Moderate*

Clam chowder, razor clams, and other seafood, plus homemade pies are featured. The long-popular family-oriented restaurant is in a cheerful dining room with casual nautical decor.

Oceanside

3 mi. N on N. Marion Av. - Gearhart   738-3554
D only. Closed Mon.   *Moderate*

Seafoods, steaks, and other standard American fare are offered in a simply furnished, airy dining room that sports an expansive window wall view of the ocean beyond low dunes.

Pig 'n Pancake

downtown at 323 Broadway   738-7243
B-L-D.   *Moderate*

All kinds of well-made pancakes are served twenty-four hours a day in summer, along with a variety of short order American fare. This family-oriented coffee shop is part of a small regional chain.

Shilo Inn

downtown at 30 N. Prom   738-8481
B-L-D.   *Moderate*

Updated American dishes, with an emphasis on regional seafoods in the evening, are served amidst appealing contemporary decor in the casually elegant dining room of Seaside's new landmark hotel. The wraparound window wall view of the Promenade, beach, and ocean is the best in town.

LODGING

An impressive assortment of accommodations has been an area feature for many decades. Tiny motels, elaborate motor hotels, and condominiums are all represented on beachfront sites. Numerous bargains are available in older inland facilities. A special part of the town's appeal is that most of the best lodgings are clustered an easy stroll from the downtown mall, the Promenade, and the beach. Many places reduce their rates by 20% and more apart from summer.

Boarding House Bed and Breakfast

downtown at 208 N. Holladay Dr.   738-9055

A Victorian boarding house on the river was handsomely converted into a seven-room bed-and-breakfast inn in 1985. Each room has a private bath and color TV, plus country-charming furnishings. A Continental-plus breakfast is included.

"The Cottage"—Victorian 1 BR cottage with
kitchen, loft, private deck on
river,   2 Q beds...$65
#5—large, overlooks river, trundle bed plus   Q bed...$54
regular room—   Q bed...$40

Bungalow City
.5 mi. NE at 1000 N. Holladay Dr.   *738-5191*
In this older, single-level **bargain** motel, each small simply furnished room has a cable TV with movies.
#2—color TV,   K bed...$34
regular room—   D bed...$30

City Center Motel
downtown at 250 1st Av.   *738-6377*
A large indoor pool and a sauna are featured in a conveniently located modern motel. Each nicely furnished room has a phone and cable color TV with movies.
regular room—   Q bed...$40

★ **Ebb Tide Motel**
downtown at 300 N. Prom   *738-8371*
This modern three-story motel has an indoor pool, whirlpool, and saunas. Each beautifully furnished unit has a phone, cable color TV with movies, refrigerator, gas fireplace, and an oceanfront view.
#221,#321—corner windows, kitchenette, great
views,   K bed...$65
#223,#225—as above, handsome blue decor,   K bed...$65
#323,#325—as above, handsome green decor,   K bed...$65
regular room—partial ocean view,   Q bed...$45

Econo Lodge
downtown at 441 2nd Av.   *738-9581*
This newer motel has a small indoor pool, whirlpool, and sauna. Each attractively furnished room has a phone and cable color TV with movies.
#123—in-bath whirlpool,   Q bed...$53
regular room—   Q bed...$49

★ **Gearhart by the Sea**
2.5 mi. N at Marion Av./10th St. (Box 2700) - Gearhart 97138 738-8331
Two large indoor pools, a whirlpool, and a (fee) 18-hole golf course are features of this six-story condominium resort complex directly above the beach. Each spacious unit has a phone, cable color TV with movies, a kitchenette, and a private balcony. For toll-free reservations in Oregon, call (800)452-9800.

#633—1 BR, kitchen, free-standing (presto-log)
        fireplace, good ocean view,   K bed...$74
#673—as above,   Q bed...$74
regular room—1 BR, limited ocean view,   Q bed...$68

★ **Hi-Tide Motel**
downtown at 30 Av. G   *738-8414*
This oceanfront motel has an indoor pool and a whirlpool. Each well-furnished unit has a phone, cable color TV with movies, and refrigerator.

#305,#205—corner, kitchenette, gas fireplace,
        great beach view,   K bed...$65
#319,#219—as above,   2 Q beds...$65
regular room —older, no view,   K bed...$54

Holladay Motel
downtown at 426 S. Holladay Dr.   *738-6529*
This older, single-level motel is Seaside's best **bargain**. Each modest room has a cable color TV with movies.

regular room—   Q bed...$25

The Lanai
1.6 mi. S at 3140 Sunset Blvd.   *738-6343*
On Sunset Beach, this modern motel has a small outdoor pool. Each spacious room has a phone, cable color TV with movies, and a kitchenette.

#41,#32—large private balcony, fine corner
        window ocean view,   Q bed...$54
#42 - #47,#33 - #38—large private balcony, fine
        ocean view,   Q bed...$54
regular room—   D bed...$43

Ocean Front Motel
downtown at 50 First Av.   *738-5661*
The only amenity in this older motel is a choice location on the Promenade. The simply furnished units (kitchens are available) have cable color TV.

upper level oceanfront—fine Prom/beach/ocean
        view,   Q bed...$52
lower level oceanfront—good Prom/beach/ocean
        view,   Q bed...$45
regular room—no view,   Q bed...$43

Ocean Vista Motel
1.1 mi. S at 241 Av. U   *738-7473*
The ocean is two blocks from this modern little motel. Each simply furnished room has color TV.

regular room—   Q bed...$34

Riverside Inn Bed-and-Breakfast
.3 mi. S at 430 S. Holladay Dr.   *738-8254*
The Necanicum River adjoins this bed-and-breakfast complex that

includes a remodeled turn-of-the-century home, cottages, and a new annex. A Continental breakfast is complimentary. Each unit has a private bath and color TV, and features casual, comfortable decor.

#4—1 BR apartment with kitchen, in house,   Q bed...$55
#9—studio in new annex, view of Tillamook Head,   Q bed...$40
regular room—small room in main house, private
             entrance,   D bed...$33

Royale Motel   *738-9541*
   downtown at 531 Av. A
This newer motel is a small, conveniently located **bargain**. Each room has a phone and cable color TV with movies.

regular room—   Q bed...$34
regular room—   D bed...$30

★ **Sand and Sea**   *738-8441*
   downtown at 475 S. Prom
Seaside's highest lodgings are in this six-level modern oceanfront condominium/motel with a small round indoor pool and saunas. Each spacious suite has a phone and cable color TV.

"oceanfront"—1 BR, kitchen, gas log fireplace,
        floor-to-ceiling windows, private
        balcony, ocean view,   Q or K bed...$100
"ocean view"—as above, but partial ocean view,   Q or K bed...$90
regular room—regular hotel room, no view,   Q or K bed...$45

★ **Seashore Resort Motel - Best Western**   *738-6368*
   downtown at 60 N. Prom
By the beach and Promenade in the heart of town, this modern motel has a large indoor pool, whirlpool, and sauna. Each nicely furnished room has a phone and cable color TV.

#38—corner, fine beach/ocean view,   Q bed...$56
regular room—   Q bed...$50

★ **Shilo Inn**   *738-9571*
   downtown at 30 N. Prom
Seaside's largest and most complete motor hotel features an indoor pool, whirlpool, steam room, sauna, and exercise room, plus a view restaurant and view lounge with live entertainment. Each beautifully furnished unit has a phone and remote-controlled cable color TV with movies. For toll-free reservations, call (800)222-2244.

deluxe suite—1 BR, kitchenette, oceanfront view,
        gas fireplace, in-tub whirlpool,
        lanai,   K bed...$137
suite—ocean view, kitchenette, fireplace, lanai,   2 Q or K bed...$127
regular room—view of town/mountains,   Q bed...$74

Sundowner Motor Inn   *738-8301*
   downtown at 125 Oceanway
This small modern motel has a tiny indoor pool with a whirlpool,

and a sauna. Each unit has a phone and cable color TV with movies.

apartment—1 BR, kitchenette,   Q bed...$56

regular room—   Q bed...$36

Surfside Condo Rentals

3 mi. N at N. Marion Av. - Gearhart 97138   738-6384

Only grass-covered dunes separate this single-level condominium complex from the ocean, and there is access to a nearby pool and an 18-hole golf course. Each plainly furnished one-bedroom unit has a phone, cable color TV, kitchen, and a wood-burning fireplace.

#207—fine beach view, skylights,   K bed...$79

regular unit—   Q bed...$79

★ **The Tides**

1 mi. S at 2316 S. Beach Dr.   738-6317

This modern motel/condominium has some fine beachfront units, plus **bargain** units. There is a large outdoor pool. Each spacious, well-furnished unit has a phone and cable color TV with movies.

#60,#50—2 BR, kitchen, fireplace, private ocean
view from corner window,   2 Q beds...$73

#53,#54,#43,#44—studio, kitchen, fireplace,
private beach/ocean view,   K bed...$54

regular room—no view,   D or Q bed...$30

White Caps

.5 mi. N at 120 9th Av.   738-5371

This small older motel has some units almost on the beach. Each simply furnished unit has cable color TV with movies.

#12—1 BR, kitchenette, good ocean view
from LR,   2 Q beds...$55

#5—some ocean view,   T & Q beds...$40

regular room #7—small, some ocean view,   D bed...$35

CAMPGROUNDS

There are only a couple of campgrounds in the area. Fortunately, the best has complete camping and recreation facilities in an unusual setting a stroll from the beautiful Oregon coast.

★ **Fort Stevens State Park**

14 mi. N: 9 mi. N on US 101 & 5 mi. NW on county road   861-1671

Oregon's largest state park includes a giant campground near the ocean. In addition, ocean beaches, two tiny lakes, a boat ramp, bicycle paths, hiking trails, and sand dunes provide opportunities for beachcombing, fishing, clamming, boating, swimming, bicycling, and hiking. Flush toilets, hot showers (fee), and hookups are available. Each well-spaced site has a picnic table and a fire area. For more information and reservations in Oregon, call (800)452-5687. Non-Oregonians add $2 surcharge to base rate.   base rate...$6

Riverside Lake Resort
3 mi. S on US 101   738-6779
This private facility is by a tiny river which is used for swimming and
fishing. Flush toilets, hot showers, and hookups are available. Most of
the closely spaced sites have a picnic table. There is a shady, separated
tent area.   base rate...$8

SPECIAL EVENTS

4th of July Fireworks   *at the Turnaround*   *July 4th*
Traditional 4th of July festivities are climaxed on the beach at the
Turnaround with a fireworks display that can be easily seen and
enjoyed by all. The Miss Oregon Pageant always takes place in Seaside
on the next weekend.

Oktoberfest   *downtown*   *late September*
Started in 1984, the festival features an outdoor beer garden (in a tent)
with German and regional food and drinks, while the Convention
Center is used to house arts and crafts and performances by bands and
dance groups from throughout the Northwest.

OTHER INFORMATION

Area Code: *503*
Zip Code: *97138*
Seaside Chamber of Commerce
  downtown at Broadway/Roosevelt Dr. (Box 7)   738-6391
  (in Oregon, call toll-free (800)452-6740)

Chelan, Washington

Chelan is the gateway to America's most extraordinary big lake. The little town is situated among apple orchards along the sunny eastern end of Lake Chelan, the largest lake in Washington, and one of the world's deepest. Grass-and-brush-covered hills provide a gentle backdrop to the photogenic site. Remarkably, the western end of the long, narrow lake is surrounded by glacier-clad peaks, lush pine forests, streams, and waterfalls in the magnificent North Cascades. The lake's great reach gives Chelan a special closeness to an enormous complex of national forests, parks and recreation areas beyond the towering mountain backdrop.

Lake Chelan even moderates the four-season climate in town, except during winters, which are cold and snowy. There are no major winter sports facilities in the nearby mountains—yet. However, cross-country skiing and snowmobiling are beginning to attract serious attention because of the scenic terrain and abundant snow. Spring features warm clear days early in the season, and the fragrance of apple blossoms in orchards along the lake. Early fall is also relatively mild. It is an uncrowded time to relish the beauty of the apple-laden countryside and to savor the quality of the fruit grown here. Summer is the only season when Chelan is filled with visitors, drawn by perfect weather and the crystal-clear warm lake. Swimming, boating, water-skiing, fishing, and lake excursions are popular. Hiking, camping, backpacking, rock climbing, horseback riding, and pack trips are enjoyed in the nearby mountains. Golf, tennis, a major new waterslide complex on a slope overlooking the lake, and well-maintained shoreline parks with sandy beaches are favorite attractions in town.

The area around the lake remained unsettled until 1879, when the U.S. government established a short-lived army post to protect settlers who were beginning to come into the valley. The townsite was platted in 1889. Passenger boat service and lake traffic were important to the local economy from the beginning. Gold and other precious metals were discovered around the turn of the century in the mountains near the lake. Ore was shipped down-lake to a railroad at Chelan until 1957, when the state's largest producing mine closed. As mining and lumber declined in importance, apple growing and tourism have become the mainstays of the area's economy.

Picturesque apple orchards blanket most of the lower slopes along the lake adjacent to town. Near the heart of town is an attractively landscaped park with expansive lawns, sandy beaches, swimming areas, marinas, and glorious up-lake views. Downtown still reflects a peaceful, hard-working past with a limited assortment of ordinary shops, restaurants, and nightlife. Numerous fine accommodations, some with luxurious resort amenities, have recently been constructed along the lakefront. Most are within an easy stroll of the small business district. So is an RV-oriented lakeside campground. A short drive along the south shore leads to one of Washington's most beautiful lakefront campgrounds.

Elevation:

1,200 feet

Population (1980):

2,802

Population (1970):

2,837

Location:

180 miles Northeast of Seattle

Chelan, Washington
WEATHER PROFILE
Vokac Weather Rating

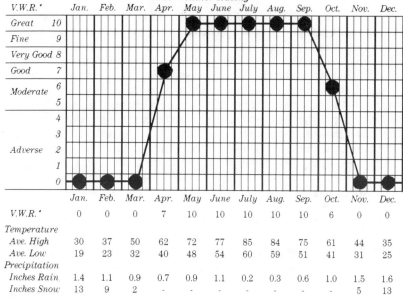

V.W.R.*	Jan.	Feb.	Mar.	Apr.	May	June	July	Aug.	Sep.	Oct.	Nov.	Dec.
V.W.R.*	0	0	0	7	10	10	10	10	10	6	0	0
Temperature												
Ave. High	30	37	50	62	72	77	85	84	75	61	44	35
Ave. Low	19	23	32	40	48	54	60	59	51	41	31	25
Precipitation												
Inches Rain	1.4	1.1	0.9	0.7	0.9	1.1	0.2	0.3	0.6	1.0	1.5	1.6
Inches Snow	13	9	2	-	-	-	-	-	-	-	5	13

V.W.R. = Vokac Weather Rating: probability of mild (warm & dry) weather on any given day.

Forecast

	V.W.R.*		Temperatures		Precipitation
			Daytime	Evening	
Jan.	0	Adverse	cold	frigid	occasional snowstorms
Feb.	0	Adverse	chilly	cold	occasional snow flurries
Mar.	0	Adverse	cool	chilly	infrequent showers/snow flurries
Apr.	7	Good	cool	cool	infrequent showers
May	10	Great	warm	cool	infrequent showers
June	10	Great	warm	warm	infrequent rainstorms
July	10	Great	hot	warm	negligible
Aug.	10	Great	hot	warm	negligible
Sep.	10	Great	warm	cool	infrequent showers
Oct.	6	Moderate	cool	cool	infrequent rainstorms
Nov.	0	Adverse	chilly	chilly	occasional showers/snow flurries
Dec.	0	Adverse	chilly	cold	occasional snowstorms

Summary

Chelan, at the eastern end of the West's most uniquely fiord-like lake, is surrounded by fruit orchards and backed by dry sagebrush-covered hills. To the west, the orchards and hills end abruptly where the lake enters the awesome escarpment of the North Cascade Range. The dramatic setting is coupled with one of the West's most usable four season climates. Chilly days and cold evenings prevail in **winter**. While occasional snowstorms provide ample snow for all winter sports, no major downhill skiing facilities are available in the nearby mountains — yet. Temperatures increase very rapidly in **spring**. Good weather accompanies blossom-time starting in April and comfortably warm days persist by May. **Summer** is outstanding. Long, hot sunny days and warm evenings are ideal for enjoying the crystal-clear lake and the alpine grandeur along its upper reaches. Pleasant weather attends the apple harvest in early **fall**, but chilly days and snowfalls return soon afterward.

196

ATTRACTIONS & DIVERSIONS

Apple Shed Tours
2 mi. SE via US 97
In season (starting in mid-September), visitors can arrange for tours of two huge sheds to observe the process of preparing premium apples for shipment nationwide. For more information, call:

Blue Chelan	682-4541
Trout	682-2591

★ **Boat Rentals**
Pleasure, sail, skiing, pontoon, and fishing boats can be rented at these small marinas:

Chelan Boat Rentals, Inc.	*1210 W. Woodin Av.*	682-4444
Ship-n-Shore Boat Rental	*1230 W. Woodin Av.*	682-5125

Boat Rides
★ **Lake Chelan Boat Co.**
1.1 mi. SW at 1418 W. Woodin Av.   682-4584
"The Lady of the Lake" is a large excursion boat that takes passengers the entire length of Lake Chelan. After cruising past orchard-covered slopes and shorelines, the boat enters a narrow canyon in the Cascade Range. Glacier-clad peaks tower overhead, and lush pine forests, waterfalls, and occasional big game seem near because the lake is never more than two miles wide. At the north end, fifty-five miles from town, passengers can have lunch or explore the tiny village of Stehekin before returning. The boat operates from 8:30 a.m.-6 p.m. daily May 15-Oct. 15, and on Sundays, Mondays, Wednesdays, and Fridays the rest of the year.

★ **Stehekin Adventure Vacation**
write: Stehekin Valley Ranch, Box 36, Stehekin, WA 98852 682-4677
During an unforgettable two-day adventure, participants enjoy: an awe-inspiring float plane ride the length of Lake Chelan to Stehekin; a shuttlebus up to Stehekin Valley Ranch for lunch and to settle into a tent-cabin; an afternoon whitewater raft trip down the Stehekin River; followed by dinner and an evening around an open fire. After breakfast the next morning, there is a guided horseback ride up to scenic Coon Lake. After lunch back at the ranch, you board "The Lady of the Lake" for the fifty-five-mile cruise back to Chelan.

Chelan Butte
5 mi. S via Chelan Butte Rd.
From the lookout tower at the top, visitors have a splendid panoramic view of Lake Chelan, orchard-covered slopes, the Cascades, the Columbia River gorge, and tawny wheat fields stretching endlessly to the east. At times, the upper (dirt portion of the) road may be closed to vehicles because of fire danger. It makes a fine hike, anyway.

Chelan Falls Gorge
4 mi. SE: .2 mi. W of jct. US 97/Chelan Falls Rd.
The Chelan River is only four miles long, but it has cut an impressive gorge through rock cliffs on its 405-foot drop from the lake to the Columbia River. A good view of the gorge and double falls is available from a primitive dirt road high above the south side of the river.

★ **Chelan Riverfront Park**
downtown between Woodin Av. Bridge/Saunders Bridge
Both sides of the Chelan River between the east end of the lake and a low dam have been attractively landscaped. Night-lighted, paved sidewalks and benches make the mile-long stroll along the picturesque shoreline a genuine pleasure any time.

Flying
Chelan Airways
1.1 mi. SW at 1418 W. Woodin Av.   682-5555
Scenic seaplane flights over the magnificent Cascade Range to Stehekin at the other end of Lake Chelan can be chartered here any time.

Golf
★ **Lake Chelan Municipal Golf Course**
1.5 mi. N via N. Lakeshore Rd. at 1501 Golf Course Dr.   682-5421
A challenging 18-hole championship golf course is located on a relatively level terrace above town with fine lake and mountain views. It is open to the public, and includes a pro shop, driving range, club and cart rentals, and a cafe for breakfast or lunch.

Horseback Riding
Cascade Corrals
55 mi. NW via Lake Chelan   682-4677
Horses can be rented for morning or afternoon trail rides, with a guide, in the beautiful mountain-rimmed valley above Lake Chelan.

★ **Lake Chelan**
One of the world's most extraordinary lakes is also the largest, longest, and deepest in the State of Washington. Well over fifty miles long and less than two miles wide, it was formed by a gigantic glacier that carved out a trough now filled by water to a depth of more than 1,400 feet. At its deepest point, the lake is actually below sea level. The town of Chelan occupies a small portion of an enormous natural dam created by the ancient glacier. No other lake on the continent has the variety of topography and climate found here. The town of Chelan, at the lake's eastern end, is surrounded by orchards and rangeland in a near-desert setting. At the lake's western end, lush pine forests line the shore, and glacier-shrouded peaks of the North Cascade Mountains rise abruptly from the water. All kinds of outdoor activities are already available on and near the crystal-clear lake, yet the area's awesome recreation potential has only been lightly tapped.

★ Lake Chelan National Recreation Area
access by Lake Chelan

The rugged mountains of the North Cascade Range that enclose the northern end of Lake Chelan are the highlight of a large natural preserve with an unbeatable range of hiking, backpacking, and rock climbing opportunities. The scenic Stehekin River and Rainbow Falls (312 feet) are favorite destinations in a vast expanse of lush pine forests and towering glacier-shrouded peaks. The only access to the area is by boat, seaplane, or hiking trails.

★ Lake Chelan State Park
9 mi. SW via US 97 & S. Lakeshore Rd.   687-3710

Spectacular up-lake views distinguish this large, well-landscaped lakeshore park. A grassy slope overlooks a sandy beach and a protected swimming area that has lifeguards in summer. Excellent docking, picnicking, and camping facilities are other features.

★ Lakeshore Park
downtown on WA 150

On the west side of downtown is a delightful park with superb lake views. Lawn-covered slopes rise above a sandy beach and a popular swimming area on Lake Chelan. Well-positioned picnic tables, plus a marina and a campground, are nearby. Miniature golf, a state-of-the-art bumper boat concession, and imaginative play equipment are also available.

★ *Moped Rentals*
Chelan Boat Rentals, Inc.
1 mi. SW on US 97 at 1210 W. Woodin Av.   682-4444

Mopeds can be rented here by the hour or longer for lakeshore jaunts and tours of the apple orchards and surrounding hills.

★ North Cascades National Park
90 mi. NW via US 97, WA 153 & WA 20   682-2549

There are no roads in this park, but a highway (WA 20) was completed between the park's two sections in 1972 through some of the most rugged mountains in the West. Numerous trails extend from this highway into both sections of the park. The major access to the southern section is via passenger ferry from Chelan to Stehekin and shuttle bus service from there to the park entrance. Within the park, many miles of trails are threaded throughout a wilderness of jagged peaks with more than three hundred active glaciers, jewel lakes hidden in luxuriant forests, and deep canyons with clear rushing streams and beautiful waterfalls. Hiking, climbing, backpacking, pack trips, fishing, and camping are popular activities.

River Running
Four Seasons Outfitters
downtown at 137 E. Woodin Av.   682-5032

Whitewater rafting and driftboat fishing on the scenic Stehekin and Methow Rivers can be arranged daily through this guide service.

St. Andrews Episcopal Church
downtown at 120 E. Woodin Av.   682-2851
The design for this log church (1898) is attributed to the noted architect, Stanford White. It is reportedly the only log church building in the Northwest in continuous use since before the turn of the century.

★ *Scenic Loop Drive*
NW on WA 150
One of the best ways to explore the picturesque apple orchards above Lake Chelan is via a twenty-eight-mile paved loop. Between Chelan and Manson, WA 150 meanders along the shore and provides sweeping views of orchards dotting gentle slopes above the lake. Beyond the village of Manson, Lakeshore Drive and Summit Boulevard climb into the heart of the apple-growing district. Then, Loop Drive continues past orchards on all sides and offers glimpses of the fiord-like middle reaches of Lake Chelan far below. Manson Boulevard and Lake Wapato Road connect back to WA 150 after passing through more miles of superabundant apple orchards and numerous dramatic overviews. The highlight of the foothills country is several small tranquil lakes backed by flourishing orchards and massive rock formations.

★ **Stehekin**
55 mi. NW via Lake Chelan   662-0151
One of the nation's most isolated communities can be accessed only by seaplane or boat from Chelan, or on foot. The tiny village is the gateway to the heart of North Cascades National Park. There are nightly park-related programs in summer. Shops have photographic and outdoor supplies, and a bakery, food, lodging, and camping facilities. Hiking, climbing, backpacking, horseback riding, riverrunning, and boating are some of the activities based here.

Warm Water Feature
★ **Slidewaters at Lake Chelan**
1 mi. SW via US 97 at 102 Waterslide Dr.   682-5751
With a splendid view from a slope near the lake, this state-of-the-art waterslide complex offers slides ranging from slow and tame to fast and scary. The inner tube river ride is especially exhilarating. Whirlpools, picnic areas, a viewing deck, and a fast food concession have also been provided. Closed from Labor Day to Memorial Day.

★ **Wenatchee National Forest**
W of town   682-2576
This vast forested area of rugged mountains includes most of Lake Chelan and part of the majestic Glacier Peak Wilderness Area. Highways and dirt roads, and an excellent trail system (including a stretch of the Pacific Crest National Scenic Trail) provide access to a myriad of brilliant glaciers and jagged peaks, streams and waterfalls, and sparkling lakes. Hiking, backpacking, climbing, boating, fishing, hunting, camping, and winter sports are seasonally popular.

Winter Sports

★ ***Cross-Country Skiing***   *682-2022*

In early 1985, groomed Nordic trails were laid at the Lake Chelan Golf Course in town. There are now more than thirty miles of groomed cross-country skiing trails at the golf course, and in Echo Valley (7 mi. N) and Bear Mountain Ranch (5 mi. W). Dry snow, easy slopes and extraordinary lake and mountain views abound.

★ ***Snowmobiling***   *682-2022*

The Lake Chelan area boasts of more than 150 miles of trails (many on Forest Service roads) that provide access to breathtaking high country scenery.

★ **Winthrop**

    61 mi. NW via US 97, WA 153 & WA 20   *996-2125*

The village nearest to North Cascades National Park is well worth a visit. Buildings downtown have been given Old West facades that look right in the mountainous setting. Besides, Owen Wister honeymooned here several years prior to writing **The Virginian**. A burgeoning assortment of shops, saloons, and restaurants line the compact main street. Three places offer notable Western-style food. The **Duck Brand Restaurant** (B-L-D—Moderate. 996-2192) serves Mexican and American fare including delicious cinnamon rolls and berry pies. The **Paddle Inn** (L-D. Closed Tues.-Wed.—Moderate. 996-2462) features carefully prepared international specialties like escargot and curry chicken at tables outfitted with full linen in a tiny cottage. **Riverside Rib** (L-D—Moderate. 996-2001) offers zesty barbecue prepared in a garden patio set with comfortably rustic tables and chairs.

SHOPPING

Chelan's small downtown area is concentrated along Woodin Avenue just east of Lake Chelan. It is an unassuming, old-fashioned town center oriented toward fulfilling the everyday needs of residents and visitors. Remarkably, no major art galleries or apple-oriented shops pay tribute to the area's scenic grandeur or premier product.

Food Specialties

★ **Judy-Jane Bakery**

    downtown at 216 W. Manson Rd.   *682-2151*

Delicious pastries, donuts, and specialty breads are displayed in Chelan's fine full-line bakery. Customers can also buy chicken snacks and other light meals to eat at several coffee tables, on a patio, or to go.

NIGHTLIFE

There isn't much life after dark in Chelan, apart from a cluster of bars downtown and a couple of comfortable lounges by the lake.

★ **Campbell's Lodge Lounge**
   downtown at 104 W. Woodin Av.   682-2561
   A delightful Victorian-style parlor with sofas and upholstered chairs
   and a flower-rimmed deck with a lake view attract patrons to the
   lounge in Campbell's Lodge.

★ **Cosina del Lago**
   2.5 mi. NW at 225 WA 150   682-4071
   Here is a fine place to enjoy an expansive view of apple orchards, Lake
   Chelan, and the Cascades. The handsome contemporary lounge also
   offers comfortable seating in front of a tiled fireplace. Upstairs, a stylish
   restaurant offers conventional Mexican-style dishes.

★ **Katzenjammers**
   8 mi. NW via WA 150 at Wapato Point - Manson   687-9541
   Live music for dancing is a periodic bonus in the comfortably furnished
   Windsurf Lounge at Wapato Point by Lake Chelan. The view is
   outstanding, especially from the lakeside patio. The adjoining dining
   room shares the scenery.

Ruby Theatre
   downtown at 122 E. Woodin Av.   682-5016
   Live theater is scheduled throughout the summer months, and at
   selected times during the remainder of the year. First-run movies are
   also shown at Chelan's downtown showplace.

Town Tavern
   downtown at 104 E. Woodin Av.   682-2436
   A card room area, several pool tables, pinball, and short order foods are
   available in a plain and popular, 1950s-style tavern.

RESTAURANTS

There are only about a dozen restaurants in Chelan, and most are
located downtown. Almost all serve relentlessly ordinary American
fare in family-oriented, plain surroundings.

★ **Campbell's Lodge Restaurant**
   downtown at 104 W. Woodin Av.   682-2561
   B-L-D.   *Moderate*
   Good American dishes are served in the large, pleasant dining room
   of Campbell's Lodge, an enduring hotel that has been Chelan's
   landmark since the turn of the century. The restaurant is still the
   most popular in town.

Cosina del Lago
   2.5 mi. NW at 225 WA 150   682-4071
   L-D. Closed Sun.-Mon.   *Moderate*
   A relatively short list of Mexican and American standards is served in
   comfortably furnished contemporary dining areas. Diners overlook
   apple orchards and Lake Chelan. A stylish cantina adjoins.

Katzenjammers

8 mi. NW via WA 150 at Wapato Point - Manson   *687-9541*
D only. Sun. brunch.   *Moderate*

Prime rib is the specialty on a short menu, and there is a salad bar. The casually elegant dining room has a panoramic Lake Chelan and Cascades backdrop. Flowering plants enhance a broad deck that adjoins this contemporary restaurant at Wapato Point.

River Park Dining

downtown at 114 E. Woodin Av.   *682-5626*
L-D. Closed Sun.   *Moderate*

Barbecued chicken and pork, and stuffed potatoes, plus soups salads, sandwiches, and desserts can be enjoyed on a deck above the picturesque new Riverfront Park.

LODGING

Several excellent resorts have choice lakefront locations, and numerous motels are in and near town. Most of the area's best accommodations are next to downtown along the eastern end of Lake Chelan. From fall through spring, rates are usually at least 30% less than those shown below.

Apple Inn Motel

.8 mi. E at 1002 E. Woodin Av. (Box 1450)   *682-4044*

This small modern motel has a hot tub and a small outdoor pool. There are a few **bargain** rooms and kitchenettes. Each unit has a phone and cable color TV.

deluxe room—wet bar/refrigerator,	K bed...$48
regular room—	D bed...$28

★ **Campbell's Lodge**

downtown at 104 W. Woodin Av. (Box 278)   *682-2561*

A historic turn-of-the-century hotel remains the major landmark downtown. Accommodations now also include cottages and many modern motel units by Lake Chelan. In addition to a sandy beach, landscaped grounds include three large outdoor pools (one beautifully sited for outstanding views by the lake), a whirlpool, a dock, plus restaurant and lounge facilities. Each spacious, well-furnished unit has a phone and cable color TV.

#314,#313—private balcony, great lake/ mountain view from	K bed...$94
#312,#311—large room, superb lake/mountain views,	K bed...$114
#214,#316,#210,#110,#310—as above,	2 Q beds...$100
#14 (in Lodge #4)—balcony, fine lake views,	Q bed...$88
#16 (in Lodge #4)—1 BR, kitchenette, patio, fine lake views,	Q bed...$106
regular room—in hotel,	Q bed...$88

★ **Caravel Motor Hotel**
downtown at 322 W. Woodin Av. (Box 1509)   *682-2715*
This modern lakefront motel has a large outdoor pool by the lake, and
a dock. Each spacious unit was recently upgraded, and has color TV.
#58,#54—in new addition, private balcony over
    water, fine lake/town view,   Q bed...$84
#111,#112—studio, kitchenette, private balcony,
    fine lake/mountain view,   Q bed...$97
regular room—   Q bed...$78

★ **Darnell's Resort Motel**
1 mi. NW at 901 Manson Rd. (Box 506)   *682-2015*
A sandy beach on Lake Chelan is a feature, along with a boat launch,
moorage, and a swimming area with a diving and slide platform.
Landscaped grounds include a large outdoor pool with a lake view, a
whirlpool, a sauna, two lighted tennis courts, pitch and putt golf, plus
complimentary bicycles, canoes, or rowboats. Each spacious unit has
cable color TV and a kitchen. In summer, no maid service is provided,
units are rented to families only, and a minimum stay of one week
required. The rates below apply before June 15 and after Labor Day
when singles and couples are welcomed.
#1,#10 (Bldg. A)—1 BR suite, ground level, lake
    view,   K bed...$65
#6 (Bldg. B & C)—private balcony, splendid
    lake/mountain view,   Q bed...$70
#8 (Bldg. B & C)—private balcony, fine lake/mt.
    view,   Q bed...$75
regular room—overlooks tennis court,   Q bed...$50

Em's Bed and Breakfast Inn
downtown at 304 Wapato (Box 206)   *682-4149*
A turn-of-the-century wood-trimmed house became a bed-and-
breakfast inn in 1983. Each very simply furnished room shares a bath. A
full breakfast is complimentary.
regular room—   Q bed...$40

Lake Chelan Motel
1.7 mi. SW at 2044 W. US 97 (Box 1969)   *682-2742*
This old cottage colony by the highway has been refurbished, and now
includes an outdoor pool. Each small, plainly furnished room has a
refrigerator and a cable color TV.
regular room—   D bed...$44

Midtowner Motel
.5 mi. E at 721 E. Woodin Av. (Box 1722)   *682-4051*
Chelan's best off-lake motel was recently expanded and upgraded.
Facilities include an indoor/outdoor pool, whirlpool, and sauna. Each
attractively furnished, spacious unit has a phone, kitchenette or
refrigerator, and cable color TV.
regular room—   Q bed...$45

Mountain View Lodge
   8 mi. NW on WA 150 (Box 337) - Manson 98831   687-9505
New in 1986, this two-level motel is a stroll from Wapato Point Resort
and Beach, and has an outdoor pool. Each nicely furnished unit has a
cable color TV.
   "Honeymoon Suite"—top (2nd) floor, end,
                 in-room whirlpool with
                 lake/mountain view,   K bed...$80
   regular room—   Q bed...$60

North Cascade Lodge
   55 mi. NW at other end of Lake (Box W)   682-4711
Operated as a leased concession by the National Park Service, this
recently remodeled complex includes a two-story alpine lodge, cabins,
and motel units on a hill overlooking Lake Chelan and the Stehekin
Valley. A rustic dining room; a boat dock; and boat, bicycle, and car
rentals are available.
   lodge room—spacious, lake view,   Q bed...$65
   housekeeping unit—spacious, lake view,
                 kitchenette,   Q bed...$68
   regular room—small,   D bed...$55

Park Lake Motel
   2 mi. SW at 2312 W. US 97 (Box 1147)   682-4396
The feature of this small cluster of old cottages by the highway is
walking proximity to a delightful lakefront park. Each tiny, well-worn
housekeeping cabin has a kitchen and cable color TV.
   regular room—   D bed...$35

Parkway Motel
   downtown at 402 N. Manson Rd. (Box 1237)   682-2822
Across from Lakeshore Park, this single-level **bargain** motel has
modest units with color TV.
   kitchen unit—kitchen, some lake view,   Q bed...$45
   regular room—small room, no view,   D bed...$30

★ **Spader Bay Condominium Resort**
   .9 mi. NW on Manson Rd. at 102 Spader Bay Rd. (Box 459) 682-5818
This big modern lakeshore condominium complex has 600 feet of
private sandy beach, a very large outdoor pool with a panoramic
lakefront view, whirlpool, saunas, boat docks, and moorage. Each well-
furnished unit has cable color TV and a patio or balcony. In summer,
daily maid service is not provided, and the minimum stay is at least
three nights.
   #8B—studio, fireplace, good lake view,   2 Q beds...$110
   #11—1 BR, fireplace, kitchen, good lake view,   Q bed...$110
   #41—1 BR, fine up-lake view,   Q bed...$110
   regular room—   Q bed...$90

★ **Wapato Point**
   8 mi. NW off WA 150 (Box 426) - Manson 98831   *687-9511*
   The neck of a peninsula on Lake Chelan has become a big lakeside
   condominium resort with a large indoor pool and two scenic outdoor
   pools; a whirlpool with an awesome lake view; six tennis courts; a long
   sandy beach and dock; (rental) canoes, rowboats, sailboats, and
   bicycles; plus a restaurant and lounge spectacularly located on the
   lake shore. Each spacious contemporary unit has a phone, cable color
   TV, wood-burning fireplace, kitchen, and a balcony or patio
   overlooking the lake. For toll-free reservations, call (800)572-9531.
   #5&#6 (Yacinde Bldgs. C & D)—upper floor,
                                  studio loft, fine
                                  lakefront view,   Q bed...$115
   #2 & #3 (Nekquelekin Bldgs.)—1 BR, fine
                                  lakefront view,   Q bed...$130
   regular room—some lake view,   Q bed...$115

Whaley Mansion
   .4 mi. S at 415 3rd St. (Box 693)   *682-5735*
   A large Edwardian wood-framed "Catalogue" house now serves as the
   area's most elaborate bed-and-breakfast inn. Thick carpets, fabric wall
   coverings, and an abundance of authentic and reproduction antiques
   and knickknacks are used throughout. Fresh local produce is
   emphasized for the complimentary full breakfast. Most of the
   elaborately furnished rooms have a private bath.
   "Frances"—large, top (3rd) floor, pleasant up-
                                  lake view,   Q bed...$85
   "Helene"—large, 2nd floor, nice up-lake view,   Q bed...$85
   "The Bridal Suite"—large, sitting room,   K bed...$95
   regular room—shared bath,   Q bed...$75

CAMPGROUNDS

There are several campgrounds in the area. One of the West's finest is a
short drive from town with complete camping and recreation facilities
in a picturesque setting by Lake Chelan.

★ **Lake Chelan State Park**
   9 mi. W: 4 mi. W on US 97 & 5 mi. W on Shore Dr. (Box 90) 687-3710
   The state has provided a large, outstanding campground along a
   scenic south shore beach by Lake Chelan. Attractions include a
   designated swimming area with a sandy beach, a grassy slope that is a
   favorite of sunbathers, a boat ramp and dock, boating, fishing, and
   waterskiing, plus nature trails. Flush toilets, hot showers (fee), and
   hookups are available. Well-spaced lake-view sites have a picnic table
   and fire grill/ring. Several especially scenic, tree-shaded tent sites by
   the lake are a few steps down a slope near the eastern end of the
   campground. Reciprocal fee.   base rate...$6

Lakeshore Trailer Park
  downtown on N. Lakeshore Dr. (Box 1669)   *682-5031*
Chelan has provided a large well-landscaped R.V. park adjacent to the
lake near downtown. Boating and fishing are popular, as is swimming
off a sandy beach that borders the south side of the park. Flush toilets,
hot showers, and hookups are available. Each closely spaced, grassy
site has a picnic table. (There are less than a dozen tent sites available
by reservation only—and they're adjacent to the highway.)
                                                    base rate...$11

SPECIAL EVENT

Harvest Festival & Appleknockers Jubilee *Chelan City Park mid-Sept.*
Apple-oriented displays, exhibits, concessions, live entertainment,
dances, contests, and a parade are all part of a weekend celebration of
the apple harvest.

OTHER INFORMATION

Area Code: *509*
Zip Code: *98816*
Lake Chelan Chamber of Commerce
  downtown at 102 E. Johnson Av. (Box 216)   *682-2022*
North Cascades National Park - District Office
  downtown at 428 W. Woodin Av.   *682-2549*
Wenatchee National Forest - Chelan Ranger Station
  downtown at 428 W. Woodin Av.   *682-2576*

La Conner, Washington

    La Conner is the hidden gem of the Pacific Northwest. It is an out-of-the-way urbane haven steeped in history and surrounded by lovely pastoral countryside. Well-preserved Victorian homes cover a gentle ridge above a vibrant little business district. Colorful shops and restaurants crowd along the mainland side of a natural channel. Across the narrow waterway is one of the many islands in Puget Sound. Rich, unfenced farmlands to the east are framed by towering peaks of the Cascade Range, and the glacial crest of majestic Mt. Baker seems to float like a glistening cloud above the peaceful landscape.

    A temperate climate prevails year-round, so hot spells and freezes are unusual. Warm weather begins in late spring and continues into early fall. This prime time for outdoor recreation is also surprisingly dry, since La Conner gets some benefit from the rain shadow caused by the Coast Range. Beachcombing, clamming, saltwater swimming, island hopping, and camping are favored along nearby shores. River running and freshwater fishing distinguish the Skagit River that empties into the Sound near town. Wilderness adventures beckon in the North Cascade National Park and vast national forest a short drive to the east. Sailing, fishing, hiking, and bicycling are popular in town, while shopping is always in vogue, even in winter when the weather is normally chilly and continuously damp.

    La Conner was founded in 1869 by John Conner, an entrepreneur who operated a trading post, dabbled in real estate, and named the town after his wife—Louisa Ann Conner. Farming, fishing, and a strategic location on water-based trade routes brought prosperity for awhile. But, when the main rail line and the county seat were established inland, La Conner became a literal backwater. The village languished for decades before cheap rent and the area's pastoral beauty began to attract artists and craftsmen. Development quickened during the 1980s, but the careful restorations and compatible new buildings still reflect the town's Victorian heritage and artistic inclination.

Today, La Conner has one of the most charming business districts in the West. Colorful landscaping and waterfront miniparks intersperse historic buildings filled with first-rate studios, galleries, antique stores, and gift shops emphasizing Northwestern collectibles. Restaurants are plentiful, with the area's best offering culinary delights equal to the finest anywhere. Several have sunny waterfront decks. Most offer fresh local seafood. The smell and appearance of fresh salmon being cooked on an open alderwood fire is one of the pleasures of strolling downtown, where a gourmet bakery, seafood markets, espresso parlors, and shops specializing in regional wines and produce are also clustered. Nightlife is confined to a few atmospheric taverns— some with waterfront view decks. Lodgings are unconventional, romantic, and scarce. There are no regular hotels or motels. But, several inviting bed-and-breakfast inns exude Victorian charm and overlook lovely countryside. Nearby, campgrounds in pine forests by tranquil waterways also capture the spirit of this special locale.

Elevation:

30 feet

Population (1980):

1,000

Population (1970):

639

Location:

70 miles North
of Seattle

WEATHER PROFILE
Vokac Weather Rating

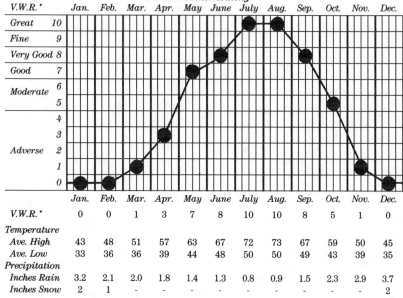

V.W.R.*		Jan.	Feb.	Mar.	Apr.	May	June	July	Aug.	Sep.	Oct.	Nov.	Dec.
Great	10												
Fine	9												
Very Good	8												
Good	7												
Moderate	6												
	5												
	4												
	3												
Adverse	2												
	1												
	0												

	Jan.	Feb.	Mar.	Apr.	May	June	July	Aug.	Sep.	Oct.	Nov.	Dec.
V.W.R.*	0	0	1	3	7	8	10	10	8	5	1	0
Temperature												
Ave. High	43	48	51	57	63	67	72	73	67	59	50	45
Ave. Low	33	36	36	39	44	48	50	50	49	43	39	35
Precipitation												
Inches Rain	3.2	2.1	2.0	1.8	1.4	1.3	0.8	0.9	1.5	2.3	2.9	3.7
Inches Snow	2	1	-	-	-	-	-	-	-	-	-	2

*V.W.R. = Vokac Weather Rating: probability of mild (warm & dry) weather on any given day.

Forecast

	V.W.R.*		Temperatures Daytime	Evening	Precipitation
Jan.	0	Adverse	chilly	chilly	frequent showers/snow flurries
Feb.	0	Adverse	chilly	chilly	frequent showers
Mar.	1	Adverse	cool	chilly	frequent showers
Apr.	3	Adverse	cool	chilly	frequent showers
May	7	Good	cool	cool	occasional showers
June	8	Very Good	warm	cool	occasional showers
July	10	Great	warm	cool	infrequent showers
Aug.	10	Great	warm	cool	infrequent showers
Sep.	8	Very Good	warm	cool	occasional showers
Oct.	5	Moderate	cool	cool	frequent showers
Nov.	1	Adverse	cool	chilly	frequent showers
Dec.	0	Adverse	chilly	chilly	frequent rainstorms/snow flurries

Summary

La Conner is tucked away on a backwater channel of Puget Sound near the mouth of the Skagit River. The location is warmed by the adjoining Sound, and receives additional benefits from the "rain shadow" of the Olympic Mountains. As a result, the village has a notably mild four season climate, and enjoys one of the West's longest growing seasons outside of California. **Winter** is uniformly chilly, and damp from frequent showers. Snowfalls are unusual, however, and rainfall is lighter than in nearby Seattle and other less protected locales. Cool **spring** days and occasional showers are ideal for nurturing the colorful fields of tulips that bloom during this season on the delta east of town. **Summer** weather is excellent. Long, warm, and normally rain-free days are just right for comfortably enjoying this tranquil hideaway. Pleasant weather continues into early **fall**, but cool days and frequent showers are the rule after Halloween.

ATTRACTIONS & DIVERSIONS

Boat Rides

★ **Chamai Motorsailer Charters**
downtown waterfront at Calhoun St. - end 466-3841

Sailing cruises to Deception Pass and beyond can be arranged any day from May through October, and overnight and longer adventures can be reserved on a thirty-two-foot sailing sloop.

★ **Chuckanut Drive**
starts 16 mi. N on WA 11

Fairhaven Park with its pretty rose gardens is at the other end of one of the Northwest's most beautiful maritime drives. A narrow paved road (once a main highway) clings to lush forested slopes above Puget Sound for a distance of about ten miles. Several turnouts give motorists excellent overviews of island-dotted waterways and the distant Olympic Mountains. A captivating state park, three excellent restaurants, and a secluded nude beach far below the highway about two miles south of Fairhaven are some of the attractions.

★ **Deception Pass State Park**
14 mi. W on WA 20 675-2417

One of the Northwest's quintessential state parks occupies forested headlands on both sides of Deception Pass—a narrow and turbulent tidal channel that separates Whidbey and Fidalgo Islands. Highlights include Rosario Beach where pine-shaded lawns tumble down to log-strewn pebbly shorelines bordering Puget Sound. Changing rooms and showers are available for hearty swimmers interested in exploring the clear cold water off several picturesque small beaches. At Deception Pass, parking lots on either side are connected to a spectacular bridge with sidewalks that provide the best views of the chasm and surrounding natural grandeur. West Beach features a large parking lot, changing areas, and a snack bar adjacent to a long pebbly beach and hiking trails along a forested shoreline. On a clear day, sunbathers have a spectacular view of the waterways, islands, and glacier-capped Olympic Mountains. Nearby is a huge and very popular campground.

Flying

★ **La Conner Seaplanes, Inc.**
downtown at 128 S. First St. (Pier 7) 466-4606

Chartered scenic sea plane rides offer an unusual and exciting perspective on the waterways, islands, and majestic peaks that surround La Conner. For a surprisingly reasonable price, you can take off from the seaway adjacent to downtown on your choice of "flightseeing" tours. For toll-free reservations in Washington, call (800)826-5580.

Gaches Mansion
downtown at Second St./Calhoun St.
La Conner's most imposing historic residence has been skillfully restored to its 1890s' elegance, and filled with period furnishings. The small Valley Museum of Northwestern Art is on the second floor.

★ **Larrabee State Park**
21 mi. NE via WA 237 on WA 11
A picturesque pebbly cove on Puget Sound is the highlight of this park on Chuckanut Drive. An expansive forested slope includes a picnic area with shelters and barbecues, a grassy area and bandshell, plus a shady campground.

★ **Mount Baker - Snoqualmie National Forest**
E of town   856-1324
All of the Cascade Range between Mt. Rainier National Park and the Canadian border west of North Cascades National Park is encompassed in the forest. Features include majestic Mount Baker, the glistening high point (10,750 feet) of La Conner's backdrop. It is an all-year recreation destination with a large, well-developed ski area—one of seven in the forest. Glacier Peak and a portion of the surrounding wilderness area is another highlight—and part of the reason why this forest contains more than one-third of the glacier-covered area in the United States outside of Alaska. Further south, the Alpine Lakes Wilderness Area is a popular destination with hundreds of crystal-clear lakes. A good network of peripheral roads and more than 1,000 miles of hiking trails (including part of the Pacific Crest National Scenic Trail) provide access to these and four newer wilderness areas. Recreation opportunities abound in this wonderland of peaks and glaciers, waterfalls and cascades, streams and lakes, emerald forests, and fields of flowers.

★ **North Cascades National Park**
68 mi. E via WA 20   855-1331
A majestic alpine wilderness area, the heart of the northern Cascade Range, is included in a national park with two sections linked by Ross Lake National Recreation Area. More than three hundred active glaciers shroud hundreds of jagged granite peaks. Countless waterfalls and cascades tumble into lakes in glacial cirques far below. A paved highway (WA 20) traverses the park and provides base camps for an extensive system of trails. Mountain goats, bald eagles, and even grizzly bear and wolverine range the high country, while moose, elk, deer, bear, and beaver are more common in lower meadows and along forested valleys. Hiking, climbing, backpacking, camping and fishing are popular throughout the park. Because of the remote location, there is an added attraction. Visitors don't have to share this sublime wilderness with crowds, even in summer.

★ **Rainbow Bridge**
   .3 mi. S on Reservation Rd.
   This award-winning span across the Swinomish Channel is the
   epitome of graceful simplicity. The russet-hued bridge is both an
   elegant landmark and a perfect prospect for viewing the seaway,
   La Conner, and farmlands extending toward distant Mt. Baker.

★ *River Running*
   Different Strokes Expeditions
   10 mi. E at 1430 S. 11th St. - Mt. Vernon   336-5486
   The Skagit River offers dramatic mountain scenery; deep, quiet
   pools; and some exciting whitewater. Trips during the warm and
   sunny months of summer are especially popular. More distinctive,
   however, are the fall floats, when trees are at their colorful best
   and salmon are spawning. Later still, the Skagit becomes the favorite
   hangout for America's national symbol. A bald eagle viewing float
   can be an unforgettable experience.

★ **Roozengaarde**
   6.2 mi. E at 1587 Beaver Marsh Rd.   424-8531
   Here is the place to learn about tulips, dahlias, and other bulb
   plants—in a tranquil exhibition garden where each flower is
   identified. A gift shop (closed Sun.) has bulbs, related gifts, and
   additional information.

   Skagit County Historical Museum
   .3 mi. E at 501 Fourth St.   466-3365
   An interesting assortment of pioneer memorabilia is showcased
   in a low-profile contemporary building on the brow of a hill. As
   an added feature, picture windows frame the farming country and
   mountains east of town. Closed Mon.-Tues.

SHOPPING

La Conner has one of the Northwest's most delightful shopping
districts. The compact main street (First St.) is lined with carefully
restored and maintained historic buildings. Inside the captivating
wood-trimmed structures, galleries, antique dealers, and specialty
shops display quality works—many by local artisans. Miniparks
overlooking the channel, sidewalk espresso parlors, waterfront
restaurants and taverns also contribute to the vitality of downtown
La Conner.

Food Specialties

Cafe Pojante
   downtown at S. First & Washington Sts.   428-7002
   In this comfortable new espresso parlor your choice of espressos
   or Italian sodas with fine homemade biscotti can be enjoyed from
   a sofa, at tables and chairs, or at sidewalk seating. Closed Tues.

★ **Calico Cupboard**
   downtown at 720 S. First St.   466-4451
   Cinnamon and caramel nut rolls, blueberry coffee cakes, assorted

croissants, muffins, pastries, scones and breads, plus pies and cookies, are as delectable as they look. All are made from scratch using quality natural ingredients, and served to go or in the cheerful dining room. Espresso and other coffee drinks are also featured.

★ **The Cheese and Wine Shop**
downtown at 717 S. First St. 466-4161
Washington wines, beers, and food products like cheese, jams, chutneys, and much more are attractively displayed in this handsome shop.

Gina's Espresso Bar
downtown on S. First St.
This classy little outdoor bar serves a good assortment of espressos and Italian sodas that can be enjoyed on an adjoining patio outfitted with log benches overlooking the channel.

★ **Larry's Alder Smoked Smokehouse**
downtown at 710 S. First St. 466-4034
Alder-wood smoking gently enhances the natural flavors of salmon, ham, poultry, and sausages. The silver salmon (samples are generously offered) and Larry's barbecue sauce are outstanding. All meats are available for dinners served at umbrella-shaded picnic tables (beyond a small dining area) on a wood deck over the channel, or to go. They will custom-smoke your fish, or ship their alder-smoked salmon anywhere.

Prize Catch
downtown at Lime Dock 466-4707
The specialty here is salmon. You can buy it fresh (in season), alder-smoked in vacuum packs, or canned. Any way—it's delicious.

★ **Washington Cheese Company**
12 mi. E at 900 E. College Way - Mt. Vernon 424-3510
Many kinds of jack and cheddar cheeses (including an unusual and tasty salmon cheddar) are made and sold in this big modern cheese factory. Visitors can observe the entire process from large second floor viewing rooms, and they can sample each of the types of cheese in the downstairs retail shop. Gift boxes will be shipped anywhere. Outstanding ice creams are also made and sold here.

Specialty Shops

★ **Earthenworks**
downtown at S. First & Washington Sts. 466-4422
La Conner's finest gallery is one of the best anywhere of Northwestern premium-quality art. Memorable pieces in ceramics, wood, woven materials, and wall hangings (ranging from watercolors to photographic murals) are beautifully displayed in two large gallery showrooms.

★ **The Fairhaven Historic District**
23 mi. N via WA 11 - Bellingham 671-7573
An assortment of surprisingly large brick buildings, clustered on a slope above Puget Sound, was the heart of a town that competed

with nearby Bellingham a century ago for dominance of the area. It lost. Fairhaven is now a suburb of Bellingham, but the remnants of the business district have been placed on the National Register of Historic Sites. Numerous picturesque Victorian structures now house a burgeoning assortment of specialty shops, restaurants, saloons, and a cinema.

★ **Gallery West**
23 mi. N at 1300 12th St. - Bellingham   734-8414
Fairhaven's best gallery offers handsome displays of museum-quality ceramics, polished wood items, jewelry, paintings, and photographs—all themed to the Northwest.

La Conner Gallery
downtown at 714 S. First St.   466-3878
Mt. St. Helens' volcanic glass, Western pewter fantasy pieces, a large assortment of glass and quartz crystal jewelry, plus Northwestern scenes and woodcrafted and ceramic art objects, lend to the appeal of this large art gallery with a picture window view of the channel.

★ **Nasty Jack's Antiques**
downtown at 103 E. Morris St.   466-3209
In a town where "century-old" and "Victorian" are frequently heard, antique shops seem especially appropriate. Nasty Jack's is the largest in a notable concentration of antique dealers on the town's main street. Everything from pedal cars for tots to a full-sized carriage, and a lot of premium-quality home furnishings in between are for sale.

Skagit Bay Books
downtown at 612 S. First St.   466-3651
This large, well-organized bookstore is highlighted by a good collection of books and maps of regional interest.

★ **Tillinghast Seed Company**
downtown at 617 E. Morris St.   466-3329
For more than a century, this handsome old clapboard building has been serving the kitchen and garden needs of Northwesterners. The interior is a museum-like showcase for everything from flower bulbs to gourmet coffee beans.

★ **Village Books**
23 mi. N at 1210 11th St. - Bellingham   671-2626
Fairhaven's bookstore is a big, engaging place highlighted by a good collection of regional titles, plus assorted light fare, ice creams, and coffees in the adjoining Colophon Cafe.

★ **The Wood Merchant**
downtown at 707 S. First St.   466-4741
One of the Northwest's finest galleries with an emphasis on premium-quality wood works offers functional pieces like rolling pins and jewelry boxes, as well as artistic pieces (wall hangings, sculptures, and jewelry).

NIGHTLIFE

After dark, peace and quiet usually prevail. Still, there are a few places with live entertainment on weekends, waterfront views, or distinctive atmosphere.

Edison
14 mi. NE at 572 & 583 Cains Court - Edison   766-6330
Edison is a tiny, trim farm town with two "locals" taverns that can also appeal to travelers. Both the **Edison Tavern** and **Longhorn Saloon** offer light meals served with tap beer, plus pool, electronic darts and shuffleboard; and the Longhorn has periodic live entertainment.

★ **La Conner Tavern**
downtown at 702 S. First St.   466-9932
Local and regional music groups occasionally play the easygoing tavern—a local favorite. Patrons can enjoy a good assortment of hamburgers and chili, plus tap beers, while shooting pool or enjoying the view in back or out on a deck overlooking the waterfront and bridge.

Lighthouse Inn
downtown at 512 S. First St.   466-3147
A vocalist or musician plays several nights each week for patrons seated in wooden armchairs in a lounge with a view of the waterfront beyond an adjoining dining room.

★ **Tony's Coffees & Teas**
23 mi. NE at 1101 Harris Av. - Bellingham   733-6319
Fine, fresh coffees (from a large assortment of bins in the next room) plus teas and natural juices are served along with sandwiches and pastries amid first-rate coffee house decor or on a new adjoining landscaped patio. Live music also happens frequently here in Fairhaven's favorite gathering place.

RESTAURANTS

Area restaurants are remarkably diverse and sophisticated. Guests can have fresh seafoods, vegetables, fruits, and berries in a wide assortment of gourmet creations served in romantic hideaways, elegant dinner houses, waterfront view restaurants, or intimate cafes in and near La Conner.

★ **Barkley's of La Conner**
downtown at 205 E. Washington St.   466-4261
L-D. Sun. brunch.   *Expensive*
The chef's skill with first-rate local seafoods and other meat, fruits, and vegetables of the region is apparent in dishes stylistically inclined toward Northern Italian. Diners have a choice of upstairs dining rooms with hardwood armchairs at tables outfitted with lanterns and fresh flowers, or tucked-away booths downstairs in a cozy wood-trimmed pub.

Black Swan
   downtown at 505 S. First St.   *466-3040*
   L-D. Sun. brunch.   *Expensive*
A short list of entrees and nightly specials plus assorted pastas are served in generous portions. Inevitably thick sauces and unusual treatments reflect the European inclinations of the chef. The simply decorated upstairs dining room provides a view of the channel from glass-topped tables set with fresh flowers and candles.

Bullie's Restaurant
   23 mi. NE at 12th & Harris - Bellingham   *734-2855*
   B-L-D.   *Moderate*
Sixteen tap beers, many of them from Washington's boutique breweries, are featured in a casual and colorful burger parlor/ bar in Fairhaven.

★ **Cafe Europa**
   9 mi. E at 516 1st St. - Mt. Vernon   *336-3933*
   L only. Closed Sat.-Sun.   *Moderate*
Homemade bread, pies, and cakes are savory accompaniments to fresh salads, hearty soups, and sandwiches offered in a country-charming restaurant accented by green plants and posters on red brick walls.

★ **Calico Cupboard**
   downtown at 720 S. First St.   *466-4451*
   B-L-tea.   *Moderate*
Delicious breads, croissants, and an assortment of cakes, cookies, and pies, plus homemade raspberry jam, are made here from scratch, as are the soups, salads, sandwiches, and egg dishes (only available for breakfast on weekends). Calico-clad waitresses serve in a winsome old-fashioned dining room with well-oiled wooden floors, hardwood tables and chairs, frilly curtains, and an appealing view of the main street.

The Channel Landing
   downtown at 116 S. First St.   *466-4737*
   L-D. B on Sat. & Sun.   *Moderate*
Old-fashioned fish and chips (breaded cod with thick-cut fries) is the highlight of a family-oriented seafood house. The casual dining room has a picture window view of the channel, and meals are served in an over-water deck when weather permits.

Chuckanut Manor Restaurant
   17.8 mi. NE at 302 Chuckanut Dr. - Bow   *766-6191*
   L-D. Closed Mon.   *Moderate*
Featured seafoods and homemade pies are routine, but they're served in a 1920s roadhouse overlooking waterways and islands. The view is best (and dinner is served) in the comfortable lounge.

The Digs Inn
23 mi. NE at 11th & Harris - Bellingham   733-2491
D only.   *Moderate*
Fresh dough and their own sauce is used for an interesting variety
of stuffed pizzas, and natural-cut fries accompany charbroiled
specialty steaks or burgers in a Fairhaven restaurant that opened
in 1986.

★ **Dos Padres**
23 mi. NE at 1111 Harris Av. - Bellingham   733-9900
B-L-D.   *Moderate*
The sauces and spices, souffle-like covering on the chili rellano,
and ground beef in the burrito suggest Fairhaven's distance from
Mexico; but it's all tasty enough to be worth going out of the way
for. The dining rooms are a similarly comfortable mix of decors
and the tiny lounge is cozy and very atmospheric. Live music
accompanies dinner every night.

Edison Cafe
14 mi. NE at 575 Main Av. - Edison   766-6960
B-L. Closed Sun.   *Low*
The regular menu is posted on a Pepsi signboard on the wall and
it's pure short order, but, the seasonally fresh pies posted on the
chalkboard are very good in this rustic roadside cafe.

★ **The Fairhaven Restaurant**
23 mi. NE at 1114 Harris Av. - Bellingham   676-1520
L-D.   *Moderate*
A long list of international entrees ranges from cioppino and crab
cakes through several homemade curries and quiches to all kinds
of half-pound burgers and homemade desserts. How about a filbert
roll, or toothsome cheesecakes with fresh fruit? The large dining
room is trimmed with a lot of neo-art deco chrome and mirrors,
while padded armchairs and a bouquet of flowers grace each glass/
wood-topped table.

Farmhouse Inn
4.2 mi. N at Whitney Rd. & WA 20 - Mt. Vernon   466-4411
B-L-D.   *Moderate*
Well-made omelets highlight some of the best breakfasts in the
area. Cinnamon rolls and assorted pies are also made here. They
are plain and hearty, like everything else served in the large family-
oriented dining rooms with comfortable farm-themed decor.

La Conner Seafood & Prime Rib House
downtown at 614 S. First St.   466-4014
L-D.   *Moderate*
Prime rib is featured on a menu that also includes a wide assortment
of other meat and seafood dishes. The bright and colorful dining
room has a picture window view of the channel, as does an adjoining
cozy lounge. A large deck over the channel is used for alfresco
dining.

Lighthouse Inn & Deli
downtown at 512 S. First St.   466-3147
B-L-D.   *Moderate*
The salmon and chicken barbecued out front over alder wood are
the best bets among an ambitious assortment of American-style
dishes accompanied by a plain salad bar and uninspired homemade
desserts. The big, informal restaurant has a window-wall view of
the waterfront. A popular view lounge adjoins. Away from the water,
on the main street, breakfast is served in an associated deli.

★ **Mountain Song Restaurant**
58 mi. E at 5860 WA 20 - Marblemount   873-2461
B-L-D.   *Moderate*
They feature tasty homemade baked goods and dishes
conscientiously prepared from their own fruits and vegetables in
this classic contemporary counterculture co-op. Meals are
wholesome, hearty, and flavorful, and can be washed down with
a choice of regional wines or beers. The dining rooms are comfortably
outfitted in rustic wood furnishings accented by fresh flowers in
local pottery on each table.

★ **The Oyster Bar**
18.5 mi. NE at 240 Chuckanut Dr. - Bow   766-6185
D only.   *Expensive*
The Oyster Bar is one of the finest dinner houses in the Western
United States—a true haven of New American cuisine. Distinctive
interpretations of regional dishes feature the freshest possible
produce and the highest quality seafoods and veal. Talent in the
kitchen is demonstrated in dishes ranging from local oysters with
pesto to salmon broiled with fresh ginger/lime sauce. Homemade
fruit sorbet, nectarine mousse, and pastries are similarly delicious.
Remarkably, the view of Puget Sound from the romantic, casually
elegant three-tiered dining room is as inspiring as the food. The
restaurant is so popular that reservations are necessary, often well
in advance.

★ **Oyster Creek Inn**
19.1 mi. NE at 190 Chuckanut Dr. - Bow   766-6179
L-D.   *Moderate*
Oysters (naturally) star among the seafoods served here, and they
are outstanding in half a dozen preparations. The dining room
is casually refined with fresh flowers and candles on each table.
Every guest enjoys an intimate view of evergreens and spectacular
hanging plants positioned by each window. The view from a
comfortable downstairs lounge is similarly romantic.

★ **Rhododendron Cafe**
15.1 mi. NE at 553 Chuckanut Dr. - Bow   766-6667
L-D. Sun. brunch. Closed Tues.   *Moderate*
An old-time roadside gas station has been artistically transformed
into a towering tribute to country cuisine. A short list of chalkboard

entrees describes dishes skillfully prepared from the freshest local ingredients. Desserts are similarly, simply delicious. Plants and wood-trimmed decor, plus flowers on each table, enhance the cozy homespun interior. An umbrella-shaded deck is also used when weather permits.

★ **Swinomish Longhouse Restaurant**

1.2 mi. W at 955 Moorage Rd.   466-4444

L-D. No L Tues.-Fri. Closed Mon.   *Moderate*

Salmon, alder-smoked Indian-style on an exhibition grill in the main dining room, is the restaurant's specialty and the thing to have, accompanied by Indian fry bread. The window-wall view across the channel of La Conner, presided over by Mt. Baker, is one of the most picturesque in the Northwest. Stylish wooden tables and chairs outfit the spacious pitched-roof dining room. There is a cozy view lounge, and a deck for alfresco dining when weather permits.

★ **Wildflowers**

13 mi. E at 2001 E. College Way - Mt. Vernon   424-9724

L-D.   *Moderate*

An ambitious menu of contemporary regional specialties includes such dishes as grilled sirloin with chili butter or stuffed chicken breast with blackberry sauce, along with homemade desserts like Grand Marnier cheesecake and frozen raspberry mousse. The food is usually very good, but the service is uneven. An older house has been converted to include an inviting dining room with a fireplace and tables set with fresh flowers and lantern/candles.

LODGING

Accommodations in La Conner are unconventional, romantic—and scarce, considering La Conner's appeal. Visitors interested in staying in town should make reservations in advance during summer, especially on weekends. Fall through spring rates are usually at least 10% less than those shown. Several standard motels are usually available in nearby Mt. Vernon.

Execulodge

11 mi. NE at 2009 Riverside Dr. - Mt. Vernon 98273   424-4141

This motor hotel has a restaurant and lounge, plus a small landscaped outdoor pool. Each of the recently remodeled rooms has a phone. A few simply furnished **bargain** rooms are also available.

mini-suite—large, in-bath whirlpool, cable color TV,   Q bed...$74

regular room—no TV or air conditioning,   Q bed...$30

Garden View Inn

12.5 mi. NE at 1617 N. 26th St. - Mt. Vernon 98273   428-5705

A modern four-story apartment complex also serves as a **bargain** motel. Each comfortably furnished unit has a full kitchen and color TV.

regular unit—1 BR, spacious, private balcony,   Q bed...$30

Heather House
  .3 mi. E at 505 Maple Av. (Box 237)   466-4675
One of the real pleasures of La Conner is the picturesque
surrounding farmlands. Heather House bed-and-breakfast inn is
sited to give guests an intimate view of the tranquil pastoral
countryside. Three bedrooms in the Cape Cod-style replica share
two baths. An ample Continental breakfast with a choice of juices
and scones or other pastries is served at a table overlooking fields
and hedgerows.
  "Master Bedroom"—large, fireplace, private view
                    of farmland & Mt. Baker,   Q bed...$65
  regular room—faces street,   D bed...$40
★ **Heron In La Conner**
  .3 mi. E at 117 Maple Av.   466-4626
The area's most sybaritic accommodations opened in early 1987
in a stylish new three-story building that captures the spirit of
Victorian La Conner. Located a short walk from downtown, the
inn occupies a lovely site, accented by fruit trees in back and
farmlands beyond extending to a skyline dominated by glistening
Mt. Baker. Guests can enjoy the scene from a porch or a hot tub.
A Continental breakfast is complimentary, as are bicycles. Each
of the twelve bedrooms is sumptuously decorated and includes
a private bath and a phone. (A color TV will be provided on request.)
  "third floor, SW corner"—spacious, fireplace, in-
                    room whirlpool,   Q bed...$85
  "third floor, SE corner"—spacious, fireplace, private
                    view of farmlands/
                    Mt. Baker from   Q bed...$85
  "third floor, NE corner"—spacious, best view of
                    Mt. Baker,   Q bed...$60
  regular room—small, 3rd floor has Mt. Baker view, D bed...$45
Katy's Inn
  downtown at Third & Washington Sts. (Box 304)   466-3366
Near the top of a bluff above downtown is a two-story house built
in 1876 as the home of a sea captain. Now it is a winsome bed-
and-breakfast inn furnished with quality antiques and iron beds.
Four rooms share two baths. Breakfast of fresh juice and fruit,
muffins, and a hot dish like ham and cheese quiche is
complimentary.
  "Blue Room"—overlooks town and the channel,
                    window/doors on two sides,   D bed...$40
  "Yellow Room"—overlooks town and the
                    channel, window/door to semi-
                    private porch,   D bed...$40
  regular room—   D bed...$40

La Conner Country Inn
downtown at Morris Av. & Second St. (Box 573)   466-3101
La Conner's landmark accommodation is a two-level wood-sided motel that captures the tranquil spirit of the area. The public rooms include a large fireplace sitting area with games. A complimentary Continental breakfast is served in the library. Each of the large, attractively furnished rooms has a private bath and a gas fireplace. A first-rate restaurant and pub adjoin.

king—	K bed...$74
standard queen—	Q bed...$65
regular room—downstairs,	T & D beds...$59

Mark II Motel
11 mi. NE at 1203 Goldenrod Dr. - Burlington 98233   757-4021
This one- and two-level motel is on a frontage road by the freeway. Each simply furnished room has a phone and color TV.

regular room—	Q bed...$35

Raymond House
downtown at 604 S. Second St. (Box 306)   466-3417
There is only one guest room, but it may have the choicest view in town. Downstairs in a private home is a modernized bedroom with a private entrance, a private bathroom, and a large private deck overlooking La Conner and the channel. No breakfast is served, but downtown is only a staircase away.

regular room—spacious, refrigerator, floor/
                          ceiling window, private balcony,   Q bed...$38

Sterling Motor Inn
12 mi. NE at 866 S. Garl - Burlington 98233   757-0071
This is a two-level motel on a busy commercial street. Each spacious room is well furnished, including recliner chairs, a phone, and cable color TV.

regular room—	Q bed...$34

Wagon Wheel Motel
1.7 mi. W via Reservation Rd. at 895 Sneeoosh Rd.   466-3687
La Conner's only motel occupies a tiny single-level building in a forest west of town. Each of the small, spartan older rooms is clean and has the basic necessities. Closed Oct.-Mar.

regular room—	D bed...$35

West Wind Motel
11 mi. NE at 2020 Riverside Dr. - Mt. Vernon 98273   424-4224
This single-level motel offers simply furnished rooms with a phone and cable color TV.

regular room—	Q bed...$35

CAMPGROUNDS

Two of the Northwest's finest public campgrounds occupy picturesque waterfront locations less than a half hour drive from town.

Bayview State Park
8 mi. N at 1093 Bayview-Edison Rd.   757-0227
A short stroll from Padilla Bay, the state has provided an attractive picnic area and campground in the pines. Nearby is a small sandy beach with picnic tables by the water. Saltwater swimmers, sunbathers, and beachcombers have a lamentably panoramic view of an oil refinery and tank farm. Flush toilets, hot (fee) showers, and full hookups are available. Each pine-shaded well-spaced site has a combination fire ring/grill and picnic table. Expansive lawns separate the RV/trailer area (with a bay-and-oil-refineries view) from the more sequestered tent/no hookup area. Reciprocal fee.   base rate...$6

★ **Deception Pass State Park**
16 mi. W on WA 20   675-2417
Just south of the "pass" (a narrow channel between islands) is a huge state-operated campground beautifully located amidst lush ferns in a spruce and pine forest. Easy trails lead a short distance to a long sandy beach. Flush toilets, hot (fee) showers, and full hookups are available. Each widely spaced, pine-shaded site is bordered by dense undergrowth, and has a fire ring/grill and picnic table. Reciprocal fee.   base rate...$6

★ **Larrabee State Park**
21 mi. NE via WA 237 on WA 11
Washington has developed a lovely campground in a luxuriant forest on a slope next to Puget Sound. Hot showers (fee), flush toilets, and full hookups are available. A pebbly cove can be easily reached via a well-marked trail. Each of the shaded, well-spaced sites has a fire ring/grill and a picnic table. Reciprocal fee.   base rate...$6

OTHER INFORMATION

Area Code: *206*
Zip Code: *98257*
Chamber of Commerce
   Box 644   466-3651
Washington State Parks (summer) information
   220 N. Walnut - Burlington   (800)562-0990

Leavenworth, Washington

Leavenworth—"the Bavarian village"—is an alpine playground for the entire family. The themed identity is apparent throughout the photogenic heart of town, and it has been remarkably successful in making Leavenworth a family-oriented tourist destination. Beyond the happy hubbub in town is the sheer beauty of the location. The village covers a flat little bench by the lovely Wenatchee River. Mountains rise abruptly on all sides. Orchards fill the broad valley downstream, while pine forests carpet valleys and slopes above town. Nearby, wilderness areas include countless lakes and glaciers sheltered among the rocky peaks of the Cascade Range.

Coupled with the surrounding natural grandeur is a dramatic four season climate. Winters are cold and snowy. Major cross-country skiing facilities have been added recently in and around town, and one of the region's largest downhill skiing complexes is in neighboring mountains to the west. Temperatures are pleasant in spring when fragrant blossoms cover orchards below town, and in fall when roadside stands display the harvest. During normally hot sunny days of summer, the clear cool river in town has a special appeal for river runners, fishermen, and swimmers. High country lakes, peaks, and glaciers attract climbers, backpackers, and others interested in wilderness adventures. Meanwhile, the Bavarian village is usually overflowing with strollers and shoppers exploring flower-filled nooks and crannies.

Settlement didn't begin until the 1890s, when the Great Northern Railway decided to establish a division point here. A lumber mill quickly followed, and the boom was on. But, in 1922 the railroad moved its division point, and a few years later the Great Depression closed the mill. The town survived—barely. In 1965, the citizenry decided to adopt a new identity—a Bavarian theme in keeping with the alpine surroundings—to make Leavenworth more inviting to tourists. Single-minded determination, private capital, and tireless labor (increasingly supported by European artisans) completely transformed the heart of town in twenty years.

Today, a manicured park with a gazebo faces solid blocks of colorful chalets sporting wooden shutters and ornate wall paintings. Old-fashioned street lamps, hand-carved signs, and benches line sidewalks, and multicolored flowers are everywhere. Loudspeakers air German music daily, indoors and out. The theme-identity is closer than ever to reality, as native European craftsmen, chefs, and shopkeepers move here in response to the village's fame and prosperity. German-in-name-only trinket parlors and restaurants must now compete with galleries displaying Northwestern and European collectibles; specialty shops emphasizing local gourmet products; and European talent and equipment in the newest and finest bakery and dining room. Lodgings are unconventional and surprisingly scarce. They now range from pensions above shops and rustic mountain lodges to luxuriously appointed motels. Numerous campgrounds near town offer outdoor family fun with locations in forests near lakes or streams.

Elevation:

1,160 feet

Population (1980):

1,522

Population (1970):

1,322

Location:

130 miles East
of Seattle

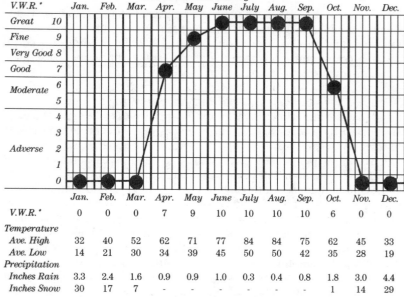

Leavenworth, Washington
WEATHER PROFILE
Vokac Weather Rating

V.W.R.*	Jan.	Feb.	Mar.	Apr.	May	June	July	Aug.	Sep.	Oct.	Nov.	Dec.
V.W.R.*	0	0	0	7	9	10	10	10	10	6	0	0
Temperature												
Ave. High	32	40	52	62	71	77	84	84	75	62	45	33
Ave. Low	14	21	30	34	39	45	50	50	42	35	28	19
Precipitation												
Inches Rain	3.3	2.4	1.6	0.9	0.9	1.0	0.3	0.4	0.8	1.8	3.0	4.4
Inches Snow	30	17	7	-	-	-	-	-	-	1	14	29

*V.W.R. = Vokac Weather Rating: probability of mild (warm & dry) weather on any given day.

Forecast

	V.W.R.*	Temperatures Daytime	Temperatures Evening	Precipitation
Jan.	0 Adverse	cold	frigid	frequent snowstorms
Feb.	0 Adverse	chilly	cold	frequent snowstorms
Mar.	0 Adverse	cool	chilly	occasional showers/snow flurries
Apr.	7 Good	cool	chilly	infrequent showers
May	9 Fine	warm	cool	infrequent showers
June	10 Great	warm	cool	infrequent showers
July	10 Great	hot	warm	negligible
Aug.	10 Great	hot	warm	negligible
Sep.	10 Great	warm	cool	infrequent showers
Oct.	6 Moderate	cool	chilly	occasional rainstorms
Nov.	0 Adverse	chilly	chilly	frequent snow flurries
Dec.	0 Adverse	chilly	cold	frequent snowstorms

Summary

Leavenworth is surrounded by massive peaks of the North Cascade Range in a sylvan canyon of the Wenatchee River. The spectacular setting is coupled with a striking four season climate. **Winter** usually involves chilly days and cold evenings. Frequent snowstorms assure ample snow cover for excellent cross-country and snowmobile courses around town and for a fine downhill ski area nearby. Temperatures increase very rapidly in **spring**, with good weather around blossom-time in April and comfortably warm weather well before Memorial Day. **Summer** is outstanding. Long, hot sunny days are ideal for enjoying the crystal-clear river in town and the fiord-like lake close by. As an added bonus of the season, rainfall is negligible, and less likely than in any of the West's other great mountain towns. Pleasant weather continues through the fruit harvest in early **fall**, but is soon followed by chilly days and increasingly frequent snowfalls.

226

ATTRACTIONS & DIVERSIONS

★ **Chelan County Museum**
    11 mi. E via US 2 at 5698 Museum Dr. - Cashmere   782-3230
More than a dozen log cabins are outfitted with pioneer memorabilia in an attractively landscaped park setting adjacent to a museum housing one of the most significant collections of Indian artifacts in the Northwest. Closed in winter.

Golf
★ **Leavenworth Golf Club**
    1 mi. SW via US 2 on Icicle Rd.   548-7267
This mountain-rimmed 18-hole golf course borders the Wenatchee River. It is open to the public with a clubhouse, rentals, and food service.

★ *Hiking*
    Der Sportsmann
    downtown at 837 Front St.   548-5623
The Cascade peaks surrounding Leavenworth are alluring enough to give even the most sedentary visitor an urge to explore a mountain trail. When you succumb, you'll need the right equipment. Topographic maps of the area are sold at Der Sportsmann, and outdoor gear can be purchased (or rented) here.

Historic Movie & Photo Gallery
    downtown at 801 Front St.   548-5434
"Leavenworth: Village of Inspiration" is a thirty-minute film explaining how and why the Bavarian theme got adopted. The free movie runs continuously in a tiny theater upstairs above Der Markt Platz.

★ *Horseback Riding*
In the valley above Leavenworth, trails ascend through sylvan forests to flower-filled meadows backed by the snow-capped peaks of the Cascade Range. Hourly and longer guided horseback rides to the high country, plus pack trips into the wilderness beyond, can be arranged at these stables:
    Eagle Creek Ranch *8 mi. NE via WA 209 on Eagle Cr. Rd.* 548-7798
    Icicle Outfitters   *19 mi. NW via WA 209 & WA 207*   763-3647

★ **Lake Wenatchee State Park**
    20 mi. NW via US 2 on WA 207
A crystal-clear five-mile-long alpine lake is the centerpiece of a superb state-operated recreation facility. A long pebbly beach has been set aside for sunbathers, and the lake is much used by swimmers, canoeists, wind surfers, and fishermen. The up-lake view of a pine-rimmed shoreline and towering peaks of the Cascades on all sides is magnificent. A bathhouse and boat ramp are available, and a large campground adjoins in a forest near the lake.

★ **The Leavenworth Loop**
   approximately 40 mi. on US 2 & WA 209
   One of the most popular scenic drives in Washington is a valley
   loop that includes WA 209 north through ranching country to Lake
   Wenatchee—a jewel of a lake surrounded by steep-sided, forested
   mountains. The return route (US 2) is highlighted by Tumwater
   canyon, where the Wenatchee River rushes down a narrow gorge.
   Along the way, aspen and other broadleafed trees are spectacularly
   colorful in fall.

★ *Mountain Climbing*
   Leavenworth Alpine Guides
   Box 699   548-4729
   Rugged granite peaks and shimmering glaciers are plentiful near
   Leavenworth. Guided rock and ice climbs, expeditions, and seminars
   led by professionals can be reserved here.

★ **Ohme Gardens**
   19 mi. E via US 2 at 3327 Ohme Rd. - Wenatchee   662-5785
   On a promontory overlooking the Wenatchee valley, nine acres of
   impressive mountain greenery have been skillfully nurtured on
   natural basalt formations. Stone pathways meander past fern
   grottoes, trickling waterfalls, and a wishing well, to a lookout point
   with a sweeping view of the Columbia River valley. The gardens
   have been evolving for more than half a century. Closed Nov.-Mar.

★ *Orchards*
   along US 2 E of town
   The broad valley of the Wenatchee River below town is filled with
   a continuous expanse of various kinds of fruit trees. Fruit stands
   are sprinkled along the highway which parallels the river for more
   than ten miles through the orchards. The drive is especially
   rewarding during the harvest in summer and fall. Then, trees are
   heavy with ripe cherries, apricots, peaches, pears, or apples, and
   visitors can stop to savor and buy whatever fresh fruits and juices
   are in season.

★ *River Running*
   Quiet Waters Outfitters
   16 mi. W at junction WA 207/WA 209   763-3733
   From April into July, river running on the Wenatchee River is very
   popular from a spectacular deep canyon west of Leavenworth to
   calmer reaches where the river approaches the Columbia River
   twenty miles to the east. Whitewater rafting trips on the upper
   reaches of the river are offered, including all equipment, meals,
   shuttle vans, and professional guides. (They also will outfit anyone
   interested in a private trip.) Canoes may be rented and put in
   here for an approximately six-mile run during summer and fall,
   when the Wenatchee is one of the best canoe waters in the
   Northwest.

Wenatchee Whitewater
11 mi. E on US 2 - Cashmere   782-2254
Professionally guided whitewater rafting trips ranging from two hours to two days on the Wenatchee River can be reserved here, with all equipment, meals, and transportation provided.

★ Rocky Reach Dam
27 mi. E on US 2 - Wenatchee   663-7522
The visitors information center in the massive dam on the Columbia River has an underwater fish-viewing gallery linked to the "fish ladder" that makes it possible for spawning salmon to go around the dam. Even more impressive are the self-guided tours of interpretive museums within the power house. The Gallery of Electricity has inventive displays explaining the whole history of electricity from Ben Franklin's kite to space age microcircuitry. Visitors can cause all kinds of electrical contrivances to make noise or give light. The Gallery of the Columbia has exhibits that highlight the geologic and cultural evolution of the area. Fifteen acres of colorful gardens and shady lawns by the dam provide inviting picnic sites.

Warm Water Feature
Public Swimming Pool
downtown adjacent to Lions Club Park on US 2
The public is invited to use this outdoor pool. There is a small sunbathing area with a splendid mountain view, plus an adjoining mini park with picnic tables and play equipment.

★ Waterfront Park
downtown at W end of Commercial St.
A lovely one-half-mile-long town park has been developed recently at the junction of the Icicle and Wenatchee Rivers. Well-lit paths wind along the forested shoreline, and a bridge leads to Blackbird Island, which is usually alive with birds. Benches, lawns, and tiny sandy beaches are pleasant places to relax and cool off on hot summer days.

Winter Sports
★ *Cross-Country Skiing*
around town
In recent years, several scenic locations in and around town have been developed for cross-country ski touring. More than twenty miles of groomed trails (some night-lighted) offer every kind of terrain, and some exceptional views. For maps, and information about equipment rentals and sales, lessons, and tours, call:

Bavarian Nordic Division   *548-5983*
Cougar Inn   *763-3354*
Leavenworth Nordic Ski Programs   *548-5165*

★ *Sleigh Rides*
Eagle Creek Ranch
8 mi. NE via WA 209 on Eagle Creek Rd.   548-7798
Sleigh rides over rolling snow-covered meadows ending at a roaring campfire with hot spiced cider are available by reservation in winter.
Red-Tail Canyon Farm
2.5 mi. N on WA 209 at 11780 Freund Canyon Rd.   548-4512
Belgian draft horses take up to thirty people on an hour-long old-fashioned sleigh ride in scenic Red-Tail Canyon. Cider pressing and cross-country skiing are other features here.

★ **Stevens Pass**
36 mi. W on US 2   973-2441
One of Washington's biggest ski areas boasts the largest variety of lighted terrain in the Pacific Northwest. The vertical rise is 1,800 feet, and the longest run is over one mile. Elevation at the top is 5,800 feet. There are six double chairlifts, and two triple chairs. All facilities, services, and rentals are available at the base for downhill skiing. A restaurant, cafe, and lounge are at the base, but all lodgings are in town. The skiing season is mid-November to mid-April.

SHOPPING

Leavenworth has earned distinction as one of the most vibrant downtowns anywhere. Today, thanks to free enterprise and architectural controls, even alleyways sport cheerful Bavarian-style facades. In addition, masses of flowers lend colorful accents to balconies, sidewalks—even lampposts. Best of all, Leavenworth has recently grown beyond its early image as an ersatz European trinket town. Browsers can now find both locally made and imported arts and crafts (like first-rate handcarved clocks, metal sculpture, ceramic figurines, etc.) competing with a still-awesome assemblage of trinket-and-T-shirt shops.

Food Specialties

★ **Aplets and Cotlets**
11 mi. E via US 2 at 117 Mission Av. - Cashmere   782-2191
Washington's most famous confection was first made here more than sixty years ago. Aplets (from apples and walnuts) and cotlets (apricots and walnuts) are as luscious as ever. Visitors are invited to sample these and other fruit candies, and to tour the spotless factory. The Country Store, in the same complex, is stocked with locally oriented gifts and gourmet foods, to go or for shipment anywhere.

Duncan Orchards
.8 mi. E at 11685 US 2   548-5984
Seasonally fresh fruit and produce has been sold here for decades, along with garden plants.

Hansel & Gretel
downtown at 819 Front St.   548-7721

This deli/cafe makes an ambitious array of pastries and pies, and also sells cold cuts, sandwiches, and ice cream to eat here or to go.

Hauff Orchards
5 mi. E on US 2

Fresh local fruits in season, plus ciders and juices and a large assortment of local jams and jellies, are displayed for sale in this roadside store. Closed Nov.-May.

Hoelgaard's
downtown at 731 Front St.   548-7514

A full line of Danish pastries is produced here, and served in the shop or to go.

★ Homefires Bakery
2.7 mi SW at 13013 Bayne Rd.   548-7362

A gifted baker, quality ingredients, and a German wood-fired masonry oven have brought authentic Old World baking to Leavenworth for the first time. It's an out-of-the-way drive from town to buy the delicious breads, cinnamon rolls, and specialty pastries, but well worth it.

★ Prey's Fruit Barn
1.8 mi. E on US 2   548-5771

All of the area's best fruits and vegetables, plus selected local cider and juices, preserves, sauces, and candies are displayed and sold here in season. Many are generously offered for sampling in one of the state's largest and friendliest roadside markets. Closed Dec.-May.

★ Rosemary's Kitchen
3.1 mi. E via US 2 at 8796 Stage Rd.   548-4166

Rosemary's apple sauce, apple filling, and preserves have a good old-fashioned taste. All are made with fruit from their own orchards, which surround the small roadside stand.

Smallwood's Harvest
3.4 mi. E on US 2   548-4196

Fresh fruit, homemade ciders, and local preserves have been coupled with antiques for sale in a large roadside building. Closed Nov.- May.

Susswaren
downtown at 733 Front St.   548-5755

This ice cream and candy store makes their own chocolates, and also makes Danish cones used for Dairy Gold ice cream.

★ Tiny's Bavarian Market
downtown at 701 US 2   548-5397

Here is a market that specializes in Washington state food products—fruits, cider, candies, preserves, and more. Because many samples are available, Tiny's is a fine place to learn about local gourmet specialties before buying or having them shipped. A dining area is also available, with ice cream and short order foods.

Specialty Shops

Bergdorf Gallerie Ltd.
downtown at 222 Ninth St.   548-4372
This inviting gallery in the Obertal Village Mall is a good place to check out the state of the art in Leavenworth. An eclectic mix of wall hangings, jewelry, wood carvings, and ceramics includes some notable works by regional artists with a Northwestern orientation.

Der Markt Platz
downtown at 801 Front St.   548-7422
The place is awash with steins, cuckoo clocks, and ceramic coats of arms, plus a couple of unusual features. A good assortment of Bavarian music (records and tapes) is offered for sale and played here (a TV screen identifies the cover of the music being played). There is also a distinctive assortment of regional jams, jellies, and food products like gingerbread houses.

Metal Sculpture Gallerie
downtown at 703 US 2
An unusual assortment of metallic wall hangings is handcrafted, displayed, and sold in a small gallery/studio in the Innsbrucker Building.

Show Haus Gallerie
downtown at 907 Front St.   548-7551
Well-done line sketches of Washington scenes, and an appealing assortment of objects of art (paintings, ceramics, polished wood, metal wall hangings, etc.) are displayed in this small shop.

Village Book and Music Shop
downtown at 215 Ninth St.   548-5911
An emphasis on Northwestern literature seems appropriate in this tiny bookstore. A good selection of new age and classical music is also for sale.

NIGHTLIFE

For all of its gemutlich, Leavenworth settles down surprisingly early at night. Live music for dancing is scarce and tame, while casual drinking places are plentiful and plain.

Gustav's Tavern
downtown at 617 US 2   548-4509
Half a dozen beers on tap and an assortment of hearty short order American and alpine-style meals are served in a handsome little wood-trimmed barroom. A sheltered adjoining patio has a fine view of the surrounding mountains.

Kristall's
   downtown at US 2 & Ski Hill Dr.   548-5267
Big mountain-framing picture windows above the bar make this the best view-lounge in town. A large stone fireplace and cozy area with comfortably padded seating are other enticements in a stylish wood-and-rock-trimmed room adjoining a family-oriented coffee shop.

Max und Moritz
   downtown at 820 Commercial St.   548-4576
Country and western music is offered on weekends in a simply furnished upstairs restaurant/bar.

Tumwater Inn
   downtown at 219 Ninth St.   548-4232
Live music for dancing is offered on weekends, and there is video dancing nightly, in a big plain room with a stone fireplace.

RESTAURANTS

A remarkable proliferation of restaurants has occurred downtown. Fortunately, since the mid-1980s, imitation-German dining rooms have been losing out to new places with talented chefs authentically trained in Europe and elsewhere.

Baren Haus
   downtown at Front/Ninth Sts.   548-4535
   L-D.   *Moderate*
An extensive assortment of hand-thrown pizzas is featured in an airy open-beam-and-brick-wall dining room fashioned out of a historic building. Steaks, seafoods, German dishes, and a salad bar are also available.

Big Y Cafe
   5.5 mi. E on US 2   548-5012
   B-L-D.   *Low*
Homemade biscuits and gravy and pies are the forte in a big, shaped-up coffee shop where everything served is all-American, plain, and plentiful.

Black Forest Restaurant
   downtown at 185 US 2   548-7130
   B-L-D.   *Moderate*
An American menu with the usual nods to German dishes is served in a family-oriented coffee shop with an interesting display of photographs showing the early history of Leavenworth.

★ **Cafe Christa**
   downtown at 801 Front St.   548-5434
   L-D.   *Moderate*
German dishes served here—like Vienna chicken—are as tasty as they are unusual. The salad dressings, sauces, preserves, and selected pastries (especially fresh strawberry pie or strudel with

whipped cream) are skillfully homemade. The dining room has the usual mural-wall-and-beer-stein decor, but there is a delightfully real, flower-bordered balcony overlooking the main street, park, and mountains beyond.

Casa Mia

downtown at 703 US 2   548-5621
L-D.   *Moderate*

An ambitious assortment of Mexican specialties is featured in a casual dining room with an appealing little alfresco dining deck.

Cougar Inn

25 mi. W via US 2 at 23379 WA 207   763-3354
B-L-D. Sun. brunch.   *Moderate*

A perfect antidote for campers with a craving for something sweet can be found up at the head of Lake Wenatchee. A variety of pies is made here, and they are very good. Conventional American meals are also served in a rustic dining room or lounge. Both have picture window views of the lake, and real working fireplaces.

Edelweiss Restaurant

downtown at 843 Front St.   548-7015
B-L-D.   *Moderate*

Simulated German dishes and similarly casually-treated American dishes are served in several family-oriented dining rooms. The largest is half-timbered with a stairway to nowhere; and a large stone fireplace set with an ersatz (electric) fire.

Garten Cafe

downtown at 320 Ninth St.   548-4412
B-L. Closed Mon.   *Moderate*

Well-made Dutch Babies or crepes may be the choice on the day's breakfast menu at the Edel Haus' restaurant (opened to the public in 1986). A limited menu is also offered for lunch in a comfortably furnished dining room or at umbrella-shaded tables on the terraced lawn.

Gustav's Tavern

downtown at 617 US 2   548-4509
L-D.   *Moderate*

Casual pub grub is served on a flower-filled patio, in a small dining room, or at a carryout window (for knackwurst, bratwurst, bockwurst, etc.).

Katzenjammers

downtown at 221 Eighth St.   548-5826
D only.   *Moderate*

A steak and seafood menu is served in a congested half-timbered dining room with a small salad bar and a large hooded fireplace that's used in winter. A cozy lounge adjoins.

Kristall's
  downtown at US 2/Ski Hill Dr.   *548-5267*
  B-L-D.   *Moderate*
The town's most successful holdout offers a large selection of casual American fare with no concessions to German cooking or decor. The big, family-oriented coffee shop is outfitted with a choice of padded booths or counter stools. Walls are decorated with local art and photographs, and waitresses are dressed in Western cowgirl garb. A plush contemporary lounge adjoins.

Lek's Thai Restaurant
  downtown at 894 US 2   *548-5935*
  D only.   *Moderate*
An appetizing assortment of authentic Thai specialties like curry with coconut milk, stir-fried vegetables with beef, or chicken with peanut curry sauce is served in a casual, comfortably furnished little dining room. Buffet dinners are featured on Friday and Saturday nights.

Mom's First at Frank's Last Stand
  5 mi. SE via US 2 on US 97   *548-4416*
  B-L-D.   *Low*
The homemade pies (including fruit pies in season like peach and apricot and blueberry) are delicious. The other reason for stopping at this small, very plain cafe is because it's next to Frank's Last Stand, a good place to get local fruits in season.

Oberland Bakery & Cafe
  downtown at 703 Front St.   *548-7216*
  B-L.   *Moderate*
The large assortment of European-style pastries is surprisingly less tasty than it looks in the bakery showcases. A few similarly ordinary breakfast and lunch dishes are also served in a casual coffee shop.

The Pewter Pot
  11 mi. E via US 2 at 124 ½ Cottage Av. - Cashmere   *782-2036*
  L-tea-D. Closed Mon. Only brunch on Sun.   *Moderate*
Beef pot pie, Cornish game hen with cranberry chutney, and apple-cured ham with rum raisin sauce are some of the traditional American specialties served with homemade desserts like Dutch Apple or pumpkin pie. The comfortably outfitted little dining room is Cashmere's finest.

Ratsstube
  downtown at 216 Eighth St.   *548-4673*
  L-D.   *Moderate*
A few Swiss and German dishes are served, but American fare predominates here. Beyond a couple of large, simply furnished dining rooms is the real feature of the restaurant, however—an outdoor deck where diners are surrounded by flowers and a panorama of peaks above town.

★ **Reiner's Gasthaus**
   downtown at 829 Front St.   548-5111
   L-D.   *Moderate*
The most authentic Austrian, Hungarian, and Bavarian dishes in
town are served here—complemented by homemade spaetzel,
savory cucumber or potato salad, and more than a dozen Bavarian
beers. The upstairs dining room is decorated with a number of
well-done murals, attractive wooden wainscoating, a beam ceiling,
and long communal tables. An accordianist plays most evenings
for dinner.

Squirrel Tree Restaurant
   15 mi. W on US 2 at junction WA 207   763-3157
   B-L-D.   *Moderate*
This roadside restaurant has the distinction of being the progenitor
of Leavenworth's architectural rebirth. It was the first (early 1960s)
Bavarian-style "redo" in the area. Casual American fare is served
in a large rough-timbered dining room with a great stone fireplace.

Tumwater Restaurant
   downtown at 219 Ninth St.   548-4232
   B-L-D.   *Moderate*
Casually treated German-named meals are the alternative to
ordinary American and even a few pasta dishes served in a historic
corner cafe with a large adjoining nightclub. The remodeled dining
room is half-timbered, with many live green plants (a welcome
alternative to murals), and a choice of padded booths, tables and
chairs, or counter service.

LODGING

Accommodations in town are surprisingly scarce. While more than
a dozen places have rooms, most are in small lodges or bed-and-
breakfast inns. Visitors seeking the individualized charm of
European-style pensions or country inns won't be disappointed,
however, nor will anyone interested in a room by a river overlooking
the mountains. Rates are often reduced as much as 20% apart
from summer and weekends.

★ **Bayern Village Motor Inn**
   .5 mi. E on US 2 at 1505 Alpen See Strasse   548-5875
The Wenatchee River is only a few feet away from this new motel
in a quiet forest. There is an outdoor pool. Each of the spacious,
well-decorated units has a fine view of the river from a private
balcony, plus a phone and cable color TV.
   regular room—   Q bed...$43

Bindlestiff's Riverside Cabins
   .6 mi. E at 11798 US 2 (Box 263)   548-5015
Cabins in a forest by the Wenatchee River are the feature here

along with an outdoor hot tub. A Continental breakfast is complimentary. Each small, modernized cabin has been simply furnished, and outfitted with a private deck overlooking the river and cable color TV.

regular room— Q bed...$38

Black Forest Restaurant & Motel
downtown at 185 US 2 548-7130
The area's only modern **bargain** motel is in a two-story building that also houses a casual restaurant and lounge. Simple contemporary furnishings are used and each room has a cable color TV.

regular room— Q bed...$30

Der Ritterhof Motor Inn
.3 mi. W at 190 US 2 548-5845
This modern motel is on landscaped grounds that include an outdoor pool, a whirlpool, and a putting green. Each nicely furnished room has a phone and cable color TV. For toll-free reservations in Washington, call (800)255-5845.

regular room— Q bed...$41

★ **Enzian Motor Inn**
downtown at 590 US 2 548-5269
Leavenworth's largest and finest lodging opened in 1984 with a pleasing combination of Bavarian architecture and decor and contemporary comforts. Landscaped grounds include a heated pool and hot tub, and a new addition features a gym and racquetball court. A Continental breakfast is complimentary. Each spacious, well-furnished room has a phone and cable color TV. For toll-free reservations in Washington, call (800)223-8511.

"Bridal Suite(s)"—wet bar, in-room whirlpool,
fireplace, Q bed...$98
"Executive Room(s)"—fireplace, K bed...$68
regular room— Q bed...$49

Europa Hotel
downtown at 833 Front St. 548-5221
In a choice location overlooking the downtown park and mountains beyond is a small European-style inn. Each of the rooms is furnished in comfortable Continental decor and has a private bath, phone, and cable color TV. A Continental breakfast is brought to the room.
#42,#40,#32,#30—overlook town park, long D bed...$46
regular room—3rd floor has mountain view
beyond rooftops, long D bed...$36

Hans Rohrbach Pension
1.2 mi. N at 12882 Ranger Rd. 548-7024
High on a slope above town is a large alpine-style lodge that captures the spirit of a European country inn. Scenic hiking trails, a swimming

pool, and hot tub are amenities, and a full breakfast is complimentary. Most of the clean little rooms open onto flower-decked balconies, and most share bathrooms.

#6—shared bath, fine valley/mountain view, balcony,	Q bed...$62
regular room—private bath, valley/mountain view,	Q or K bed...$65
regular room—shared bath, mountain view,	D bed...$55

McClain's Bed and Breakfast
.3 mi. E at 1226 Front St.   *548-7755*

Leavenworth's best-equipped bed-and-breakfast inn is an easy walk from downtown. Amenities in the adults-only facility include an outdoor pool, a whirlpool, and a game room. Bicycles are complimentary, as is a full breakfast. Each of the rooms is nicely furnished.

"Bridal Suite"—private bath, waterbed,	K bed...$69
regular room—private bath,	Q bed...$69
regular room—shared bath,	Q bed...$55

River's Edge Lodge
3.8 mi. E at 8401 US 2   *548-7612*

By the banks of the Wenatchee River is a modern motel with an outdoor pool. Each unit has a river view beyond a public walkway, and a cable color TV.

#214—end unit, newer, well-furnished, phone, gas fireplace, windows on 2 sides,	Q bed...$60
2nd floor—newer, spacious, well-furnished, phone, gas fireplace,	Q bed...$48
regular room—older, simply furnished,	Q bed...$45

Tyrolean Inn
downtown at 633 Front St.   *548-4119*

A small hotel over a restaurant and lounge was upgraded in 1986 by new owners. Each of the well-equipped rooms has a private bath, phone, and cable color TV.

#2 "Bridal Suite"—2 BR, mountain-view windows on 2 sides, large whirlpool,	2 Q beds...$65
"Whirlpool Room(s)"—in-bath whirlpool,	Q bed...$45
regular room—	D or Q bed...$35

Village Inn
11 mi. E via US 2 at 229 Cottage Av. - Cashmere 98815   *782-3522*

In a quiet residential area near downtown Cashmere is a small modern motel. Each simply furnished room has a phone and cable color TV.

regular room—	Q bed...$42
regular room—	D bed...$38

CAMPGROUNDS

Several campgrounds are conveniently located near town. The best have complete facilities (except hookups) in forested locations near a lake or river.

Chalet Park
.8 mi. E on US 2
This small private campground by the highway is a short stroll from the Wenatchee River. Flush toilets, hot showers, and full hookups are available. A lawn area has been set aside for tenters. Each of the closely spaced sites has a picnic table. base rate...$8.50

KOA Pine Village Campground
1.3 mi. E: .8 mi. E on US 2 & .5 mi. N on county road   548-7709
The Wenatchee River adjoins this large privately operated campground. It can be reached via a private access down a bluff. There is also a large outdoor pool. Flush toilets, hot showers and full hookups are available. Some of the closely spaced sites are shaded, others are on a lawn, and each has a picnic table. An area has been set aside for tenters.   base rate...$15

Lake Wenatchee State Park Campground
20 mi. W via US 2 on WA 207
A short stroll above a very popular beach at the east end of Lake Wenatchee, Washington has provided a large campground with flush toilets and (fee) hot showers but no hookups. The pine-shaded sites are relatively closely spaced and lack privacy, but each has a fire ring/grill and picnic table. Reciprocal fee.   base rate...$6

Nason Creek Campground
19 mi. W via US 2 on WA 207
Well-spaced shaded sites are clustered along both side of Nason Creek near Lake Wenatchee. There are chemical toilets and no hot water. Each of the sites has a fire ring/grill and picnic table. Several overlook the creek.   base rate...$5

Tumwater Campground
8.7 mi. W on US 2
Operated by the Forest Service in a heavily wooded location by the Wenatchee River is a large campground with flush toilets, but no hot water or hookups. Each of the widely spaced shady sites is isolated by undergrowth from others and has a picnic table and fire ring/grill. All are by or near Chiwaukum Creek or the river.   base rate...$6

SPECIAL EVENTS

★ **Mai Fest**   *downtown*   *mid-May*
Spring is welcomed with the traditional maypole dance during a celebration that's always the second weekend in May. Other

festivities include a grand march, music in the bandstand, and art in the park. Best of all, if the fruit trees are in bloom down-valley, visitors can enjoy a fragrant floral extravaganza.

★ **Autumn Leaf Festival**   *downtown*   *late September*
A Bavarian Oktoberfest seems especially appropriate here from the last weekend in September through the first weekend in October. German music, dancing, and beer enliven downtown, while "fall color" contributes to the grandeur of the surrounding mountains, and apple orchards await the harvest in the valley.

★ **Christmas Lighting**   *downtown*   *early December*
Thousands of lights outlining many of the downtown buildings are turned on simultaneously on the first and second weekends in December. It is a beautiful sight—especially when snow blankets the rooftops and icicles hang from the eves.

OTHER INFORMATION

Area Code: *509*
Zip Code: *98826*
Leavenworth Chamber of Commerce
  downtown at 703 US 2 (Box 327)   *548-7914*
Wenatchee National Forest Ranger Station
  downtown at 600 Sherbourne St.   *782-1413*

Long Beach, Washington

Long Beach is a playful town with a claim to fame spelled out in the name. Bordering the casual little community on the west is a broad beach of smooth driveable sand that extends for twenty-eight miles along the Pacific Ocean. It is the longest anywhere. Beyond is "The Graveyard of the Pacific" where hundreds of boats have been lost to the hazards of crossing the bar into the mouth of the Columbia River south of town. Low dunes of soft sand parallel the beach for its entire length along a two-mile-wide peninsula. On the other side, a forested shoreline borders the calm waters of Willapa Bay.

Temperate weather prevails year-round, along with one of the Northwest's longest growing seasons. As a result, rhododendrons flourish in a vast nursery near town and in private gardens throughout the peninsula. While freezes are rare, so are hot spells—or even very warm spells. Summer days are usually cool and breezy, so there is less fog than farther north along the coast. It's perfect weather for flying a kite; surfcasting; clamming; or exploring miles of hard sandy beach in a car, on a moped or bicycle, or on foot. Even the hearty don't swim here, however, and sunbathers are scarce except on the few calm, warm days. Sportfishing for salmon off the nearby mouth of the Columbia River is renowned. From fall through spring, almost continuous rainfall increasingly attracts storm-watchers to witness the spectacle of huge windlashed surf pounding the beaches.

Lumber, fishing, and oysters fostered settlement at several

peninsula locations beginning in the 1840s, decades after Lewis and Clark first viewed the Pacific Ocean near here during their historic journey in 1805. Long Beach didn't get started, however, until the 1890s when coastal steamers and a narrow gauge railroad made this a "summering place" for vacationers. Over the years, the railroad and steamers were replaced by highways and the car. With its strategic location, the town gradually became both the recreation and business center for the peninsula.

Long Beach is still a small town with a big assortment of activities for the whole family. A free museum full of strange stuff, an amusement zone with updated rides and games, and moped rentals are downtown features. Miniparks in the heart of town sport a gazebo, restrooms, and several large new wood sculptures that capture the town's playful spirit. Close by, a new mural depicting a cranberry harvest (the area's major crop) graces a building in a tiny business district with a nucleus of specialty shops that includes two excellent bakeries. Nightlife is rustic and rudimentary. Surprisingly, there are no ocean-view lounges or dining rooms in or near town, but several of the area's many restaurants feature outstanding Northwestern cuisine in individualistic surroundings. Lodgings are plentiful, ranging from historic small hotels to large modern motor hotels with expansive ocean views. Campers are also well looked after in a superb facility by an ocean beach near the mouth of the mighty Columbia River.

Elevation:

10 feet

Population (1980):

1,199

Population (1970):

968

Location:

110 miles Northwest of Portland

Long Beach, Washington
WEATHER PROFILE
Vokac Weather Rating

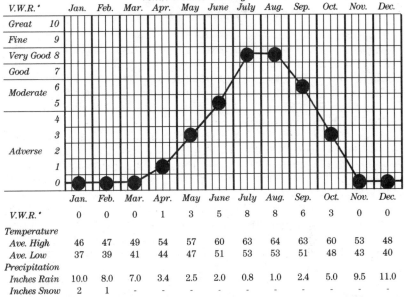

V.W.R.*	Jan.	Feb.	Mar.	Apr.	May	June	July	Aug.	Sep.	Oct.	Nov.	Dec.
V.W.R.*	0	0	0	1	3	5	8	8	6	3	0	0
Temperature												
Ave. High	46	47	49	54	57	60	63	64	63	60	53	48
Ave. Low	37	39	41	44	47	51	53	53	51	48	43	40
Precipitation												
Inches Rain	10.0	8.0	7.0	3.4	2.5	2.0	0.8	1.0	2.4	5.0	9.5	11.0
Inches Snow	2	1	-	-	-	-	-	-	-	-	-	-

V.W.R. = Vokac Weather Rating: probability of mild (warm & dry) weather on any given day.

Forecast

	V.W.R.*	Temperatures Daytime	Evening	Precipitation
Jan.	0 Adverse	chilly	chilly	continual downpours
Feb.	0 Adverse	chilly	chilly	continual rainstroms
Mar.	0 Adverse	chilly	chilly	continual rainstorms
Apr.	1 Adverse	cool	chilly	continual showers
May	3 Adverse	cool	cool	continual showers
June	5 Moderate	cool	cool	frequent showers
July	8 Very Good	cool	cool	occasional showers
Aug.	8 Very Good	cool	cool	occasional showers
Sep.	6 Moderate	cool	cool	frequent showers
Oct.	3 Adverse	cool	cool	frequent rainstorms
Nov.	0 Adverse	cool	chilly	continual rainstorms
Dec.	0 Adverse	chilly	chilly	continual downpours

Summary

The Pacific Ocean, Willapa Bay, and the mouth of the Columbia River nearly surround this seaside village. As a result of their warming influence, Long Beach benefits from a longer growing season than any other great town in the Northwest. Unfortunately, the unsheltered Long Beach peninsula is also one of the wettest places in the West during **winter**. Freezes and snowfall are rare, but the weather is uniformly chilly and continuously rainy. **Spring** remains unpleasantly cool and wet, with gradually increasing temperatures and decreasing rainfall. Suitable weather for comfortably enjoying most outdoor activities finally arrives in mid-**summer**. Consistently cool days and evenings are usually fog-free because of prevailing breezes, and showers only occasionally mar beach fun. The weather becomes more brisk through **fall**, and continual rainfall begins again after Halloween.

243

ATTRACTIONS & DIVERSIONS

★ *Bicycling*

The long narrow peninsula between the Columbia River, the Pacific Ocean, and Willapa Bay has many scenic byways and—good news for bikers—few hills. Bicycles can be rented by the hour or longer at:

Bicycle & Moped Rentals *10.1 mi. N at Park/Bay Avs. - Ocean Park*
Sea View Bike Shop   *1 mi. S on WA 103 at 48th Pl. - Seaview*

Clarke Rhododendron Nursery
   6 mi. NE via WA 103 on N. Sand Ridge Rd.   *642-2241*
One of the world's largest rhododendron and azalea nurseries is especially beautiful in May when the colorful shrubs are in fullest bloom.

★ **Fort Canby State Park**
   6.7 mi. S via WA 103 - Ilwaco   *642-3078*
The rocky headlands that mark the natural northern boundary of the Columbia River's mouth provide a dramatic backdrop to one of the state's most complete parks. There are hiking trails to two lighthouses; fishing on the north jetty where the Columbia River empties into the ocean; the only safe ocean swimming in the area (off a picturesque sandy cove at Waikiki Beach); as well as a giant campground.

★ **Fort Columbia Historical State Park**
   11.5 mi. S on US 101 - Chinook   *777-8221*
This well-developed park on a promontory overlooking the Columbia River's bar has an interpretive center, picnic areas, and viewpoints interconnected by short trails. Nearby are the gun batteries that guarded the river's mouth between 1896 and the end of World War II. The emplacements and turn-of-the-century fort buildings including the commanding officer's quarters have been carefully preserved and outfitted with interpretive signs and memorabilia.

Fun Zone
   downtown on Pacific Av. S.
A cluster of commercial entertainment places along the main highway through town features skill games, electronic amusements, and rides.

★ *Horseback Riding*
Skipper's Horse Rental
   .3 mi. S at S. 10th St. & S. Boulevard   *642-3676*
You can rent a horse here any day for hour-or-longer rides on the nearby hard sand beach.

★ **Lewis & Clark Interpretive Center**
   7 mi. S via WA 103 - Ilwaco   *642-3029*
Fort Canby's gun emplacements, used to protect the entrance to the Columbia River between the Civil War and World War II, have

become the site of a very informative visitors center. Lewis & Clark's journey across the continent to this spot is described in murals, models, and movies. Visitors have a superb view of the river's mouth from a terrace in front of the interpretive center.

★ **Long Beach**
  borders downtown on W side
The town of Long Beach is aptly named for the area's renowned feature—the world's longest driveable beach. Beyond low dunes along the western boundary of town, a broad hard sand beach extends in either direction for a total distance of twenty-eight driveable miles along the Pacific Ocean.

Long Beach Go Cart
  downtown at WA 103 & S. 10th St.
One of the more raucous amusements in downtown Long Beach is a well-equipped little go-cart track.

★ **Marsh's Free Museum**
  downtown at 409 Pacific Av. S.   *642-2188*
Since 1921, the privately owned Marsh Museum has welcomed visitors to rummage amongst collections of sea shells and glass balls, old-time music boxes and peep shows, and displays of some of the strangest stuff in the Northwest. It's free family fun, supported by the largest selection of souvenirs in Washington.

★ *Moped Rentals*
For effortless and exhilarating tours of the peninsula's beach and back country, a moped is the way to go. To rent one for an hour or longer, contact:
  Long Beach Moped Co.   *downtown at 620 Pacific Av. S.*
  Sea View Bike Shop   *1 mi. S on WA 103 & 48th Pl. - Seaview*

★ **North Head Lighthouse**
  6 mi. S via WA 103 - Ilwaco
High on a solid rock bluff overlooking the Pacific Ocean and the mouth of the Columbia River is a picturesque lighthouse that protects the "graveyard of the Pacific." Still in operation, it was constructed in 1898 because Cape Disappointment Lighthouse, built nearby in 1856, had limited visibility to the ships approaching from the north. A parking lot has been provided and a short trail to the lighthouse includes some scenic overlooks.

Oysterville Historic District
  14 mi. N on WA 103
Tucked away on the remote northern shore of Willapa Bay are the remnants of a village that was an oyster-harvesting boomtown shortly after the Civil War. All of the (primarily residential) structures were included on the National Register of Historic Places in 1976.

★ ***Sportfishing***
  3.5 mi. S via WA 103 & US 101 at Baker Bay - Ilwaco
Tiny Ilwaco is the home port of a major sportfishing fleet—moored in a protected bay near the mouth of the Columbia River. Charters are available for bottom fish (April thru October) and salmon and tuna during the summer season. Custom canneries near the docks will prepare your catch for same-day use or shipment. You can also reserve scenic cruises. The following operators, all professionals located along the waterfront at Ilwaco, offer sportfishing and scenic trips, and provide all necessary equipment.

A-1 Tuna Salmon Charters	*642-3734*
Coho Charters	*642-3333*
Hobo Charters	*642-2300*
Ilwaco Charter Service	*642-3232*
Pacific Salmon Charters	*642-3466*
Reel-em-in Charters	*642-3511*
Tidewind Charters	*642-2111*

SHOPPING

A tiny nucleus of distinctive shops is developing in the heart of Long Beach. Apart from this concentration, specialty shops are sprinkled along the highway that runs the length of the peninsula.
Food Specialties
Cornell's Crab Pot
  .8 mi. S at 1917 S. WA 103   *642-2524*
Local fish and shellfish (especially Dungeness crab) are featured in a variety of foods offered to go or in a casual fast food dining area in the back.

★ **Cottage Bakery**
  downtown at 118 Pacific Av. S.   *642-4441*
The breakfast pastries and donuts, plus assorted pies and cakes, are as delicious as they look in Long Beach's full service bakery.

★ **Milton York**
  downtown on Pacific Av. S. & Bolstad Av.   *642-2352*
Saltwater taffy and other candies, plus ice creams, preserves, and baked goods are made here. Many are from recipes that go back more than a hundred years at this location.

Ocean Fresh Crab & Seafood Market
  9.7 mi. N on WA 103 - Ocean Park   *665-5200*
Fresh crabs, oysters, steamed clams, and other seafoods, plus smoked salmon or sturgeon are among the specialties that you can buy to go at this roadside market.

The Old Salt Wine Cellars
  downtown at 610 Pacific Av. S.
A small wine selection, including selected Northwestern wines, is

featured, and tasting is available. Cheese and other foods are also sold, along with gift items.

★ **Uncle Bob's**
   3.5 mi. S via WA 103 & US 101 at Baker Bay - Ilwaco   *642-2508*
Here is the best cannery-smokehouse-gift shop complex on the peninsula. They will can or smoke your catch. In addition, fresh, canned, smoked, and jerky salmon, plus sturgeon and other seafoods, are sold to go, or in gift packs for shipment anywhere. Unusual sea-and-shore souvenirs are also available.

Specialty Shops

The Book Vendor
   downtown at 100 Pacific Av. S.   *642-2702*
Books of regional interest are available in this convenient little shop, along with books to curl up with on a rainy night.

Grayhouse Gallery, Gifts, & Gourmet
   downtown at 105 Pacific Av. S.   *642-2889*
Local arts and crafts; imported and antique gifts; and coffees, teas, and other food specialties are all displayed in a shop full of eclectic collectibles.

Long Beach Kites
   downtown at 104 Pacific Av. N.   *642-2202*
Breezes and beaches make Long Beach a natural for a kite festival. But, anyone can take a fly at the sport, now that there's a shop in town with a large array of colorful kites, plus a TV screen showing kites in action.

The Sea Chest Gallery
   1.1 mi. S at 46th Pl./WA 103 - Seaview   *642-2189*
A small cottage has been converted into an inviting studio/showroom to display fine watercolors of Northwestern scenes by the well-known owner/artist.

NIGHTLIFE

A homespun fun zone and some unpretentious taverns are the primary destinations for a night on the town. No atmospheric, surf-view lounge exists to date.

Long Beach Tavern
   downtown at Pacific Av. S. & S. 3rd St.   *642-3235*
The best of the area's many workaday taverns is nicely furnished with padded booths, a very popular bar, a fireplace, and a couple of pool tables.

RESTAURANTS

Restaurants are plentiful on the Long Beach peninsula. Most offer ordinary American fare in family-oriented surroundings. The few exceptions feature outstanding Northwestern regional specialties in individualized surroundings. Surprisingly, the area has no notable surf-view dining rooms to date.

★ **The Ark Restaurant**
11.5 mi. N on WA 103 - Nahcotta   665-4133
L-D. Sun. brunch. No L on Tues. Closed Mon.   *Expensive*
Many of the regional seafood specialties prepared here (especially Willapa Bay oysters pan-fried, in stew, burgers, etc.) are described in cookbooks written by the two women who are owners and chefs of this famous restaurant. Guests seated at comfortably furnished tables have a panoramic window-wall view of Willapa Bay and an oyster cannery from the spacious dining room and from a small lounge.

B.J. Squidley's
10 mi. N on WA 103 - Ocean Park   665-5261
B-L-D.   *Low*
Casual cookery is supplemented by a limited selection of baked goods from the Cottage Bakery in Long Beach. Interesting rough-cut log decor is offset by a homely kitchen in full view of the simply furnished dining room.

Kopa Welcoma
10.1 mi. N at WA 103 on beach access road- Ocean City
L-D.   *Moderate*
Willapa Bay oysters are featured—grilled for dinner or in a sandwich with homemade bread. Also, clam chowder is offered in several sizes in a homespun, nautically themed coffee shop by the Ocean Park access to the beach.

★ **Milton York**
downtown on Pacific Av. S. & Bolstad Av.   642-2352
B-L-D.   *Moderate*
All-American dishes are given careful attention and complemented by fine breads, pastries, cakes, pies, and ice creams. All are homemade in the same location that has been producing sweet treats for more than a century. Casually outfitted tables crowded around delicious-looking displays of their candies and baked goods are usually fully occupied by crowds who come here to enjoy first-rate old-fashioned American food.

★ **My Mom's Pie Restaurant**
.4 mi. S on WA 103 at S. 12th St.   642-2342
L only. Closed Mon.   *Moderate*
In season, the strawberry, raspberry, peach, and wild blackberry pies are luscious. Cream pies and fruit pies, available any time, are also delicious, as are the chili, clam chowder, meat pot pies, and salads. As a result, there is frequently a wait for a table in one of the plain little dining rooms of this increasingly renowned luncheon haven.

Red's Restaurant
   3.2 mi. S at 1st & Lake Sts. - Ilwaco   *642-3171*
   B-L.   *Low*
The down-home-style food preparation is as humdrum as the paper-and-plastic decor in Ilwaco's steak-n-seafood eatery.

Sanctuary Restaurant
   9.5 mi. S on US 101 at Hazel St. - Chinook   *777-8380*
   D only. Sun. brunch. Closed Mon.-Tues. in winter.   *Moderate*
Specials on fresh local seafood are a nightly highlight of a Continental menu that also features homemade desserts. A turn-of-the-century church building has been skillfully converted into a popular dinner house enhanced by soft lights and stained glass windows.

★ **The Shelburne Restaurant**
   1.1 mi. S on WA 103 - Seaview   *642-4142*
   L-D. Sun. brunch.   *Expensive*
The long-established restaurant at the Shelburne Hotel has achieved national acclaim. To continue to earn it, the menu is changed frequently according to seasonally available regional produce and the chef's whims. The kitchen gives nods to New American cuisine among classic Continental specialties. The sumptuous wood-toned decor in the dining room is evocative of an earlier, more extravagant time, while the furnishings are simply homespun.

The Tides
   downtown at 111 Pacific Av. S.   *642-9297*
   B-L-D.   *Low*
Two very good places for breakfast in the area adjoin each other downtown—Milton York and The Tides. Specialties include local seafoods in hangtown fry, omelets, etc. with support from delicious homemade biscuits. The tiny casual coffee shop sports some local art on the walls. A cozy firelit lounge is in back.

LODGING

Numerous accommodations have been sprinkled along the peninsula for many decades. Tiny highway-fronting motels, a small historic hotel, motor hotels, and condominium complexes are all represented. The best are by the dunes near the beach. Bargains are very scarce in summer. Many places reduce their prices by 25% and more from fall through spring.

Anchorage Motor Court
   1.2 mi. N on WA 103 (Box 581)   *642-2351*
There are only eight cabins in this tiny older oceanfronting complex. But, each is meticulously maintained and comfortably furnished, including a kitchen and cable color TV. Best of all, each unit has

a fine ocean view from every room.

regular room— Q bed...$44

Boulevard Motel

downtown at 301 Boulevard N. (Box 400) 642-2434
Both downtown and the beach adjoin this older cottage/motel complex with an indoor pool. Each simply furnished unit has color TV. For toll-free reservations, call (800)248-6273.

ocean-view cottage—2 BR, kitchen, fireplace, 2 D beds...$45
regular room—sand dunes/ocean view, Q bed...$35

The Breakers

1.4 mi. N on WA 103 (Box 428) 642-4414
The area's first large condominium complex (four three-story buildings) was built on grassy dunes by the beach. Toward the back of the minimally landscaped grounds is a fenced enclosure with an outdoor pool and whirlpool. Each unit has a private balcony or patio and routine modern furnishings, including a phone and cable color TV. None of the units is aimed directly at the ocean.

"Suite"—1 BR, kitchen, (duralog) fireplace in LR,
some ocean view, D or Q bed...$63
#425,#125—efficiency & 1 BR (if available),
kitchen, (duralog) fireplace, fine
ocean view, 2 Q beds...$78
regular room—small, Q or K bed...$37

★ **Chautauqua Lodge**

1 mi. N via WA 103 at 304 14th St. NW (Box 757) 642-4401
The area's most complete motor hotel is a big, modern three-story complex in an isolated spot fronting on low dunes by the beach. Amenities include a large indoor pool, two whirlpools, a sauna, and a recreation room, plus a casual restaurant and lounge with live music for dancing on weekends. Each comfortably furnished unit has a private balcony, a phone, and cable color TV.

#332 thru #335 "Honeymoon Suites"— newer
building, in-bath whirlpool, gas
fireplace, fine ocean
view across grassy dunes
from K bed...$85
regular room—no view, Q bed...$35

Edgewater Inn Motel

.4 mi. S at 409 10th St. SW (Box 793) 642-2311
All of the rooms are beachfronting in Long Beach's newest motel. Each tastefully furnished room in the three-story building has a phone and cable color TV with movies.

#301—2 BR, top, corner, fine ocean view, 2 Q beds...$52
regular room— Q bed...$42

The Lighthouse Motel
3 mi. N on WA 103 (Box 527)　　　　　　　　　*642-3622*
This tiny single-level motel fronts on dunes adjoining the ocean beach. Each unit offers attractively personalized decor, a complete kitchen, a private deck with a dunes-and-ocean view, plus color TV.

　#9—2 BR, end, fireplace, fine private ocean view,　2 D beds...$43
　one-bedroom with fireplace—　　　　　　　　　　　　D bed...$38
　regular room—1 BR,　　　　　　　　　　　　　　　D bed...$32

Ocean Lodge
downtown at Bolstad Av. & N. Boulevard (Box 337)　　*642-2777*
This small motel has a prime location in the heart of town adjoining the main approach to the beach. Facilities include an indoor pool, whirlpool, sauna, and exercise room. A few units have a view of dunes by the beach. Each unit has a color TV.

　#30—1 BR, large, gas fireplace, some ocean view,　　Q bed...$48
　#8,#4—1 BR, large, wood-burning fireplace,
　　　　　ocean view beyond parking lot,　　　　　　Q bed...$52
　regular room—without kitchen,　　　　　　　　　　Q bed...$36

★ Our Place
.5 mi. S at 1309 S. Boulevard (Box 226)　　　　　*642-3793*
Here is a small, modern motel in a quiet location by dunes a short stroll from the beach. Amenities include two whirlpools, a sauna, steam room, and a fully equipped exercise room for adults only. Each of the attractive, well-furnished units has a phone, refrigerator, and cable color TV with movies.

　#111—end, 2 BR, kitchen, LR with brick fireplace
　　　　　and private dunes/ocean view,　　　2 T & Q beds...$49
　#230—top (2nd) floor, corner windows with
　　　　　distant ocean view,　　　　　　　　　　Q bed...$37
　regular room—no view,　　　　　　　　　　　　D bed...$32

Pacific View Motel
downtown at 203 Bolstad Av. & N. Boulevard (Box 398)　*642-2415*
Adjacent to the main beach access archway downtown is a well-maintained older cottage complex. Each unit fronts on dunes by the beach and has a cable color TV.

　#11,#10—top (2nd) floor, spacious, town/
　　　　　beach view windows on 2 sides,　　　　　Q bed...$36
　regular room—　　　　　　　　　　　　　D or Q bed...$34

Ridge Court Motel
downtown at 3rd St. N. & N. Boulevard (Box 483)　　*642-2412*
An older cottage colony adjacent to low dunes beyond the beach is the only **bargain** downtown. There is an indoor pool. Each simply furnished room has a cable color TV.

　regular room—　　　　　　　　　　　　　　　Q bed...$29

Seaview Coho Motel

1.3 mi. S on US 101 (Box 198) - Seaview 98644   *642-2531*
Bargain rooms are available in an older motel near the highway.
Each of the small, plain rooms has a cable color TV.
regular room—   Q bed...$25

★ **Shaman**

downtown at 115 3rd St. SW (Box 235)   *642-3714*
One of the area's finest accommodations is a modern motel that
borders several attractive miniparks to the east, and dunes that
extend to the beach on the west side. There is an outdoor pool.
Each attractively furnished, spacious unit has a phone and cable
color TV with movies.
#40 thru #31—top floor, free-standing fireplace,
                    ocean view beyond walkway,   Q bed...$45
regular room—   Q bed...$36

The Shelburne Inn

1.1 mi. S on WA 103 (Box 250) - Seaview 98644   *642-2442*
Here is the last of the turn-of-the-century Peninsula hotels that
still accommodates guests. The highway-fronting building (on the
National Register) has been refurbished and expanded, and now
serves as a bed-and-breakfast inn. A well-known restaurant
occupies the first level, along with a gift shop. Each of the small
rooms is individually decorated. A full country breakfast is
complimentary.
room with private bath—   D or Q bed...$85
regular room—shared bath,   D bed...$60

CAMPGROUNDS

Many small, private campgrounds are sprinkled along the highway
(WA 103) that runs the length of the Peninsula. None compares
to Washington state's campground at Fort Canby State Park—one
of the largest and most skillfully developed facilities in the
Northwest.

★ **Fort Canby State Park**

6.7 mi. S via WA 103 (Box 488) - Ilwaco 98624   *642-3029*
The state has provided an enormous, beautifully sited campground
near the mouth of the Columbia River by the Pacific Ocean. A
boat launch and ramps on Baker Bay; trails to forested headlands
and the north jetty; and miles of sandy beaches and coves are
other park features. Sites at the north end are nicely spaced, have
a feeling of privacy because of dense shrubbery, and (many) border
the beach. Hot showers (fee), flush toilets, and full hookups are
available. Each site has a picnic table and fire ring/grill. Reciprocal
fee. For toll-free reservations in Washington, call (800)562-0990.
                                                       base rate...$6

SPECIAL EVENT

★ **Washington State International Kite Festival** *in town late Aug.*
Almost from the beginning (1981) this has been one of the biggest
kite-flying gatherings in America. During the third week in August,
more than 10,000 people per day gather on the beach to watch
competitive events, culminating in a mass kite fly-in. The American
record was probably broken in 1986 when more than one thousand
kites were in the air at one time.

OTHER INFORMATION

Area Code: *206*
Zip Code: *98631*
Long Beach Peninsula Visitor's Bureau
  Box 562   *642-2400*

Olympia, Washington

Olympia is an appealing medley of casual urbanity and ideal surroundings. It sprawls around beautiful Budd Inlet at the extreme southern end of Puget Sound. Mt. Rainier towers above luxuriant forests that frame the eastern skyline, while the Olympic Mountains loom along the northwestern horizon. Well-tended lawns, gardens, and parks complement a wealth of bays, lakes, and streams throughout the large community. A boldly handsome cluster of buildings atop a skillfully landscaped promontory mark this as Washington's capital city. Below, the revitalized downtown is bordered by picturesque shorelines and marinas.

The sheltered maritime location assures a relatively mild four season climate. It's chilly, and it rains—a lot—from fall into spring. But, snow and freezes are unusual enough that fan palms grow outdoors here along with a flourishing array of native plants. Summer, with long warm days and very little rain, is the year's busy season. Waterfront parks in the heart of town provide bicycle and hiking paths, picnic sites and play areas, sandy beaches for swimming and sunbathing, a tidewater promenade, and beyond—sailing, cruising, and sportfishing on Puget Sound. Nearby, sylvan trails border an alluring stream with several waterfalls including enchanting Tumwater Falls. Olympic National Park, Mt. Rainier National Park, Mt. St. Helens National Volcanic Monument, and Pacific Ocean beaches offer virtually unlimited recreation opportunities within a two-hour drive.

Olympia, Washington

A strategic location at the southern end of Puget Sound and vast pine forests first attracted settlers to this site. The town was founded in 1851, and soon boasted both a deep sea port and a lumber mill. Two years later, Washington Territory was formed (from part of Oregon Territory) with Olympia as the capital. In 1905, the economy diversified further when a brewery opened close by Tumwater Falls to take advantage of the pure artesian waters. In recent years, major public improvements downtown, around the capitol, and by the falls have made Olympia an increasingly popular visitor destination.

The capitol group is the most popular attraction in Washington these days, and the natural park by the falls is the most underrated. The fully revitalized downtown is a favorite destination for shoppers and strollers—with a good assortment of specialty shops and galleries. It is also one of the West's gourmet havens. Classic bakeries and other purveyors of toothsome treats are here, along with the Olympia Public Market, the second largest farmer's market in the state and a peerless source of local produce. Nightlife is diverse, too, ranging from a landmark theater complex to a funky cluster of taverns, clubs, and espresso parlors downtown. Restaurants are plentiful and varied, with several specializing in innovative uses of fresh local fruits, vegetables, and seafoods like exquisite Olympia Oysters. Lodgings are neither rife nor distinctive, with a few notable exceptions. Visiting campers can opt for a site in the woods by a warm clear lake at several nearby campgrounds.

Elevation:

90 feet

Population (1980):

27,447

Population (1970):

23,296

Location:

60 miles Southwest of Seattle

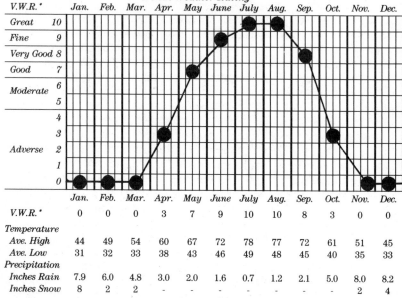

V.W.R.*		Jan.	Feb.	Mar.	Apr.	May	June	July	Aug.	Sep.	Oct.	Nov.	Dec.
V.W.R.*		0	0	0	3	7	9	10	10	8	3	0	0
Temperature													
Ave. High		44	49	54	60	67	72	78	77	72	61	51	45
Ave. Low		31	32	33	38	43	46	49	48	45	40	35	33
Precipitation													
Inches Rain		7.9	6.0	4.8	3.0	2.0	1.6	0.7	1.2	2.1	5.0	8.0	8.2
Inches Snow		8	2	2	-	-	-	-	-	-	-	2	4

*V.W.R. = Vokac Weather Rating: probability of mild (warm & dry) weather on any given day.

Forecast

	V.W.R.*	Temperatures Daytime	Evening	Precipitation
Jan.	0 Adverse	chilly	chilly	continual rainstorms/snow flurries
Feb.	0 Adverse	chilly	chilly	continual rainstorms/snow flurries
Mar.	0 Adverse	cool	chilly	continual rainstorms
Apr.	3 Adverse	cool	chilly	frequent showers
May	7 Good	warm	cool	frequent showers
June	9 Fine	warm	cool	occasional showers
July	10 Great	warm	cool	infrequent showers
Aug.	10 Great	warm	cool	infrequent showers
Sep.	8 Very Good	warm	cool	occasional showers
Oct.	3 Adverse	cool	cool	frequent rainstorms
Nov.	0 Adverse	cool	chilly	continual rainstorms
Dec.	0 Adverse	chilly	chilly	continual rainstorms/snow flurries

Summary

Olympia lies along the forested shores of beautiful Budd Inlet at the extreme southern end of Puget Sound. The town enjoys a relatively mild four season climate, thanks to the maritime influence of Washington's inland sea and the sheltering effect of nearby mountain ranges. **Winter** is uniformly chilly, and rain is continual. Snow flurries happen occasionally, but hard freezes are rare. Temperatures increase and rainfall diminishes rapidly through **spring**. Good weather for outdoor recreation usually prevails well before Memorial Day. **Summer** weather is excellent. Long warm days and cool evenings infrequently marred by showers are ideal for making good use of the surrounding countryside. Colorful foliage in early **fall** heralds the change from mild weather to cool days and increasingly frequent rainstorms as winter approaches.

ATTRACTIONS & DIVERSIONS

Bicycling

★ **Olympic Outfitters Ltd.**
downtown at 117 N. Washington St.   943-1997
Bicycles and related gear can be rented here by the hour or longer to tour the lakes and inlet on miles of designated bikeways. Camping equipment and sailboards can also be rented, and all kinds of sporting goods and apparel are available for sale.

★ **Capitol Group**
.5 mi. S on S. Capitol Way   753-3269
Washington state has developed a resplendent campus of architecturally engaging governmental buildings sprinkled on vast expanses of emerald-green lawns. The Legislative Building is the centerpiece, topped by an imposing stone masonry dome 287 feet high. When completed in 1928, it was the fourth largest dome in the world. Fountains, sculptures, and seasonal gardens are artistically located throughout the beautiful grounds to enhance the visual distinction of Olympia's most popular attraction.

★ **Capitol Lake Park**
downtown on W. 5th Av. at Water St.   753-8384
A trail runs for miles along the landscaped shore of Capitol Lake, giving bicyclists, joggers, and hikers scenic outlooks of the lake, town, Capitol, and Mt. Rainier. Several picnic areas have been provided in lawn or tree-shaded areas, and a supervised swimming beach and model boat basin border the heart of town.

Golf

★ **Tumwater Valley Golf Club**
3 mi. S at 4611 Tumwater Valley Dr. - Tumwater   943-9500
The area's most scenic golf course is a public 18-hole course that straddles the Deschutes River. Features include a pro shop, practice range, club and cart rentals, and a clubhouse with food service.

★ *Library*
downtown at E. 8th Av. & S. Franklin St.   352-0595
The Olympia Timberland Library occupies a large contemporary structure built around a striking plant-filled atrium that also showcases a fine rock sculpture of an otter by a Northwestern artist. The well-furnished interior includes padded armchairs conveniently located near a good assortment of magazines and newspapers. Closed Sun.

Millersylvania State Park
11 mi. S via I-5 & 113th Av. at 12245 Tilly Rd S.   753-1519
The state has provided ramps for boating and fishing, plus several sandy beaches with fenced-off swimming areas (and lifeguards in summer) along the heavily wooded shore of tiny Deep Lake. Bathhouses, a food concession, and a complete campground are also present.

★ Mt. Rainier National Park
65 mi. SE via WA 510, WA 702 & WA 706   569-2211

Mt. Rainier is the pre-eminent landmark of the Pacific Northwest. Looming 14,410 feet above sea level, the magnificent ice-clad volcano can be seen (on a clear day) along the southeast horizon from Olympia, and from most of Washington. Rainier's thirty-five square miles of glaciers, which completely cover the peak and extend well below timberline, form the largest single-mountain glacial system in the contiguous United States. Dozens of waterfalls and small lakes are tucked into dense forests and meadows lush with wildflowers on the surrounding slopes. Mountain goats, herds of elk and deer, bear, bobcats, coyotes, and dozens of other species of animals live in the park. More than three hundred miles of hiking trails (including the aptly named Wonderland Trail which encircles the mountain) are usually open from June into October, when heavy snows close all higher trails and roads until summer. Climbing, backpacking, hiking, fishing, and camping are popular recreation activities. Four visitor centers on the south and east sides of the park have exhibits, illustrated talks, guided walks, information, gift shops, food service, and decks for observing the sublime grandeur of the mountain.

★ Mount St. Helens National Volcanic Monument
70 mi. SE via I-5 exit 63, WA 505 & WA 504   696-7500

On May 18, 1980, a volcanic explosion of incredible force blew off the top 1,300 feet of Mount St. Helens. The blast laid waste to a vast forest; clogged river valleys with mud and logs; dammed Spirit Lake and raised its water level hundreds of feet; and cast a pall of ash that darkened the sky for days before covering parts of three states with fine grey powder. Since then, the world's most closely monitored volcano has settled down again. A visitor center has opened at Lewis and Clark State Park (I-5 exit 68—south of US 12), and the Spirit Lake Memorial Highway (WA 504) has reopened to a point a dozen miles northwest of the volcano. Anyone with proper permits can now climb what's left of the mountain. Of course, the area remains subject to closure at any time.

Old State Capitol Building
downtown at 600 S. Washington St.   753-6740

The Thurston County Courthouse, built in 1892, served as the site of state government between 1901 and 1928. On the National Register of Historic Places, the building is now used for education administration. The house/senate chambers have been converted into offices, but the graceful stairways and hardwood trim are intact, and (it's said) the ladies' restrooms are showcases of polished granite. Anyway, the rough-hewn granite facade is imposing and the adjoining square is a well-landscaped haven of tranquility downtown.

★ Olympia Brewery
2.2 mi. S at Custer/Deschutes Ways - Tumwater   754-5000

One of the largest and most attractive breweries in the West occupies a picturesque site by Tumwater Falls. Everyone is invited to enjoy forty-minute tours that provide a good review of the attractively landscaped grounds and brewery facilities. Samples are provided at the end of each tour, and there is a gift shop. Open daily 8 a.m. - 4:30 p.m.

★ **Olympic National Park**
   93 mi. NW via WA 8, US 12 & US 101   *452-4501*
The natural grandeur of the Olympic Peninsula has been preserved in more than 1,400 square miles of sublime wilderness that extends from glacier-clad peaks to ocean shores. The breathtaking Hurricane Ridge Highway provides unforgettable panoramas of Mt. Olympus (the highest peak at 7,965 feet) and dozens of glaciers that lend a shimmering brilliance to the rugged peaks at the top of the peninsula. Far below in the western river valleys, the wettest climate in the coterminous United States (averaging 140 inches of precipitation per year) has resulted in luxuriant coniferous forests with fir and cedar more than two hundred feet tall and a warm green overgrowth of ferns and mosses. One of these, the Quinault Rain Forest, is close to the southern entrance nearest Olympia. Wildlife is abundant, including elk, deer, bear, mountain goats, and bald eagles. Seals are common on the fifty-seven-mile strip of primitive Pacific coastline. No roads reach far into the interior, but several hundred miles of trails crisscross the entire wilderness and provide access to scores of glaciers, waterfalls, streams, and lakes. Hiking, backpacking, mountain climbing, pack trips, fishing, and camping are popular, as is swimming at Sol Duc Hot Springs.

★ **Percival Landing Park**
   downtown N of State Av. & Water St.   *753-8380*
One-half mile of linear wooden deck begins at the extreme southern end of Budd Inlet and extends along the waterfront to a wooden observation tower with a spectacular view of the harbor, downtown, and surrounding evergreen hills and (on a clear day) Mt. Rainier. Sculptures, fountains, benches, floral plantings, restrooms, and moorage are other features of the picturesque park.

Priest Point Park
   2.5 mi. N on East Bay Dr.
Budd Inlet is the western boundary of Olympia's largest park, and there is a saltwater beach. Nature trails, gardens, recreation and picnic areas are other features of the heavily wooded park.

State Capitol Museum
   1 mi. S at 211 W. 21st Av.   *753-2580*
Pioneer artifacts and Indian exhibits related to Washington state history are housed in a Spanish-stucco mansion. Closed Mon.

★ **Trail's End**
   6 mi. SE via 79th Av. SE at 7842 Trails End Dr.   *754-4908*
"The most complete equestrian center in the Pacific Northwest"

is a special haven for horses, their owners, and their fanciers. Facilities include big indoor and outdoor arenas, a saddle shop, hundreds of box stalls and overnight stabling, plus RV hookups, a restaurant, and a saloon with live entertainment nightly. Horse shows are sponsored every weekend throughout the year.

★ **Tumwater Falls Park**
2.4 mi. S on Deschutes Way - Tumwater   943-2550
The most delightful water feature in the area is a series of small scenic waterfalls along a heavily wooded gorge of the Deschutes River between the Olympia Brewery and Capitol Lake. Carefully sited paths along both sides of the river give strollers access to the entire falls area. There are numerous places to stop and contemplate the tranquil beauty of the scene, or to have a picture-perfect Northwest-style picnic. An added attraction is the fall salmon run up the man-made fish ladders by the waterfalls.

Tumwater Historical Park
2.5 mi. S at 602 S. Deschutes Way - Tumwater   753-8583
The centerpiece of Tumwater's early settlement is a small, nicely landscaped park by a pond backed by the original Olympia brewery and a distant view of Tumwater Falls. Several restored historic structures (not including the old brewery) on the grounds are occasionally open to visitors.

★ **Wolfhaven**
12 mi. SE via Capitol Bl. at 3111 Offut Lake Rd. - Tenino 264-2775
The only nationally recognized sanctuary for wolves in the western United States welcomes visitors year-round. Guides discuss the myths and realities of wolves during tours of the refuge. Don't miss the "howl-ins" on Friday nights in summer.

SHOPPING

During the mid-1980s, major civic improvements including a waterfront park, performing arts center, and community center have helped to restore downtown Olympia to its historic status as the commercial heart of the area. Strollers and shoppers alike can enjoy both the public developments and a burgeoning array of galleries, specialty stores, and gourmet food shops.

Food Specialties
★ **Batdorf & Bronson Coffee Roasters**
downtown at 513 S. Capitol Way   786-6717
They roast their own coffee beans, and serve all kinds of fresh-brewed coffees, espresso, cappuccino, or teas with scrumptious pastries and cheesecakes (made just for them). The stylish decor of the new shop is enhanced by a background of classical music. Assorted coffee beans are sold by the pound. Closed Sun.

★ **Bayview Market Place**
downtown at 516 W. 4th Av.   352-4901
The state of the art in Northwestern grocery stores recently opened downtown by Budd Inlet. In addition to artfully arranged displays of the usual supermarket items, the big, well-lighted store offers excellent selections of: premium-quality meats and cheeses; gourmet regional and international delicacies; well-stored Northwestern and other wines; plus full lines of baked goods and deli items made here. Patrons can enjoy an upstairs dining area with a terrific view of Budd Inlet, or picnic tables by the building on a waterfront deck. Olympia's quintessential market is open twenty-four hours a day.

★ **Chattery Down**
downtown at 209 E. 5th Av.   786-5006
Scones, brioche, and pies served here with tea or coffee are delicious. The unusual dining area in a gift shop is enhanced by tables set with full linen and fresh flowers. New age music provides a nice background to high tea or an afternoon break. Closed Sun.

Chez Francois French Bakery
downtown at 201 E. 4th Av.   754-0391
French breads in a variety of shapes, and plain or filled croissants are served in a cheerful corner cafe, or to go. Closed Sun.

★ **Drees Great Addition**
downtown at 113 E. 5th Av.   357-7177
Prodigious croissants and other homemade pastries are served with coffee, espresso, or Italian sodas in Olympia's newest haven for gourmets. A tempting assortment of made-in-Washington food specialties is also displayed. Closed Sun.

★ **Lattin's Country Cider Mill**
9.4 mi. SE at 9402 Rich Rd. SE   491-7328
It's tucked away on a remote country road, but worth finding. Especially on Monday or Tuesday, when the apple sorter and presses are working, the aroma alone is worth the drive. Visitors can taste samples of apples or ciders from apple, blackberry, and other fruits pressed on the premises any day. Assorted apples or cider are sold in any quantity at a retail counter in the little factory. Closed Sun.

Olympia Cheese Company
7.5 mi. E via I-5 at 3145 Hogum Bay Rd. NE   491-5330
They've been making a variety of cheese here for more than twenty years. Visitors can taste and purchase a dozen different cheeses at a tiny entryway tasting/retail counter from 9 a.m. to 5 p.m. Closed Sun.

★ **Olympia Farmers Market**
downtown at Thurston Av. & Columbia St.
The City of Olympia has constructed a distinctive shade structure to house the state's second largest regular farmers market. It's

a delightful place to experience the superb fresh produce that is a hallmark of the Pacific Northwest. Open Thurs. thru Sun. from April to December.

★ **Pioneer Sourdough Baking Company**
  downtown at 105 W. Legion Way   352-8329
  Savory sourdough breads are the irresistible feature of a culinary shrine that opened in Olympia during the fall of 1986.

★ **Wagner's European Bakery and Cafe**
  downtown at 1013 S. Capitol Way   357-7268
  Several kinds of delicious cinnamon rolls are just one of the highlights in an outstanding full-line bakery that has been pleasing Olympians and travelers alike for almost half a century. Everything's served to go or with coffee, soup, salads, and sandwiches in the next room. Closed Sun.-Mon.

Specialty Shops

★ **Childhood's End Gallery**
  downtown at 222 W. 4th Av.   943-3724
  All kinds of arts and crafts, including some works by Northwestern artists, are nicely displayed and accompanied by classical music in a multi-room gallery.

Cornerstone Pottery
  downtown at 202 E. 4th Av.   352-9534
  Talented local potters display a variety of pottery styles and shapes in this cheerful corner shop. Closed Sun.

Fireside Book Store
  downtown at 116 E. Legion Way   352-4006
  This inviting little bookstore has comfortable armchairs for browsers. Closed Sun.

Pat's Bookery
  downtown at 522 S. Capitol Way   352-0202
  An extensive magazine selection, plus newspapers, books, and cards are sold in this well-organized, brightly lighted store.

★ **Yard Birds Shopping Center**
  downtown at 500 N. Capitol Way   943-1623
  Superabundant assortments of nautical gear and sporting goods are displayed in a sprawling complex where it's fun to browse as well as buy. This is also a good source for regional books and topo maps.

NIGHTLIFE

Olympia has a good diversity of nightlife. Numerous places feature live entertainment and dancing. Symphonies, concerts and live theater are scheduled throughout the year in the performing arts center. Nightcaps can be enjoyed in romantic firelit settings, or in plush lounges overlooking waterfalls or the inlet.

Bailey's
   2.6 mi. E at 3333 Martin Way   491-7515
There is live country/western music most nights in a very plain room next door to a steakhouse.

Carnegie's
   downtown at S. Franklin St. & E. 7th Av.   357-5550
A pianist is usually joined by others to entertain on weekends in a capacious lounge that was once part of a Carnegie library. A handsome bar has been added, but the fireplace still works and high windows still frame a view of Washington's one-time capitol.

Ebb Tide Inn
   1 mi. N at 1525 N. Washington St.   943-7770
Live music is available most nights, but in Olympia's best waterfront lounge, a window-wall view of Budd Inlet and the green hills beyond is an attraction any time.

Falls Terrace
   2.4 mi. S at 106 S. Deschutes Way - Tumwater   943-7830
This comfortably furnished lounge adjoining a fine restaurant has a close-up view of Tumwater Falls and the Olympia Brewery.

Fireside Inn
   5.8 mi. E at 7321 Martin Way - Lacey   456-6650
Live country/western music and dancing and the padded-plastic, 1950s decor appeals to an older crowd.

Malibu Fun Pub
   downtown at 118 E. 5th Av.   754-9222
On the raucous edge of the heart of town is a dark and noisy nightclub that offers whatever is the latest in live music for dancing/listening, plus occasional special events—exotic nude dancers, lip wars, etc.

Migel's
   3 mi. S at 4611 Tumwater Valley Dr. - Tumwater   352-1575
Mexican and other specialty drinks are served to patrons on sofas, plush chairs, or barstools in a greenery-filled lounge, or on a patio overlooking a golf course and the Deschutes River.

★ **The Washington Center for the Performing Arts**
   downtown at 512 S. Washington St.   753-8586
Throughout the year, Olympia's landmark theater (which opened in 1985) plays host to a full range of dramatic and musical productions, as well as performances by ballet companies, symphony orchestras, recording artists, and others.

★ **Westwater Inn**
   1.9 mi. SW at 2300 Evergreen Park Dr. SW   943-4000
Live entertainment and dancing are available most nights in the most comfortable lounge in town. Guests seated in contemporary chrome/fabric armchairs can also enjoy the fine view of Capitol Lake and green hills beyond a landscaped outdoor pool.

RESTAURANTS

Restaurants are abundant throughout the area, and many of the best are concentrated downtown. Enough feature fresh local seafood, fruits, and vegetables in light, innovative dishes or classic preparations to qualify Olympia as a budding gourmet haven. Several provide views of the area's natural charms like Budd Inlet, Tumwater Falls, and Mount Rainier.

Ben Moore's
downtown at 112 W. 4th Av.   357-7527
B-L.   *Moderate*
Olympia oysters and geoduck, when they're in season, are a couple of reasons for trying this good, old-fashioned bar and grill.

Carnegie's
downtown at E. 7th Av. & S. Franklin St.   357-5550
L-D. No L on Sat. & Sun.   *Moderate*
Seafood, steaks, and fowl are simply prepared, and served in one of the area's most unconventional dining rooms. The airy main level of a handsome one-time Carnegie library is now furnished with hardwood dining tables and armchairs, but diners are still surrounded by books and a working fireplace in the main dining room or the adjoining lounge.

★ **Crackers**
downtown at 317 E. 4th Av.   352-1900
B-L-D.   *Moderate*
All of the items on an eclectic menu—ranging from burgers through cobb salad to oysters marinara—are well brought off in a big stylish update of a 1940s diner. Good food, lush plants and wood-toned decor, an exuberant exhibition kitchen, and a main street view help explain why Crackers is usually crowded. As an added attraction, cappuccino, desserts, and meals are served into the wee hours on weekends.

Dad's Place
downtown at 303 E. 4th Av.   943-9093
B-L. Closed Sat.-Sun.   *Low*
Homemade pies like French apple, blackberry, and lemon meringue are the forte among uncomplicated American meals served in a shaped-up, very plain cafe with a choice of booths or counter service.

Ebb Tide Inn
1 mi. N at 1525 N. Washington St.   943-7770
L-D.   *Moderate*
A contemporary American menu includes some regional seafoods, but the primary feature of this land's end restaurant is an expansive picture window view of Budd Inlet and evergreen hills beyond.

★ **Especially Yogurt**
downtown at 101 N. Capitol Way   754-6480
B-L-D. No B on Sun.   *Moderate*
Bowls of seasonally fresh berries and fruits, plus humongous

homemade muffins distinguish this updated yogurt parlor, which also serves croissant sandwiches and a variety of flavors of frozen yogurt.

★ **Falls Terrace**
  2.4 mi. S at 106 S. Deschutes Way - Tumwater   943-7830
  L-D.   *Moderate*
The chef has a way with a wok and also does delicious work with a long list of dishes including many regional specialties. Big, stylish dining rooms are perfectly sited to give most diners an outstanding view of Tumwater Falls, a landscaped park, and buildings of the Olympia Brewery. The food is consistently very good and plentiful. The deservedly popular restaurant is usually full, yet service is surprisingly fast and friendly. A comfortable view-lounge adjoins.

★ **Fleur de Lys**
  .4 mi. E at 901 E. Legion Way   754-6208
  L-D. No L on Sat. Closed Sun.-Mon.   *Moderate*
Classic French dishes are skillfully prepared from fresh local products, and new delights have been created from regional specialties like geoduck and Olympia oysters. Delicious desserts made here are also served amid an aura of refinement in a converted house.

★ **Gardner's**
  downtown at 111 W. Thurston Av.   786-8466
  L-D. Closed Sun.-Mon.   *Moderate*
The fresh local seafoods (Olympia oysters, geoduck, salmon, etc.) are unforgettable. Other entrees and support dishes are also masterfully prepared from the freshest and finest available ingredients in one of Washington's most sophisticated restaurants. Wood accents, quality wall hangings, plants, and fresh flowers contribute to the romantic appeal of the intimate dining room.

★ **Jo Mamas**
  .6 mi. E at 120 N. Pear St.   943-9849
  L-D.   *Moderate*
Delicious pizzas are served here—made with a combination of whole wheat and white flour dough, and homemade tomato sauce. Several fine regional tap beers, plus homemade bread and ice creams, also contribute to the appeal of a remodeled house filled with a series of artistically constructed wooden booths, each with a feeling of privacy.

★ **La Petite Maison**
  1.1 mi. W at 2005 Ascension NW   943-8812
  L-D. No L on Sat. Closed Sun.   *Expensive*
Continental and New American cuisine are both apparent in tasty renditions of Northwest seafoods and produce emphasized on a menu that changes with the seasons. A turn-of-the-century cottage has been transformed into a series of small, nicely appointed dining rooms.

265

Little Richard's
downtown at 117 E. 5th Av.   357-6808
B-L. Closed Sun.   *Moderate*
Good homemade muffins and pies are featured, and there is an ice
cream counter, soups, salads, and sandwiches in a room where wood-
tones and stained glass are a pleasing change from the usual bright and
boring deli decor.

★ **Mason Jar**
1.8 mi. S at 478 Cleveland Av. - Tumwater   754-7776
L only.   *Moderate*
The Toll House pie here is a towering tribute to a chocolate chip
cookie. Other desserts like the peach dumplings and blueberry
cordial pie are also among the finest anywhere. For each day of
the week, different and delicious soups, salads, and sandwiches
are served, along with distinctive specials. Woven napkins and
mason jar drinking glasses contribute to the homespun atmosphere
of the wood-toned dining room.

Migel's
3 mi. S at 4611 Tumwater Valley Dr. - Tumwater   352-1575
L-D. Sun. brunch.   *Moderate*
Purists might argue that the product isn't as authentic as the
promise of the elaborate Mexican menu, or that the sauces are
too tame. But, the food is tasty and plentiful, and the big dining
rooms are comfortable—outfitted with padded booths and
armchairs at tables set with fresh flowers. Greenery is abundant,
both in the dining rooms and lounge, and beyond on a golf course
visible through picture windows.

Olympia Oyster House
downtown at 320 W. 4th Av.   943-8020
L-D.   *Moderate*
New owners have breathed life back into the area's oldest restaurant.
Oysters are the notable specialty, and the succulent little Olympia
oysters are appropriately highlighted in season. Food preparation and
decor are conventional, and there is a pleasant view of the south end of
Budd Inlet and the Promenade. A small lounge adjoins.

Pat's
5 mi. E at 6011 Pacific Av. - Lacey   459-0256
B-L.   *Low*
Pat creates delicious pies (like fresh peach in season), cinnamon rolls
(both frosted and sticky buns), and breads that make this little short
order coffee shop worth a stop.

The Place
3.5 mi. W via US 101 at 244 Madrona Beach Rd. NW   866-8213
B-L-D.   *Moderate*
Homemade biscuits, cinnamon rolls, and pies complement a wide range
of American dishes and some Mexican specialties in a little roadside
cafe with a choice of padded booth or counter service.

Prime Connection
4.8 mi. E at 5815 Lacey Blvd. SE - Lacey   *459-1515*
L-D.   *Moderate*
Alder-smoked barbecue and rock-salt prime rib are reasons enough for a visit. This newer restaurant offers casual contemporary decor in both the dining room and lounge.

Seven Gables Restaurant
1 mi. NW at 1205 W. Bay Dr.   *352-2349*
L-D. Only brunch on Sun. Closed Mon.   *Moderate*
The American dishes served here are colorful, but uninspired. A Victorian home above Budd Inlet was converted into a restaurant with decor that still reflects some of the charm of an earlier time. A couple of tables offer a nice harbor view.

Smithfield Cafe
downtown at 212 W. 4th Av.   *786-1725*
B-L-D.   *Moderate*
Coffees, pastries, and sandwiches are served in an easygoing coffee house with funky furnishings epitomized by a colorful piano.

★ **Sonny's Capital City Cafe**
downtown at 1023 S. Capitol Way   *754-5152*
B-L-D. Closed Sun.   *Moderate*
Traditional 1950s food (burgers, meat loaf, etc.) is balanced by contemporary dishes (croissant sandwiches, pasta salads, etc.). Fresh ingredients are used, and baked goods and pies are homemade. The recently opened restaurant is an artful update of post-war diner decor.

★ **The Spar**
downtown at 114 E. 4th Av.   *357-6444*
B-L-D.   *Moderate*
Generous, well-prepared offerings of homestyle American foods are complemented by an assortment of breads, pastries, and pies made on the premises. The classy old cafe with a long horseshoe counter retains much of the spirit of its turn-of-the-century origins augmented by a series of historic area photos. A bar and card room adjoin.

Urban Onion Restaurant
downtown at E. Legion Way & S. Washington St.   *943-9242*
B-L-D. Closed Sun.   *Moderate*
An eclectic assortment of contemporary dishes ranging from wok stir-fry to Mexican specialties is offered in a restored dining room of the historic Olympian Hotel.

★ **Vandees**
2.1 mi. W at 1520 Black Lake Blvd. SW   *754-4900*
B-L-D.   *Moderate*
Well-prepared, generous servings of freshly made dishes are offered, and the delicious cinnamon rolls, biscuits, and pies are all home-baked. Several Dutch-originated pancake dishes carry out the theme of the large comfortable coffee shop, and help explain why Vandees is a contender for "the best breakfast in town."

LODGING

Olympia has a wealth of natural and civilized attractions, yet accommodations are relatively scarce, and uniformly ordinary with two exceptions. Most places reduce their rates approximately 10%, apart from summer.

Aladdin Motor Inn - Best Western
downtown at 900 S. Capitol Way 352-7200
Conveniently located near both the waterfront and Capitol, this large modern motor hotel has convention facilities, a dining room and lounge, and a small outdoor pool. Each comfortably furnished room has a phone and cable color TV with movies. For toll-free reservations, call (800)528-1234.

regular room—refrigerator,	K bed...$46
regular room—	Q bed...$44

Bailey Motor Inn
2.6 mi. E at 3333 Martin Way 491-7515
This older **bargain** motel has a large indoor pool plus a restaurant and lounge. Each of the simply furnished rooms has a phone and cable color TV with movies.

newer room—	Q bed...$29
regular room—small, no air conditioning,	D bed...$27

Carriage Inn Motel
.9 mi. SE at 1211 S. Quince St. 943-4710
This modern two-level motel has a small outdoor pool. A coffee shop and lounge adjoin. Each room provides routine comforts, including a phone and cable color TV.

regular room—	Q bed...$37

Golden Gavel Motor Inn
downtown at 909 S. Capitol Way 352-8533
The best-located **bargain** motel in town is a stroll from both the waterfront and the Capitol. Each nicely furnished room in the modern, two-level motel has a phone and cable color TV.

regular room—	Q bed...$28

Governor House Hotel
downtown at 621 S. Capitol Way 352-7700
Downtown's landmark hotel is a large eight-story facility across from a park in front of the old state capitol. The complex includes convention facilities, Sylvester's dining room and bar, a coffee shop, and an outdoor pool above a parking garage. Each simply furnished room has a mini-balcony and floor-to-ceiling windows, plus a phone and cable color TV.

#703—spacious, refrigerator/wet bar, park & bay views,	Q bed...$51
8th floor lake views (several)—fine views of Capitol Lake,	Q bed...$51
regular room—	Q bed...$47

Holly Motel
2 mi. E at 2816 Martin Way   *943-3000*
An outdoor pool is the feature of this older single-level **bargain** motel. Each of the small, plain rooms has a phone and cable color TV with movies.
regular room—   Q bed...$25

Motel 6
3.3 mi. S at 400 W. Lee St. - Tumwater 98502   *943-5000*
The **bargain** chain is represented locally by a large, modern two-story motel with an outdoor pool. Each routinely furnished room has a TV.
regular room—   D bed...$23

Super 8 Motel
3.9 mi. E at 4615 Martin Way - Lacey 98503   *459-8888*
Another national chain is represented locally by a newer three-level motel. Each simply furnished room has a phone and cable color TV.
regular room—   Q bed...$35

★ **Vance Tyee Motor Inn**
3.5 mi. S at 500 Tyee Dr. - Tumwater 98502   *352-0511*
A park-like setting lends to the appeal of one of the area's largest and finest motor hotels. Sprawling modern buildings contain the casually elegant Chantrell's dining room and a lounge with live entertainment; Muffins Coffee House; a gift shop; and meeting rooms. A tennis court and an outdoor pool are in a garden setting. Each spacious, well-furnished room has a phone and cable color TV. For toll-free reservations in Washington, call (800)552-7122; elsewhere (800)426-0670.
#151,#152,#157,#158—large whirlpool in
                     separate room,   2 Q beds...$105
regular room—   1 or 2 Q beds...$50

★ **Westwater Inn**
1.9 mi. SW at 2300 Evergreen Park Dr. SW   *943-4000*
Olympia's biggest and best motor hotel is in a choice site on the heavily wooded west bluff above Capitol Lake. Attractively landscaped grounds include a large outdoor pool and whirlpool, a posh contemporary restaurant and lounge with some of the best views in town, plus convention facilities and a gift shop. Each of the spacious, well-furnished rooms has a phone and cable color TV. For toll-free reservations in Washington, call (800)562-5635; in other Western states (800)551-8500.
#102,#152—in-bath whirlpool, wet bar, lake
                     view,   K bed...$95
#318,#312—private lake, pool and hills view,   K bed...$61
regular room—   D or Q bed...$51

CAMPGROUNDS

Several campgrounds are tucked into the forests around town. The best offer complete facilities in the woods by lakes that are warm enough for swimming in the summer.

★ **Millersylvania State Park**
   11 mi. SE via I-5 & 113th Av. at 12245 Tilly Rd. S.   753-1519
   The state operates this campground in a luxuriant forest of pines
   a stroll from picturesque mile-long Deep Lake. Several beaches and
   bathhouses are provided along with fenced-off swimming areas.
   Full hookups, flush toilets, and hot (fee) showers are available.
   Each of the widely spaced sites is tree-shaded, and has a picnic
   table and fire ring/grill. Sites near the lake are surrounded by lush
   ferns. Reciprocal fee. For toll-free information (summer only) in
   Washington, call (800)562-0990.   base rate...$6

Salmon Shores Resort
   6 mi. SW at 5446 Black Lake Blvd.   357-8618
   Five hundred feet of shoreline on pretty, three-mile-long Black Lake
   is the feature of this privately owned campground. Fishing boats,
   canoes, rubber rafts, and "fun bugs" can be rented, and there is
   a boat launch. A swimming area is roped off by a grassy slope.
   Hot showers, flush toilets, and hookups are available. The closely
   spaced sites lack privacy, but each is shaded by large pines and
   has a picnic table and fire ring.   base rate...$8

SPECIAL EVENTS

Lakefair   *Capitol Lake*   *mid-July*
The park next to Capitol Lake comes alive during the second
weekend in July with a carnival, arts and crafts displays, and a
twilight parade. Hydroplane races on the lake and fireworks round
out the celebration.

★ **Harbor Days**   *downtown*   *late August or early September*
On the weekend before Labor Day, Waterfront Park and the
downtown harbor are the setting for a delightful maritime
celebration highlighted by a colorful tugboat rendezvous. Many of
the vintage and modern tugs are open for tours at Percival Landing
before the tug races. Arts, crafts, food and beer gardens, the Olympia
Farmers Market, and continuous entertainment are also part of
the fun on the waterfront.

OTHER INFORMATION

Area Code: *206*
Zip Code: *98501*
Olympia/Thurston County Chamber of Commerce
   1000 Plum St.   357-3362
Visitor Convention Bureau
   1000 Plum St.   357-3370
Washington State Division of Tourism *information hotlines*
   in Washington, call toll-free   *(800)562-4570*
   elsewhere (Mon.-Fri.) call toll-free   *(800)541-WASH*

Port Townsend, Washington

Port Townsend is a showcase for the arts in a town that time forgot. Here on the remote northeastern tip of the Olympic Peninsula is one of the West's finest collections of Victorian architecture. The appealing human scale of the unspoiled old town, and a sublime waterfront location backed by lush pastoral countryside, contribute to the magic of this special place.

Even the climate is a pleasant surprise. During the mild winters, snowfall and hard freezes are unusual. Precipitation is relatively light throughout the year because Port Townsend is in the "rain shadow" of the nearby Olympic Mountains. Vacationers fill the town to capacity in summer when warm sunny days are perfect for comfortably enjoying the area. Nearby to the southwest is the rugged grandeur of Olympic National Park. To the east, a remarkable diversity of open water, natural canals, and tiny hidden harbors in Puget Sound has been developed with parks, beaches, and marinas offering every kind of maritime recreation. Boating, fishing, clamming, beachcombing, hiking, and camping are popular near town, and there are several scenic golf courses in the area.

In 1792, Captain George Vancouver came ashore and named this site Port Townsend in honor of an English nobleman. Almost sixty years went by before settlers erected the area's first log cabin. By the 1880s, the town was booming with logging and maritime activity. New wealth was quickly translated into substantial brick and stone buildings in the waterfront business district and mansions on the adjacent bluff. During the 1890s, however, the boom collapsed as Port Townsend lost the race for shipping and railroad preeminence to Seattle and other towns. Intermittent activity at the adjoining fort and construction of a paper mill two miles away kept the town alive through a period of benign neglect which lasted for well over half a century. In 1972, the Army deeded its turn-of-the-century military complex to the Washington State Parks and Recreation Commission. Artists and craftsmen began to rediscover the natural beauty of the area at about the same time, and to skillfully restore and use the legacy of Victorian structures.

Solid rows of nineteenth century brick buildings still line the downtown waterfront. Many house studios and shops displaying excellent locally produced arts and crafts. A cluster of restaurants with a special penchant for fine breakfasts, plus several atmospheric bars, lend additional distinction. Even the adjoining fort site has been converted into a major cultural and recreational asset. It is now the home for Port Townsend's arts festivals and symposiums. There are only a couple of conventional lodgings in town. As a delightful alternative, many splendid century-old homes and mansions on the blufftops have been carefully restored to serve as charming bed-and-breakfast inns filled with authentic period pieces or locally made art objects. Visitors who want to sleep closer to nature will find an excellent in-town campground at a peaceful beachfront site near the fort.

Elevation:

100 feet

Population (1980):

6,067

Population (1970):

5,241

Location:

50 miles Northwest
of Seattle

Port Townsend, Washington
WEATHER PROFILE
Vokac Weather Rating

V.W.R.*		Jan.	Feb.	Mar.	Apr.	May	June	July	Aug.	Sep.	Oct.	Nov.	Dec.

		Jan.	Feb.	Mar.	Apr.	May	June	July	Aug.	Sep.	Oct.	Nov.	Dec.
V.W.R.*		0	0	2	4	7	8	10	10	8	5	1	0
Temperature													
Ave. High		44	47	51	57	63	67	71	71	67	59	50	46
Ave. Low		35	36	38	41	45	49	51	51	49	45	40	37
Precipitation													
Inches Rain		2.2	1.7	1.6	1.2	1.4	1.4	0.7	0.7	1.1	1.6	2.4	2.4
Inches Snow		3	1	-	-	-	-	-	-	-	-	-	1

*V.W.R. = Vokac Weather Rating: probability of mild (warm & dry) weather on any given day.

Forecast

	V.W.R.*	Temperatures Daytime	Evening	Precipitation
Jan.	0 Adverse	chilly	chilly	frequent showers/snow flurries
Feb.	0 Adverse	chilly	chilly	frequent showers
Mar.	2 Adverse	cool	chilly	frequent showers
Apr.	4 Adverse	cool	chilly	frequent showers
May	7 Good	cool	cool	occasional showers
June	8 Very Good	warm	cool	occasional showers
July	10 Great	warm	cool	infrequent showers
Aug.	10 Great	warm	cool	infrequent showers
Sep.	8 Very Good	warm	cool	occasional showers
Oct.	5 Moderate	cool	cool	frequent showers
Nov.	1 Adverse	cool	chilly	frequent showers
Dec.	0 Adverse	chilly	chilly	frequent showers

Summary

Carved out of a splendid evergreen forest at the isolated northeastern tip of the Olympic Peninsula lies Port Townsend. The town has a surprisingly mild four season climate including one of the West's longest growing seasons outside of California. Even fan palms flourish outdoors in this favored location—warmed by the adjoining strait and protected by the "rain shadow" of the neighboring Olympic Mountains. **Winter** is persistently chilly, and damp from frequent showers and rare snow flurries. **Spring** temperatures are cool, but frost-free, so frequent drizzles engender luxuriant new growth and flowers relatively early in the season. **Summer** weather is excellent. Long warm days, cool evenings, and infrequent sprinkles invite exploration of this seaside hideaway and its tranquil environs. Warm, sunny days continue into **fall**, but cool weather and frequent showers begin again after Halloween.

ATTRACTIONS & DIVERSIONS

★ *Bicycling*
Port Townsend Emporium (Coast to Coast Store)
downtown at 1102 Water St.   *385-5900*
An excellent system of tree-shaded byways provides access to hidden
harbors, sandy beaches, and tiny coastal villages. For leisurely
explorations, bicycles can be rented here by the hour or day.

★ **Chetzemolka Park**
.7 mi. N at Blaine/Jackson Sts.
On a bluff overlooking Admiralty Inlet is a large town park named
after a friendly Indian chief. It features panoramic marine views
with snow-capped Mt. Baker in the distance; access to a long rocky
beach; well-spaced picnic facilities; and beautifully landscaped
grounds with meandering streams, ponds, flower gardens, and a gazebo.

★ **Coupeville**
30 min. ride via Keystone Ferry plus 5 mi. N on WA 20 678-5434
Here is a tiny seaside village with much that is beautifully preserved
from a long and colorful history. Concentrated along the waterfront
are a picturesque wharf; carefully restored Victorian homes and
a blockhouse; plus a worthwhile assortment of specialty shops. **The
Coupeville Harbor Store** (678-3625) at the end of the wharf rents
boats and bicycles and sells provisions and light meals. **Toby's
Tavern** (678-4222) is a shaped-up, nearby source of tap beer and
short order foods, plus pool and a picture window view of the
cove from several padded booths. Coupeville's notable restaurants
and lodgings are listed elsewhere in this chapter.

★ **Courthouse**
.5 mi. SW at Jefferson/Walker Sts.
Built in 1891, this monumental brick building is a masterwork of
Victorian overstatement. The 124-foot-tall clock tower is an
enduring source of pride for residents, and a landmark for mariners.
One of the two oldest courthouses in the state, the building still
serves as it always did. Visitors marvel at the expansive interior
spaces and unadulterated Victorian craftsmanship that convey a
museum-like quality in contrast with the building's continuing
governmental role.

★ **Customs House**
downtown at Washington/Van Buren Sts.
This imposing stone building, constructed in 1893, is another
showcase of "living history." The post office and federal offices are
housed behind public areas that remain relatively untouched by
time—with polished redwood trim, inlaid marble floors, curved glass
windows, and elaborate wrought-iron staircases. Topping stone
columns at the south entrance are faces of the friendly Indian
chief "Duke of York" and his wife.

Fort Flagler State Park
20 mi. SE off WA 20 on Morrowstone Island   385-1259
Established in the 1890s, the fort was deactivated in 1937. The waterfront site features sandy beaches, picnic facilities, a campground, boat launch and moorage (rental boats are available), nature study trails, and a lighthouse. Recreation opportunities include beachcombing, saltwater swimming, fishing, and boating.

★ **Fort Worden State Park**
2 mi. N via Walker & Cherry Sts.   385-4730
The state now operates the fort, built just before the turn of the century, as a center for cultural workshops and symposiums. Carefully maintained structures lining the parade ground include a number of imposing Victorian houses that were officers' quarters. They are available for vacation rentals. Within easy walking distance are dense forests bordered by long expanses of beach. Gun emplacements overlooking Puget Sound, and the Point Wilson Lighthouse (built in 1870 and operated by the Coast Guard), are highlights of shore hikes. The Marine Science Center (housed on the dock) has "wet tables" where local sea creatures may be viewed and touched, plus many glass tanks. A popular campground has been provided near the beach.

Golf

★ **Port Ludlow Golf Course**
18 mi. SE off WA 20 - Port Ludlow   437-2222
Lush fairways are flanked by towering firs at this beautifully designed 18-hole championship course overlooking Admiralty Inlet. Washington's top-rated golfing facility is open to the public and includes a pro shop, putting green, driving range, club and cart rentals, and a restaurant and lounge in the Resort at Port Ludlow.

★ **Haller Fountain**
downtown at Washington/Taylor Sts.
At the bottom of a long scenic stairway that connects downtown with the blufftop is a tiny garden park with a wonderfully old-fashioned fountain sculpture. The bronze sea nymph "Innocence" has been here since 1909.

Hiking

★ **Port Townsend Bay Co.**
downtown at 1042 Water St.   385-5279
The best way to experience the wealth of historic structures, parks, beaches, and forests in and around town is on foot. Here is the area's best outfitter, with fine selections of U.S.G.S. topographic maps, books about the area, outdoor equipment, and clothing.

★ *Historic Buildings*
Authentic Victorian structures are everywhere in the Northwest's most unspoiled concentration of late-Victorian architecture. Many are listed on the "National Register of Historic Places." Most are

still in use either for their original purposes or for compatible adaptations. An easily followed brochure with a map and descriptions of historic sites is available at the Chamber of Commerce.

★ **Langley**
30 min. ride via Keystone Ferry & 23 mi. SE via WA 525 321-6765
This lovely village by the sea is so picturesque that it was recently used as the setting for a major motion picture. The compact town center has an appealing assortment of arts and crafts and antique shops, plus an impressive market (the **Star Store**) and a bookstore (the **Moonraker**) with a desirable regional collection. The after-hours social center of the area is the **Dog House**, a captivating tavern that is more than the sum of a handsome wood back bar, waterfront view, good casual food, tap beer, pool, and darts. Langley's notable restaurants and lodgings are listed elsewhere in this chapter.

★ *Library*
.3 mi. NW at 1220 Lawrence St.   *385-3181*
The Port Townsend Public Library, one of the few Carnegie libraries still used as a public building, was built in 1913. It exudes nostalgia, especially in the periodical reading area, with upholstered sofa and chairs in front of a wood-burning brick fireplace. Closed Sun.-Mon.

★ **Olympic National Forest**
28 mi. SW via WA 20 & US 101   *765-3368*
Surrounding Olympic National Park are lush rain forests; one of the world's heaviest stands of Douglas fir; abundant wildlife— including Roosevelt elk; and sparkling lakes, streams and rivers in picturesque canyons far below glacier-capped peaks. Hundreds of miles of hiking trails and self-guided nature trails lead to camping, hiking, hunting, fishing, river running, and swimming sites.

★ **Olympic National Park**
55 mi. SW via WA 20 & US 101   *452-9235*
More than 1,400 square miles of awe-inspiring wilderness extends from glacier-clad peaks to ocean shores. The wettest climate in the coterminous United States (averaging 140 inches of precipitation a year) has created luxuriant coniferous rain forests in the western river valleys. From the spectacular Hurricane Ridge Highway, there are breathtaking panoramas of Mt. Olympus (the highest peak at 7,965 feet) and dozens of glaciers that lend a shimmering brilliance to the extremely rugged mountains at the top of the peninsula. Wildlife is abundant, including elk, bear, deer, and bald eagles. Seals are common on the rocky fifty-seven-mile strip of primitive Pacific coastline. Hundreds of miles of trails (including many self-guided nature trails) provide access to scores of lakes, streams, and waterfalls. Hiking, backpacking, mountain climbing, horseback and pack trips, fishing, and camping are popular, as is swimming at Sol Duc Hot Springs.

★ **Port Gamble**
   28 mi. SE via WA 20 & WA 104   *297-2311*
Founded in 1853, this tiny nineteenth century town was built by
a logging company that still owns it. What may be the oldest
continuously operating sawmill in America is here. The company
has restored/preserved more than thirty Victorian homes, churches,
and commercial buildings on a picturesque site overlooking Puget
Sound. Even street lights have been replaced with gas lamp replicas.
There is a historical museum, and a sea-and-shore museum with
an outstanding shell collection.

Poulsbo
   34 mi SE via WA 20, WA 104 & WA 3   *779-4848*
This picturesque little harborside community has a distinctive
Scandinavian flair. There are numerous specialty shops, and **Sluys
Bakery** with a tempting full line of baked goods. Several casual
restaurants overlook the marina. The **Scandia Garden
Smorgasbord** is an all-you-can-eatery in a converted landmark,
and the **Ruptured Duck Tavern** is a popular sports bar with pool,
ping pong, foosball, darts, and electronic games.

Sportfishing
Charter boat services feature scenic tours, salmon fishing in season,
and year-round bottom fishing. All bait and tackle are provided.
For reservations, contact:
   Calm Sea Charters *.3 mi. NE at Point Hudson*   *385-5288*
   Dogfish Charters *1 mi. SW at Port of Port Townsend*   *385-3575*

★ **Whidbey Island**
   30 min. ride via Keystone Ferry   *385-0550*
The Port Townsend-Keystone ferry leaves frequently for the half
hour trip to Whidbey Island—the largest in Puget Sound. Numerous
scenic byways are well worth exploring by car, bicycle, or on foot.

★ **Whitney Rhododendron Gardens**
   35 mi. S on US 101 - Brinnon   *796-4411*
Especially in May when these giant shrubs are in fullest bloom,
this garden nursery is a floral wonderland. Closed Dec.-Jan.

Winery
   Neuharth Winery
   32 mi. W via US 101 on Still Rd. - Sequim   *683-9652*
Since 1979, classic varietals and several specialty grape wines have
been produced here, primarily from grapes purchased from eastern
Washington growers. Neuharth is the nation's most northwesterly
winery with a tasting room. Tasting, tours, and sales (normally)
9:30-5:30 Wed.-Sun.

SHOPPING

Downtown, on Washington and Water Streets between the
waterfront and a nearby bluff, is one of the most picturesque

concentrations of Victorian structures anywhere. Rows of solid brick buildings now house distinctive gift and gourmet shops, antique stores, and arts and crafts studios, as well as restaurants, bars, and lodgings.

Food Specialties

★ **Aldrich's**
.3 mi. NW at 940 Lawrence St. 385-0500
Occasionally, neighborhood grocery stores develop a style that transcends their status as a source of staples. This one has—with everything from premium regional produce and international food specialties to an appetizing selection of gourmet takeout foods produced by an extraordinary local caterer. It's a fine place to assemble the right stuff for a first-class picnic or for any culinary festivity.

★ **Bread and Roses Bakery**
downtown at 230 Quincy St. 385-1044
The beauty of the roses out front is matched by the quality of the breads and pastries made in one of the finest full-line bakeries in the West. Scones, galettes, and traditional baked goods like cinnamon rolls, croissants, and muffins are available to go, or they may be enjoyed with savory coffee and homemade preserves on a pleasant rear deck shaded by an apple tree.

★ **Elevated Ice Cream Company**
downtown at 627 Water St. 385-1156
Many flavors of homemade ice cream, fruit-based Italian ices, delicious baked goods, and hand-dipped chocolates made here are served to go, or in a charming parlor with artwork lining the walls. There is also an espresso bar and a sundeck overlooking the bay in this contender for "the best ice cream parlor in the West."

Showcase Bakery
downtown at 229 Taylor St. 385-2500
This full-line carryout bakery features delicious pastries, cookies, donuts, and breads. Closed Sun.

★ **The Wine Seller**
downtown at 940 Water St. 385-7673
A fine selection of Northwestern wines heads an extensive premium wine collection. There are also many imported beers, roasted coffees, teas, and cheeses. A tasting bar for wines and espresso is available daily in this attractive shop on the main street.

Specialty Shops

★ **Earthenworks**
downtown at 1002 Water St. 385-0328
A collection of fine pottery, wood works, wall hangings, jewelry, and woven goods created primarily by local and regional artists is beautifully exhibited on two levels of a large, century-old building.

★ **Great Expectations**
  downtown at 630 Water St.   385-3091
Bentwood straw brooms; sculptured candles (including a big one
shaped like a whale); "permanent" sand castles; ceramic faces; pot
pets; kaleidoscopes; cut glass oil lamps; and many other unusual
handmade collectibles are skillfully showcased. Bare brick walls
and the wooden floor of a historic building enrich the displays'
appeal.

Imprint Bookstore
  downtown at 820 Water St.   385-3643
Books of regional interest are a feature among many well-organized
displays in an inviting shop.

Liz's Loft
  downtown at 1010 Water St.   385-0773
A Northwestern theme unites a potpourri of arts and crafts by
regional artists and others in a historic building.

★ **North by Northwest**
  downtown at 630 Water St.   385-0955
Indian arts and crafts ranging from baskets and sculptures to wool
sweaters and hats, plus a good collection of books regarding
Northwestern Indians, are nicely displayed in a converted Victorian
building.

★ **Port Townsend Art Gallery Bookstore**
  downtown at 725 Water St.   385-1926
Multimedia art works and a fine selection of books, maps, and
magazines about the Northwest are highlights. The full-line
bookstore is in a high-ceilinged, brick-walled room with a waterfront
view.

NIGHTLIFE

Distinctive places for evening entertainment and refreshments
range from casual, comfortably furnished taverns in restored
century-old buildings to posh view lounges in contemporary resorts.

Manresa Lounge
  1.7 mi. SW at Sheridan/7th Sts.   385-5750
When it's working properly, the computer-operated grand piano
is an eerie but pleasant surprise in a cozy tucked-away lounge
outfitted with padded armchairs, sofas, and barstools.

Paddington's Pub
  downtown at 923 Washington St.   385-6536
Live entertainment is offered nightly in this multilevel hideaway
tavern, and there is an outdoor beer garden.

★ **The Resort at Port Ludlow**
  18 mi. SE off WA 20 - Port Ludlow   437-2222
Downstairs from the Harbor Master Restaurant is the Wreck Room,
a large modern lounge with a spectacular window wall overlooking

a picturesque bay. Live music for listening or dancing is offered almost every night.

★ **Sea Galley**
  downtown at 106 Taylor St.   *385-2992*
Live entertainment attracts crowds on weekends for dancing, but the real feature is that this is the only on-the-water lounge in town. Large windows give maximum exposure to a tranquil waterfront scene, and there is a small adjoining deck over the water. A seafood restaurant adjoins.

★ **Town Tavern**
  downtown at Water/Quincy Sts.   *no phone*
Periodic live entertainment and dancing draw crowds to Port Townsend's classic old-time tavern. This unspoiled Victorian showplace captures the community's spirit with its well-worn wooden floor, high ceiling and tall windows adorned with hanging plants, resplendent polished wood back bar, much-used pot-bellied stove, cozy balcony seating area, and an arresting painting of a nude lady; plus pool tables, more than a half dozen beers on tap, and wines by the glass.

RESTAURANTS

Port Townsend has become a haven of homestyle American cuisine emphasizing fresh local seafood and produce. Several of the best restaurants are in artistically restored Victorian structures, and some dining rooms provide fine views of Puget Sound.

★ **The Bayview**
  .3 mi. SW at 1590 Water St.   *385-1461*
  B-L-D.   *Low*
Homemade breakfasts, including an assortment of tasty crepe-style omelets, contribute to the enduring popularity of this wood-and-fabric, contemporary cafe/dining room. The restaurant was built over the water, and the panoramic view is one of the most beguiling anywhere.

★ **The Captain Whidbey**
  30 min. on ferry & 7 mi. N via Shoreline Hwy.- Coupeville 678-4097
  B-L-D.   *Moderate*
Northwestern specialties with an emphasis on freshness and quality ingredients are prepared by a chef with an excellent background in Continental cuisine. A beach-stone fireplace and intimate cove view lend appeal to the romantic wood-trimmed dining room of the venerable inn.

Fountain Cafe
  downtown at 920 Washington St.   *385-1364*
  L-D. Closed Sun.   *Moderate*
Homemade soups and desserts, unusual sandwiches and salads, and daily fresh seafood specials are all reasons for trying this

charming little dining room. Extra touches—like fresh flower bouquets—reflect the owners' concern for details.

The Half Shell Restaurant
downtown at 630 Water St.   *385-6677*
D only.   *Moderate*
Fresh seafoods and vegetables are simply prepared and served amidst eclectic decor in a converted historic building.

★ **La Fonda**
.7 mi. SW at 2330 Washington St.   *385-4627*
L-D. No L on Sat. & Sun.   *Moderate*
Traditional and contemporary Mexican-style dishes are conscientiously prepared and generously served with homemade salsas and chips. Whitewashed stucco, tile, and carved wood trim, plus high-backed wooden chairs, fresh flowers and candles, give the terraced dining rooms a genuine south-of-the-border feeling.

Landfall Restaurant
downtown at 412 Water St.   *385-5814*
B-L-D. No D on Mon.-Thurs.   *Moderate*
Fresh ingredients are used in an assortment of omelets in the morning, and in local seafoods and Mexican dishes. A handcrafted "greenhouse" room with a metal fireplace and picnic tables, as well as the original rustic little cafe, have an intimate view of an adjacent marina.

Lanza's
.3 mi. NW at 1020 Lawrence St.   *385-6221*
D only. Closed Mon.   *Moderate*
A wide assortment of pizzas and traditional Southern Italian dishes are served in a modish dining room where live music is periodically offered with dinner.

Le Quai
30 min. on ferry & 25 mi. SE at 4813 S. WA 525 - Clinton 321-1071
D only. Closed Mon.   *Moderate*
A soup tureen and fresh salad accompany a selection of French-country entrees ranging from prawns provencale to pepper steak or beef Wellington. The simply furnished little dining room is enhanced by fresh flowers and candles at each table.

★ **Lido's Restaurant & Inn**
downtown at 925 Water St.   *385-7111*
L-D.   *Moderate*
Fresh local seafoods (like pink scallops from Port Townsend Bay or salmon stuffed with Dungeness crab) are featured—broiled, baked, sauteed, or in chowders or stews—along with homemade pastas. The popular restaurant was recently expanded and remodeled in a century-old building that now has dining on two levels (including a harbor-view room); a cellar lounge; and an upstairs inn.

Manresa Castle
1.7 mi. S at Sheridan/7th Sts. 385-5750
B-L-D. *Expensive*
Conventional Continental dishes are served in a large, casual dining room. A smaller (nonsmoking) dining room/bar is a well-preserved example of Victorian decor with glossy wood paneling, hardwood trim and brass fittings, and high double-hung windows with a view of Port Townsend and the bay. A piano lounge is downstairs.

Michael's
30 min. on ferry & 5 mi. N via WA 20 - Coupeville 678-5480
L-D. No L on Tues.-Fri. Closed Mon. *Expensive*
Northwestern seafoods, beef, and chicken dishes are prepared by the talented-but-unpredictable chef-owner of this casual dining room tucked away in the back of a small shopping complex.

Mike's Place
30 min. on ferry & 23 mi. SE via WA 525 - Langley 321-6575
B-L-D. *Low*
Cinnamon rolls, biscuits, and good-looking pies compensate for the really plain decor and lack of view in this popular eatery.

★ **Nancy's Place**
8 mi. SE at 2380 Rhody Dr. - Hadlock 385-5285
B-L-D. *Moderate*
Scrumptious homemade breakfast pastries, breads, and dessert pies all contribute to the appeal of an all-American roadside coffee shop where "from scratch" still means something.

★ **Quilcene Cafe**
25 mi. S on US 101 - Quilcene 765-3541
B-L-D. *Low*
Superb homemade almond rolls, cinnamon rolls, biscuits, seasonally fresh fruit and berry pies, and breads (available to go), plus flavorful Quilcene oyster dishes, are highlights of an unaffected old-fashioned roadside cafe with a choice of booths, tables and chairs, or counter stools.

The Resort at Port Ludlow
18 mi. SE via WA 20 & Oak Bay Rd. - Port Ludlow 437-2222
B-L-D. *Expensive*
The Harbormaster Restaurant offers a contemporary American menu (salmon, monkfish, prime rib, New York steak, etc.), tables set with fresh flowers and chrome candles, and "perfect" Northwestern scenery through windows on three sides of the dining room.

★ **The Salal Cafe**
downtown at 634 Water St. 385-6532
B-L. *Moderate*
Some of the best breakfasts in the Northwest are served here from fresh local ingredients skillfully prepared with a light touch. A cheerful solarium-style back room is decorated with excellent locally produced wall hangings.

Sea Galley
downtown at Water/Taylor Sts. — 385-2992
B-L-D. — Moderate
Seafoods, steaks, and a salad bar are featured, along with nautical decor and marine views in a contemporary wharfside dining room. Lunches are also served in a comfortable lounge with an even better view of Puget Sound.

The Sea Gull
30 min. on ferry & 5 mi. N via WA 20 - Coupeville — 678-6865
B-L-D. Only brunch on Sun. — Moderate
Simply prepared local fresh seafoods and produce are featured throughout the week, and showcased during the Friday night seafood buffet. This restaurant (new in 1986) is on the downtown waterfront with picture window views of Penn Cove and Mt. Baker from two comfortably furnished dining levels.

Sea Shanty Inn
downtown at 711 Water St. — 385-1336
B-L. Closed Mon. — Moderate
American favorites are simply prepared, and served in a comfortable little wood-trimmed coffee shop with a view of the main street.

★ **Sunshine Grill & Bar-B-Q**
.3 mi. NW at 1025 Lawrence St. — 385-7588
B-L-D. — Low
Alder-smoked barbecue is the specialty—used to prepare beef and pork ribs, turkey, chicken, and all kinds of burgers. Breakfast omelets with homemade biscuits are also delicious, as are homemade pies from fresh seasonal fruit. The wood/brick/green plants decor is warm and cheerful, and each table is set with fresh flowers.

Three Crabs
38 mi. W: 33 mi. W via US 101 & 5 mi. N - Dungeness — 683-4264
L-D. — Low
Local Dungeness crab is the specialty—cracked, on toast, in omelets, etc. It is served fresh in season (October-March) along with other fresh seafood, including geoduck—a giant local clam. A family-oriented fish shack has grown into a large, easygoing restaurant with several dining rooms with a bay view beyond the parking lot.

Timber House Restaurant
26 mi. S on US 101 - Quilcene — 765-3339
L-D. Closed Tues. — Moderate
Local oysters and other seafoods (many breaded and deep-fried) are featured, along with steaks and chicken dishes, in this long-established roadhouse. The large, rough-hewn dining room is outfitted with comfortable armchairs and plastic-coated, etched plank tables, plus many green plants. There is a pleasant forest view from many windows, and a cozy lounge adjoins.

Tyee Restaurant
30 min. on ferry & 4 mi. N at 405 S. Main St. - Coupeville 678-6616
B-L-D. Low
Tasty homemade muffins and pies complement American-style
dishes in a nostalgic roadside cafe attractively outfitted with
chrome-stooled counter tables set with fresh flowers.

Waterfront Pizza
downtown at 951 Water St. 385-6629
L-D. Moderate
The regular, sourdough, or whole wheat crusts are homemade, like
the sauce—and very good. It's available by the slice or more, mostly
to go since there's only counter stool seating in the tiny room.

★ **Water Street Deli-Restaurant**
downtown at 926 Water St. 385-2422
L-D. Moderate
Design-your-own-sandwiches are featured, along with homemade
soups (the clam bisque is superb) and salads for lunch, while dinners
range from hunter's steak to baked salmon. A tantalizing array
of homemade desserts is displayed all day, along with assorted
Northwest premium wines and beers. A century-old building has
been converted into a distinctive deli with hardwood floors; church
pew, movie house, and other unusual seating; plus eclectic bric-
a-brac and wall hangings.

LODGING

With an unsurpassed collection of Victorian structures, it is not
surprising that Port Townsend has become one of the West's bed-
and-breakfast capitals. There are very few conventional motels or
other accommodations. From late fall through early spring, rates
are usually at least 10% less than those shown apart from weekends.

Bishop Victorian Guest Suites
downtown at 714 Washington St. 385-6122
An old apartment building in the heart of town was recently
thoroughly upgraded. Each spacious unit has some period pieces,
plus a phone, cable color TV, and a kitchen.

#18,#20—1 BR, corner, intimate town/water view, D bed...$60
#22—1 BR, corner, fine bay view, D bed...$60
regular room— D bed...$60

★ **The Captain Whidbey**
ferry & 7 mi. N via Shoreline Hwy. - Coupeville 98239 678-4097
On a bluff over Penn Cove is a charming turn-of-the-century inn
made entirely of distinctive madrona logs. Both the lobby and dining
room have a big beach-stone fireplace, and a picturesque view of
the cove and mountains beyond. A full range of accommodations
is available, and all are furnished, in part, with antiques and plush

feather beds.

cottage—small 1 BR cabin, pvt. bath, fireplace, cove view,	D bed...$75
lagoon room—spacious, pvt. bath, pvt. veranda, cove view,	D bed...$65
regular room—shared bath,	D bed...$57

Caroline's Country Cottage

ferry & 23 mi. SE: 215 6th St. (Box 459)-Langley 98260 221-8709
On a hill that's a bit of a hike from the cove is a very handsome bed-and-breakfast inn. Carefully manicured grounds include an outdoor hot tub and a delightful gazebo in a garden. Complimentary breakfasts and appetizers with wine in the afternoon are prepared by the gourmet hostess. Each beautifully furnished room has a private bath and a view of the sea.

regular room—	Q bed...$60

The Coupeville Inn

ferry & 5 mi. N: 200 NW Coveland - Coupeville 98239 678-6668
Coupeville's first downtown motel is in an inviting little two-story building on a slope above the waterfront. Continental breakfast is complimentary. Each spacious, tastefully furnished room has a phone and cable color TV.

view room—pvt. balcony, fine town/harbor/Mt. Baker view,	Q bed...$65
regular room—forest view,	Q bed...$44

Fort Worden State Park

2 mi. N via Walker & Cherry Sts. (Box 574)   *385-4730*
This beautifully sited ex-military base includes a remarkably intact cluster of turn-of-the-century buildings. Several of the large officer's houses (ranging from two to six bedrooms) have been refurbished as vacation rentals. While you can't rent the commanding officer's house (now a museum), you can get an isolated, simply refurbished blue bungalow that overlooks it and has a panoramic view of Admiralty Inlet.

"Blissful Vista"—1½ BR cottage, kit., raised brick fireplace, LR with view windows on 3 sides, tiny extra BR, sea view from	T & Q beds...$49
regular unit—2 BR house, some water views,	2 T & D beds...$59

Heritage House Bed & Breakfast

.3 mi. SW at 305 Pierce St. at Washington St.   *385-6800*
A stately century-old residence near a bluff above downtown and the bay has been skillfully converted into an elegant bed-and-breakfast inn. Each of the guest rooms is exquisitely furnished in authentic Victoriana. A Continental breakfast is complimentary.

"Lily"—full bath, French doors to semi-pvt. balcony, windows on 3 sides, marine view from 4-poster	D bed...$76

"Lilac"—corner, spacious, blue tones, fine bay view,   D bed...$51
"Peach Blossom"—foldaway tin clawfoot tub,
                high Victorian   D bed...$66
regular room—tiny, garden view,   D bed...$38

★ **The James House**
downtown at 1238 Washington St.   *385-1238*
This grand Victorian mansion, the first bed-and-breakfast inn in the Northwest, commands a sweeping view of downtown and the waterways from a blufftop location. All rooms are furnished in period antiques. A complimentary Continental breakfast is served.
"Bridal Suite"—clawfoot tub bath, fireplace, pvt.
              balc., bay windowed sitting
              room, fine bay view,   D bed...$85
#3—shared bath, several windows, fine harbor
    views,   D bed...$60
regular room—shared bath,   D bed...$52

Lizzie's
.4 mi. W at 731 Pierce St.   *385-4168*
An Italianate Victorian residence has been carefully restored into a charming bed-and-breakfast inn. All rooms feature period furnishings, and a gourmet Continental breakfast is complimentary.
"Lizzie's Room"—fireplace, bay window alcove,
              clawfoot tub, half-canopied   Q bed...$79
"Daisy's Room"—shared bath, bay view from
              4-window alcove,   K bed...$55
regular room "Hope's Room"—shared bath,   D bed...$42

Manresa Castle
1.7 mi. S at Sheridan/7th Sts.   *385-5750*
The town's largest lodging facility is a landmark mansion with more than forty rooms. Built by the town's first mayor in Victorian times, it was acquired by Jesuits in the 1920s and enlarged to serve as a seminary. In the last decade, it has been restored to some of its turn-of-the-century distinction, with formal gardens, antiques, a restaurant, and a lounge. Each room has some period furnishings, a phone, color TV, and a private bath. For toll-free reservations in Washington, call (800)732-1281.
#302 "Skyline Tower Suite"—extraordinary
              round room with 5 large
              rounded windows, brass
              bed overlooks town/water, D & Q beds...$90
#200 "Honeymoon Tower Suite"—stately round
              room with 3 rounded
              town/water view windows, K bed...$90
regular room—   D bed...$65

Palace Hotel
downtown at 1004 Water St.   *385-0773*
A handsome, nearly century-old brick building in the heart of town is now a small Victorian-style hotel. All rooms feature antiques and have a cable color TV.
"Marie's Suite"—lg. BR/parlor, kitchenette,
        fireplace, great main street &
        harbor view,   Q bed...$62
#9A—private bath,   D bed...$38
regular room—shared bath,   D bed...$32

Port Townsend Motel
.3 mi. SW at 2020 Washington St.   *385-2211*
This conventional motel has a convenient location near downtown and the bay. Each of the nicely furnished rooms has a phone and cable color TV with movies.
view rooms—spacious, 2nd (top) fl., distant
        marine view,   Q bed...$54
regular room—   Q bed...$44

★ **The Resort at Port Ludlow**
18 mi. SE at 781 Walker Way - Port Ludlow 98365   *437-2222*
Naturalistic contemporary architecture and decor distinguish this large bayside resort. Amenities include two pools (an indoor pool, and a large outdoor pool with a fine bay view), sauna, squash court, recreation room with pool and ping pong tables, seven tennis courts, beach and saltwater swimming lagoon; plus (a fee for) an 18-hole championship golf course, rental bicycles, rental boats of all kinds, fishing gear, and sail or powered boat charters at the marina. There is also a large and elegant harbor-view dining room and a view lounge with entertainment. Each beautifully furnished unit has a phone and cable color TV. For toll-free reservations in Washington, call (800)732-1239.
#610—1 BR loft suite, stone fireplace, private
        deck, kitchen, fine bay view,   Q bed...$126
#223,#158—deluxe waterside BR, excellent bay
        view, private deck,   K bed...$99
#607,#611—deluxe waterside BR, fine bay view,
        pvt. deck,   Q bed...$99
regular room—view of landscaped grounds,   Q bed...$89

The Tides Inn
.4 mi. SW at 1807 Water St.   *385-0595*
This modern little single-level motel offers the only conventional accommodations right on the water. Each comfortably furnished unit has a phone and cable color TV.
#20—kitchenette, shared deck, several
        windows view downtown/bay,   Q bed...$75

#25—private water view from corner windows, deck,   Q bed...$65

#26,#27,#28—front windows have pvt. water view, deck,   Q bed...$65

#31—private corner window view of water, deck,   Q bed...$50

#24—water view,   Q bed...$45

regular room—   Q bed...$40

★ **Whidbey House**
   ferry & 23 mi. SE: 106 1st St. (Box 156)-Langley 98260 221-7115
   For a romantic retreat, this secluded bed-and-breakfast inn in the heart of Langley is unbeatable. Quality antiques, fresh fruit and flowers, a Continental breakfast, and a sherry decanter in every room are among the special touches. Five beautifully furnished guest rooms are tucked away on a hillside by the waterfront. Each has a private bath and a waterfront view.

   upstairs suites—fireplace,   Q bed...$65

   regular room—lower level, deck,   Q bed...$65

CAMPGROUNDS

There are few campgrounds in the area. The best adjoins town and offers complete camping and recreation facilities on a picturesque sandspit next to Puget Sound.

★ **Fort Worden State Park**
   2 mi. N via Walker & Cherry Sts.   *385-4730*
   The state has provided a well-situated campground at the base of a heavily wooded hill between two sandy beaches overlooking Puget Sound. Features include saltwater swimming (for the hearty) and fishing, scuba diving, beachcombing, clamming, boating, a boat ramp, and nature trails. Flush toilets and hot showers are available. All sites have a picnic table, fire ring/grill, and hookups. Reciprocal fee.   base rate...$9

SPECIAL EVENTS

★ **Rhododendron Festival**   *in and around town*   *mid-May*
   A flower show; coronation and dance; sports events; arts and crafts fair; sailing, balloon, and bed races; parades; fireworks; and a fish fry are all included in a nine-day celebration that coincides with the peak bloom of the Northwest's loveliest shrubs.

★ **Celebration of American Arts** *Ft. Worden St. Pk. mid-June to Sept.*
   A series of special events attracts nearly one thousand professional and amateur participants from around the U.S. and Canada to workshops conducted by luminaries in the disciplines of dance, writing, jazz, chamber music, and traditional folk music. The public is invited to attend exhibits, readings, dances, and performances.

★ **Wooden Boat Festival** *on the waterfront in town* *early Sept.*
A fine display of boats is the highlight of a celebration that brings
seafarers and marine craftsmen together for nautical festivities and
a series of workshops, symposiums, films, and demonstrations.

OTHER INFORMATION

Area Code: *206*
Zip Code: *98368*
Port Townsend Chamber of Commerce
  .8 mi. SW at 2437 Sims Way *385-2722*

Index

About the Author

David Vokac, born in Chicago, grew up on a ranch near Cody, Wyoming. His zest for the West has continued in a career coupled to locations through the region. During summers while an undergraduate, he served as an airborne fire-spotter for the Shoshone National Forest next to Yellowstone National Park. He taught courses in land economics while completing a Master's degree in geography at the University of Arizona in Tucson. In Denver, Colorado, Vokac was in charge of economic analysis for the city's first community renewal program, and later became Chief of Neighborhood Planning. He moved to the West coast during the mid-1970s to prepare San Diego County's first local parks plan, and stayed to act as Park Development Director.

Mr. Vokac is now a full-time writer, and founder of a Western travel and leisure advisory service. During the past year, he logged almost fifty thousand miles in a silver Audi criss-crossing Oregon and Washington while investigating and writing about all of the great towns of the Pacific Northwest. When not researching, speaking, or consulting, he can be found traveling for the sheer joy of it somewhere in the West.

Books Available in the "Great Towns" Series

The "Great Towns" series of travel guidebooks is intended to give you complete, accurate information about favorite out-of-the-way destinations throughout the West. All notable attractions, restaurants, lodgings, nightlife, shops, campgrounds, and special events are described and rated for each exciting locale. In addition to the 1987 publication:

THE GREAT TOWNS OF THE PACIFIC NORTHWEST,
by David Vokac $8.95

the series also includes:

THE GREAT TOWNS OF CALIFORNIA
by David Vokac $8.95

This guide, published in 1986, has more detailed information than any other to help you plan and enjoy your visits to exceptional places beyond the bustling cities of the Golden State. The handy 304-page book includes 50 illustrations and photos.

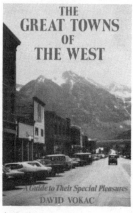

THE GREAT TOWNS OF THE WEST
by David Vokac $14.95

The first comprehensive travel guidebook about fifty special towns in spectacular, remote settings from the California coast to the Canadian Rockies was published in 1985. The convenient, 464-page book includes more than 100 illustrations and photos.

Ask for them at your favorite bookstore, or order direct.
West Press will pay postage and handling.
Mail your check or money order to:
WEST PRESS
P.O. Box 99717
San Diego, CA 92109